T0329985

Public Investment and Regional Economic Development

Public Investment and Regional Economic Development

Edited by:

Daniel Felsenstein
Hebrew University of Jerusalem, Israel

Ronald McQuaid
Napier University, Edinburgh, UK

Philip McCann
University of Reading, UK

Daniel Shefer
Technion - Israel Institute of Technology, Haifa, Israel

Edward Elgar
Cheltenham, UK • Northampton, MA, USA

Published by
Edward Elgar Publishing Limited
Glensanda House
Montpellier Parade
Cheltenham
Glos GL50 1UA
UK

Edward Elgar Publishing, Inc.
136 West Street
Suite 202
Northampton
Massachusetts 01060
USA

A catalogue record for this book
is available from the British Library

Library of Congress Cataloguing in Publication Data
Public investment and regional economic development / edited by Daniel
Felsenstein... [et al.].
    p. cm.
Includes bibliographical references and index.
1. Public investments. 2. Regional planning. I. Felzenshtain, Daniyel.

HC79.P83 P83 2001
338.9—dc21   2001040356

MIX
Paper from
responsible sources
FSC FSC® C013604
www.fsc.org

ISBN 978 1 84064 715 0

Printed and bound by CPI Group (UK) Ltd, Croydon, CR0 4YY

Contents

Figures

Tables

Contributors

Raphael Bar-El is Professor of Regional Economic Development and chairs the Department of Public Policy and Administration, Ben-Gurion University of the Negev, Israel.

Peter Batey is Lever Professor of Town and Regional Planning and Dean of the Faculty of Social and Environmental Studies at the University of Liverpool, England.

Fatemah Bazzazan is a Lecturer in the Department of Economics, Azzahra University, Iran and Ph.D. candidate in the Department of Civic Design, University of Liverpool, England.

Daniel Felsenstein is Senior Lecturer in the Department of Geography and Director of the Institute of Urban and Regional Studies, Hebrew University of Jerusalem, Israel.

Amnon Frenkel is Senior Lecturer in the Faculty of Architecture and Town Planning at the Technion - Israel Institute of Technology, Haifa, Israel.

Kevin Heanue is Research Associate in Economics at Dublin City University Business School, Ireland.

Geoffrey J.D. Hewings is Professor of Geography at the University of Illinois, Urbana, Illinois, USA.

David Jacobson is Associate Professor in Economics at Dublin City University Business School, Ireland.

Scott Leitham is a consultant with ME&P, Cambridge, England

Moss Madden was, until his death in February 2000, Professor of Planning and Regional Science in the Department of Civic Design, University of Liverpool, England.

Peter Maskell is Professor of Business in the Department of Industrial Economics and Strategy, Copenhagen Business School, Copenhagen, Denmark.

Philip McCann is Reader in Regional Economics in the Department of Economics, University of Reading, England.

Ronald McQuaid is Professor in Economics and Director of the Employment Research Institute, Napier University, Edinburgh, Scotland.

Ziene Mottiar is Lecturer in Economics at the Dublin Institute of Technology, Ireland.

John D. Nelson is Senior Lecturer and Head of Transport Engineering in the Department of Civil Engineering, University of Newcastle-upon-Tyne, England.

John B. Parr is Professor of Regional and Urban Economics in the Department of Urban Studies, University of Glasgow, United Kingdom.

Joseph Persky is Professor of Economics at the University of Illinois, Chicago, USA.

Boris A. Portnov is Senior Researcher at the Centre for Desert Architecture and Urban Planning, Jacob Blaustein Institute for Desert Research, Ben Gurion University of the Negev, Israel.

Stephen Roper is Assistant Director of the Northern Ireland Economic Research Centre, Queen's University Belfast, Northern Ireland.

Daniel Shefer holds the Lunenfeld-Kunin Chair in Urban and Regional Economics and is Dean of the Faculty of Architecture and Town Planning at the Technion - Israel Institute of Technology, Haifa, Israel.

Stephen Sheppard is Professor of Economics, Williams College, Williamstown, Massachusetts, USA.

Yoram Shiftan is Senior Lecturer in the Department of Civil Engineering, at the Technion - Israel Institute of Technology, Haifa, Israel.

Michael Sonis is Professor of Geography, Bar-Ilan University, Israel and Adjunct Professor, Regional Economic Applications Laboratory, Department of Geography, University of Illinois at Urbana USA.

Elia Werczberger is Associate Professor of Urban Planning in the Public Policy Program, Tel Aviv University.

In Memoriam

Moss Madden

Moss Madden, who tragically died after a short illness contracted a few days before the Jerusalem Regional Science Symposium in February 2000, was a leading figure in planning education and regional science research whose reputation extended throughout the world. Based in the Department of Civic Design for almost thirty years, he pursued a highly successful academic career at the University of Liverpool which took him to the top of his profession.

Although he was not a native of the city, Moss spent the whole of his adult life in Liverpool. He chose initially to study civil engineering at the University, before deciding on a career in planning. In 1970 he took up a place on the Master of Civic Design course, attracted by the prospect of studying planning in a stimulating, multidisciplinary environment. Like several of his contemporaries, Moss opted to specialise in quantitative planning techniques. Upon graduating, he accepted the offer of a university research assistantship to study simulation modelling. This was the first step on an academic ladder which led, eventually, in 1993 to the award of a Personal Chair in Planning and, four years later, to the Headship of the Department of Civic Design.

Most of Moss's research was in the interdisciplinary field of regional science. It involved fruitful collaborative work with economists, geographers and mathematicians, as well as with other planning academics. First with Peter Batey and later with others including John Dewhurst, Geoff Hewings, Andrew Trigg, Yoshio Kimura and Michael Sonis, he developed new approaches to demographic-economic modelling which allowed regional population and economic change to be analysed (and predicted) within an integrated framework based on extended input-output analysis. Subsequently he went on to explore new types of impact multiplier and to examine the relationships between Extended Input-Output Models and Social Accounting Matrices and Computable General Equilibrium Models. This fundamental and original research received widespread recognition in North America, Japan and Australia, as well as in Europe, and formed the basis of his international reputation. It led, in recent years, to more applied work where the new models were used as part of socio-economic impact assessments of large infrastructure projects such as airports and barrages. In fact, one of Moss's last publications was a volume of invited essays on *Regional Science in Business*, edited jointly with Graham Clarke. The book focuses on a wide range of practical applications of regional science methods.

The outlet for many of the papers Moss produced was the Regional Science Association, with its supranational groupings in Europe, North America and the Pacific, and national sections throughout the world. Moss was a key figure in the British and Irish Section, serving as chairman in the mid-1990s, organising conferences, editing proceedings, and generally providing strong academic leadership. He greatly valued the international links that the Association provided and showed himself to be an enthusiastic and highly effective networker. Moss had exceptional organisational and administrative skills which he put to good use in the various facets of his work. He was particularly proud of the productive links he helped to establish between British and Israeli regional scientists, reflected in several highly successful joint meetings in the two countries. Those of us who worked with Moss, in Liverpool and in many other parts of the world, will greatly miss his sharp, incisive mind, breadth of vision and understanding, warm companionship and sense of fun. The regional science community has lost a remarkable leader, scholar and friend.

Peter Batey
Lever Professor of Town and Regional Planning
Dean of the Faculty of Social and Environmental Studies, University of Liverpool

1. Introduction

Daniel Felsenstein, Ronald McQuaid, Philip McCann and Daniel Shefer

The relationship between public investment and regional economic development is of perennial interest to researchers, policy makers and students. Public investment is often seen as a possible method for 'jump-starting' lagging regional economies and allowing them to catch up. Therefore a key issue is the need to re-assess the relationship between public investment and regional growth. One fruitful avenue of investigation that has emerged from this interest has been the development of Endogenous Growth Theory and its application to regional economic development (Nijkamp and Poot 1998; Martin and Sunley 1998). By stressing the endogeneity to the growth process of those factors traditionally treated as exogenous in neoclassical models (such as human capital and technology), this approach underlines the way in which some regions create an internal mechanism for promoting or perpetuating their growth. Endogenous growth can thus be a self-reinforcing process whereby knowledge and skills are continuously embellished and the region's competitive base is enhanced.

Public investment in physical and human capital may be one way of facilitating the development of increasing returns and spillover effects, the hallmarks of endogenous regional growth. Allocating public funds to improving the regional knowledge infrastructure and upgrading the level of local human capital is often perceived as likely to set in motion those forces that result in regional growth. The question arises, however, as to the exact form of public investment ('hard' or 'soft') and its method of delivery ('direct' or 'indirect'). 'Hard' public investment refers to public allocations to physical and capital stock such as buildings, equipment and especially public infrastructure such as roads and transportation networks. Conventional wisdom is that the public provision of these investments will allow lagging regions to mobilise production factors more efficiently, thereby realising their full potential (Aschauer 1989; Biehl 1991). Empirical evidence of this effect however, is far from conclusive (Button 1998).

1

'Soft' investment refers to public involvement in developing human resources, business support services and a region's innovation and entrepreneurial base. Again, the commonly-held perception is that this form of investment complements public support for hard infrastructure. The rising stock of productive assets in a region and increasing capital and labour productivity can be further enhanced by raising the skills and competencies of the local labour force and by assisting the creativity and resourcefulness of entrepreneurs through business support systems (Townroe and Mallalieu 1991). As this kind of infrastructure investment is of a more ephemeral nature, assessments of its relative effectiveness are piecemeal. While studies that look at the impact of public investment in particular support programmes do exist (for example, Marshall et al. 1993; Smallbone et al. 1993), these are generally individual and non-comparable case studies employing an array of differing methodologies and foci. As such, we still know relatively little about the aggregate regional effects of public investment in 'soft' infrastructure.

While both 'hard' and 'soft' public investment aim at reducing costs to producers, the main issue at stake from a regional economic development perspective is whether the benefits arising from this investment are appropriated solely by these recipients or whether they also filter through as externalities and spillovers to the wider regional economy. This is further underscored by the method of delivery of public investment. On the one hand this investment can be 'direct', that is delivered through the producer, household or individual in the form of business subsidies, tax concessions, transfer payments or training schemes (Fisher and Peters 1998). On the other hand it can be 'indirect', in the sense that it is aimed at creating an aggregate change in a region through the provision or subsidy of roads, communications networks, schools and higher education institutions (Bartik 1991). The benefits of these investments are not solely internalised by the individual firm or household.

Of course, these categories are not mutually exclusive and are all interconnected with each other. Public investment in road infrastructure or in industrial R&D may at the same time benefit both the individual firm and the wider regional economy. The main question would seem to be which of the alternative approaches generates a higher rate of return in the region and enhances local productivity more efficiently. While this has been dealt with in terms of 'hard' public investments such as roads (Aschauer 1989; Biehl 1991), much less is known about softer forms of investment such as public support for education, training and business assistance.

This volume does not try to conclusively solve these issues. It does, however, present a variety of perspectives on public investment and regional economic development and analyses a range of types of investment, from transport and housing infrastructure to education and innovation. Regional growth and competitive advantage are based on overlapping factors, which relate to dynamic connections between infrastructure, capital and labour and so on. These factors include: flexible production and specialisation; capabilities to develop and utilise new technologies (products and production processes); competition with rival firms and pressure from customers; specialised suppliers and factor inputs such as labour; agglomeration economies and economies of scale (as discussed by Marshall over a century ago); and dynamic inter-industry clusters. The networks of formal and informal relations between organisations can be important for regional growth and small business formation, as are the development of human capital and the operation of labour markets, public institutions and the creation of knowledge and other resources. Hence regional policies and public investment in regions need to take account of this wide range of complex factors and their inter-relationships.

The four parts of this volume address the various forms in which public investment can impact on regional growth. Echoing the recent influence of both endogenous growth theory and the burgeoning literature on the role of infrastructure in contributing to regional convergence or divergence (Button 2000), the three empirical parts of the book deal with innovation and knowledge creation, human capital and physical infrastructure. The first part deals with the tools of analysis of regional economic change and with policy lessons arising from past experience. In this part, two chapters suggest extensions to input-output analysis, the workhorse model of regional analysis. A further chapter revisits the notion of 'regional economic planning', discussing policy failures due to misdirected emphases, uncritical reliance on conventional wisdom, and unwillingness to consider alternative approaches.

The second part considers the central policy issues of innovation and knowledge creation. These are increasingly recognised as key endogenous factors in regional economic growth. In most advanced economies, public investment in innovation and technology attempts to influence the rate and direction of technological change and, in some cases, tries to steer this growth into particular places. The part considers the way in which innovative activity impacts on regional growth and examines the efficacy of the public policy instruments that have been used.

A further factor promoting endogenous regional growth is human capital. Ever since the seminal work of Lucas (1988), public investment in human capital has been acknowledged as generating spillover effects that increase the productivity of the general labour force and of the regional physical capital stock. Part Three illustrates the complex nature of the relationship between human capital investment and regional labour markets. The chapters consider the links between human capital gains and employment changes, both within regions and between regions, from different perspectives.

Part Four considers the role of investment in physical infrastructure, long seen as a both a cause and a consequence of economic development in a region. Infrastructure investments are often considered to be a stimulant for promoting self-perpetuating growth in a region. In this respect endogenous growth theory is linked to investments in regional infrastructure endowments. Four chapters consider the importance of road, housing and building infrastructure for regional development, using a range of models and techniques to explore the complex two-way interaction between investment and economic behaviour.

Taken together, the chapters in this book combine to increase our understanding of the relationships between public investment, regional economic development, and the behaviour of individuals, firms and governments. The approaches and techniques employed here point to ways of furthering our understanding of the inter-relatedness of these issues. A sound understanding of this relationship is necessary to ensure that public policy can be effective as a means of promoting regional development. Some answers are provided but, of course, many new questions arise. As addressed in the individual chapters, there still remains a need to further develop our models and techniques.

The origins of this book lie in the Israeli-British and Irish regional science workshop that was held in Jerusalem in February 2000. This was the third in a series of bi-national regional science meetings involving these two sections of the Regional Science Association International that began in 1990. Moss Madden was a key figure in promoting these seminars and had been intimately involved in the organisation of each one. Unfortunately, he was unable to attend the Jerusalem meeting that he had helped arrange and sadly passed away the day after the workshop ended. This book is a modest tribute to his foresight and vision in promoting international regional science linkages and cross-national collaboration.

The Jerusalem workshop was made possible due to the support of the British Council; the Israeli and British-Irish sections of the Regional Science Association International; the Authority for Research and Development, the Faculty of Social Sciences, the Institute for European Studies and the Levi Eshkol Institute for Economic, Social and Political Research - all at the Hebrew University of Jerusalem; the School of Management at Ben Gurion University of the Negev and the Sego Fund at the Technion-Israel Institute of Technology.

Co-ordinating a volume comprising fifteen chapters and twenty-three authors is never an easy task. We would like to thank Michal Stern for her sterling work in converting multiple manuscript files into one standard format and preparing the final manuscript for press. In addition we would like to acknowledge the administrative support provided by the Employment Research Institute at Napier University, Edinburgh. Finally, thanks go to Peter Batey for kindly writing the front piece in memory of our dear colleague, Moss Madden.

REFERENCES

Aschauer D.A. (1989), 'Is public expenditure productive?', *Journal of Monetary Economics*, **23**, pp. 177-200.

Bartik T.J. (1991), *Who Benefits from State and Local Economic Development Policies?*, Kalamazoo, MI: W.E. Upjohn Institute for Employment Research.

Biehl D. (1991), 'The role of infrastructure in regional development', in R.W. Vickerman (ed.), *Infrastructure and Regional Development*, London: Pion.

Button K.J. (1998), 'Infrastructure investment, endogenous growth and economic convergence', *Annals of Regional Science*, **32**, pp. 145-62.

Button K.J. (2000), 'New approaches to spatial economics', *Growth and Change*, **31**, pp. 480-500.

Fisher P.S. and A.H. Peters (1998), *Industrial Incentives: Competition Among American States and Cities*, Kalamazoo, MI: W.E. Upjohn Institute for Employment Research.

Lucas R.E. (1988), 'On the mechanics of economic development', *Journal of Monetary Economics*, **22**, pp. 3-42.

Marshall N., N. Alderman, C. Wong and A. Thwaites (1993), 'The impact of government-assisted management training and development on small and medium-sized enterprises in Britain', *Environment and Planning C*, **11** (3), pp. 331-48.

Martin P. and P. Sunley (1998), 'Slow convergence? The new endogenous growth theory and regional development', *Economic Geography*, **74** (3), pp. 201-27.

Nijkamp P. and J. Poot (1998), 'Spatial perspectives on new theories of economic growth', *Annals of Regional Science*, **32**, pp. 7-38.

Smallbone D., D. North and R. Leigh (1993), 'The use of external assistance by mature SME's in the UK; some policy implications', *Entrepreneurship and Regional Development*, **5**, pp. 279-95.

Townroe P.M and K. Mallalieu (1991), 'Infrastructure for regional development: advice and support to new small businesses', in R.W. Vickerman (ed.), *Infrastructure and Regional Development*, London: Pion.

PART ONE

Modelling and Planning

Introduction to Part One

Regional economic modelling and planning involves the attempt to understand the structure and the ability to change the future course of the economic environment. While planning is thus essentially oriented to the future it recognizes that in its absence the world will continue to develop and change. It is further assumed that in the absence of conscious action some of this change may produce results that are not generally desired. Regional economic planners, therefore, attempt to devise policies which can influence development in desired directions, using means and incurring costs acceptable to the region as a whole. These policies are concerned with increasing the efficiency and use of resources to meet objectives considered to be socially desirable.

Part One consists of three contributions by eminent regional scientists. In Chapter 2, John Parr claims that along with successful regional economic planning there are numerous failures and mistakes. He attributes these failures to misdirected emphases, uncritical reliance on conventional wisdom and unwillingness to follow alternative approaches. Undoubtedly, important lessons can be drawn from such failures and mistakes. Analysing some of the seminal works in regional planning, Parr claims that several basic issues that must be dealt with, one of which is the task of goal formation and dealing with conflicting goals, such as efficiency and equity.

The choice between place prosperity and people prosperity is one that most nations have not pondered carefully enough. Similarly, dominance of spatial regional economic policy over sectoral strategy or *vice versa* sometimes leads to unsatisfactory results and an inefficient allocation of scarce resources. Here too, Parr advocates the design of a mixed strategy in spatial and sectoral terms. He discusses three neglected issues in regional economic planning: transmission mechanisms, transfer payments and preferential expenditures and compensation mechanisms. The author suggests that regional planners in developing nations have much to learn. Nevertheless, he warns, an in-built danger exists of replicating past mistakes taken from the developed world to the context of the developing world. What appears to be lacking in developing nations is a good model of regional economic planning, from which a working copy could be fashioned.

Modelling the linkage between industrial and household activity, especially at the regional level, has been one of the major areas of development in the field of input-out analysis. A dynamic form of the extended input-output model is presented in Chapter 3 written by Peter Batey, Fatemeh Bazzazan and Moss Madden. Four types of general models are presented in the chapter and two are presented in dynamic form. One of these takes account of different household income groups while the other differentiates between employed and unemployed workers. The extended input-output model involves the closure of the model with respect to households. Thus the household sector becomes endogenous to the model like any other industrial sector. Madden, in collaboration with Batey and others, made a significant contribution to the extended input-output model, particularly in respect to the linkage between the economic-demographic and demographic-economic interface. This included examining the impact of transfer payments, such as social security received by unemployed, semi-employed and retired persons, on the regional economy.

In the dynamic extended input-output model households are disaggregated into income groups and employed and unemployed workers. Concomitantly, household savings (or household capital formation) by income groups and employment status are also incorporated into the model. Thus dynamic extended input-output models are wider in scope than conventional dynamic input-output models, since they include the study of household savings, profits and industrial investment. The principal advantage of the dynamic extended input-output model lies in the calculation of more realistic impact multipliers and forecasts. In general, industrial investment has a positive effect on the size of the multipliers while household saving reduces consumption and thus has a negative effect on the size of the multipliers.

Miyazawa's scheme of the matrix inter-relational income multiplier is explored in Chapter 4 by Michael Sonis and Geoffrey Hewings. The authors successfully attempt to incorporate labour and capital income, savings, consumption and investment into the Miyazawa model. This extension utilizes the 'onion-skins' approach with several layers of labour and capital, savings, consumption and investments. This approach facilitates the inclusion of the Miyazawa income generation and propagation mechanism in the Sraffa-Leontief model and thus helps explain the interconnection of Miyazawa's ideas with those independently elaborated within the Pyatt-Round social accounting scheme.

2. Regional Economic Planning: Learning from Past Experience

John B. Parr

2.1 INTRODUCTION

It would be fair to claim that over the last six or seven decades the field of regional economic planning has achieved more than a few successes. Against this record, however, must be set the various failures and mistakes, these taking the form of misdirected emphases, reliance on conventional wisdom, unwillingness to follow alternative approaches and so on. The intention of this chapter is to examine certain of these failures and to consider what lessons might be drawn from such experience. Focusing primarily on the situation in Western Europe and North America, consideration will be given to those features of regional economic planning which have been either overemphasised or seriously neglected. First, however, it is necessary to comment briefly on the general environment within which regional economic planning takes place.

It is fairly obvious that regional economic planning (along with other concerns such as health and education policies, for example) has to take second place to other economic concerns of a national government such as macroeconomic stabilisation, monetary targets, fiscal policy and international economic relations, involving trade, capital movements and exchange rate stability. But even here it is worth bearing in mind that the pursuit of a policy of this type need not be wholly oblivious to regional considerations. Thus given policy (for example international trade policy) may be followed in alternative ways, all achieving broadly the same results, but certain of these alternatives may be less injurious to problem regions than others. On certain occasions, at least, there exists the possibility of tailoring a national policy in such a way that the primary objective can be achieved, while at the same time attaining a desired multi-regional outcome. There is, of course, no denying the fact that regional economic planning is one of a number of economic policies that a nation might wish to pursue. These usually exist in a competitive relationship with one another (most obviously with respect to resource expenditure), although it is sometimes the case that the relationship is a complementary or mutually re-enforcing one, in which case the opportunity exists for regional economic planning to have an important co-ordinating aspect to it, particularly at the sub-national level.

One further comment by way of introduction concerns the fact that regional economic planning may be conducted at various levels. It is frequently implemented by the central government, although this responsibility is sometimes devolved to a lower level of government or to a regional-development agency. In federal systems there may be an important regional (provincial or state) competence in the initiation and implementation of regional policy. Underlying this is the question as to which level of government is the most appropriate for identifying the regional problem and for implementing regional economic policy. There are no clear answers here, and for the majority of nations the responsibility is divided among national, regional and local levels of government. This sometimes works in a satisfactory manner, but on other occasions it becomes the source of tension, conflict and inefficiency. It is not, however, simply a question of the appropriate level of responsibility or the appropriate distribution of responsibility among levels. Regional economic planning at all three levels (and certainly at the highest two) is often in the hands of more than one department or agency, the division being along functional lines, for example infrastructure provision, the granting of financial assistance, the undertaking of direct investment and so on. This, too, can be the source of difficulties.

2.2   THE DESIGN OF REGIONAL PLANNING: SOME BASIC ISSUES

The stage prior to the implementation of regional economic planning involves the identification and diagnosis of the regional problem. In relative terms, identification is the easy part, since it is not difficult to observe an economic phenomenon which is the cause for concern, whether this involves localised unemployment, rural depopulation, or substantial interregional differences in income (welfare) levels. The reasons for the problem, in a sense the diagnosis of the problem, are much harder to come to grips with. This diagnosis should involve the application of the fairly impressive battery of analyses that have been developed within economics, regional science and related fields. The emphasis should be on the general causes of the problem and not on specific conditions, important as these may appear.

But the identification and diagnosis of a regional problem (to say nothing of its treatment) depends very heavily on the availability of data, the acquisition of which may be a time-consuming and costly business. Central to the problem of data availability in this particular context is the question of regionalisation (Friedmann 1956). The economic region, as a division of the national space economy, is a convenient but artificial construct, though probably not much more so than a sector of economic activity, representing a division of the national industrial economy. To a large extent we are prisoners of the past, inasmuch as the opportunity for changes in the system of regionalisation occurs only rarely. Moreover, a particular regionalisation scheme may cause the regional problem to be perceived in a particular way, so that in the extreme the regional problem becomes a function of the regionalisation scheme being used (change this, and the nature and extent of the problem are changed). But what general considerations ought to be borne in mind? Early attempts at regionalisation placed considerable emphasis on river basins, where rivers were seen as agents which unified space rather than divided it. This was particularly evident in the studies by Sir Patrick Geddes, following on from the much earlier work of Frédéric Le Play. In the first half of the twentieth century there was a tendency to emphasise homogeneity in the delineation of regions, and this was apparent with the interest in crop or commodity regions and manufacturing zones or belts. A more sophisticated attempt at dealing with this question was contained within the work of North (1955), who suggested that a region might be defined in terms of area with a common export base. In the developed world, however, the very complexity of regional economic structure renders the task of identifying homogeneity in these terms a very difficult assignment.

The concept of the homogenous region eventually gave way to that of the functional region or community-of-interest region. The city region (Dickinson 1947), the metropolitan community (McKenzie 1933), and the *région polarisée* (Boudeville 1966) were all very much in this mould. Typically, such an economic region consists of a large city or metropolitan area (often a transportation node) and an area to which this centre provides goods and services (its market area), and/or from which it draws its imports (its supply area), but more generally an area over which the centre/node exerts an influence with respect to ownership, decision making (public and private), control and the exchange of information. Such a functional or nodal region is becoming an increasingly dominant feature of the space economies of developed nations. It comes very close to meeting the requirement, set down by Hoover and Fisher (1949), that a region should represent an area within which there is a high degree of interdependence of incomes. In a variety of respects such a region would seem to be an appropriate one for the purposes of conducting regional economic policy. Ideally, economic regions should correspond to political regions, but the latter are sometimes drawn up or emerge as a result of considerations other than economic ones. While it would be unwise to minimise the significance of political/administrative regions, the frequent lack of correspondence between economic and political regions is one that has bedevilled regional economic planning in an uncomfortably large number of nations. This is a problem that we probably have to live with!

Finally, in dealing with these basic issues, a word or two is in order on the nature of goals or objectives for regional economic planning. For a number of fairly obvious reasons there is a reluctance to think in terms of concrete (measurable) goals, and policy makers are much more comfortable with broad emphases or directions (Leven 1964). But it is the specification of a consistent set of goals (whether among regions of a nation or among districts of a region) which underlies not only the formulation of a strategy and the concomitant allocation of resources, but also the *ex post* evaluation of policy. Policy makers thus operate behind a screen which partially shields them from scrutiny. A further reason for the failure to commit to goals is related to the unwillingness of policy makers (or their political masters) to confront the problem of conflict of goals, most notably between efficiency and equity (at both the inter-regional and intra-regional levels). The task of goal formulation, however, is an extremely important one, the evasion of which generally involves significant efficiency losses.

2.3   PREOCCUPATIONS IN REGIONAL ECONOMIC PLANNING

This section considers the difficulties that may arise as a result of a particular emphasis being pursued, whether this involves a policy objective, an instrument of policy, or a given strategy. There is a pronounced tendency in virtually every nation to approach regional policy in terms of particular emphases, usually representing the continuation of past practice. As an illustration, we may consider the question of objectives. In Germany, for example, the emphasis has tended to involve incomes (ensuring as low a dispersion as possible in the variation of incomes among regions). By contrast, in France the goals have typically related to the inter-regional distribution of investment, while in the UK the concern has largely been with differences in unemployment. To a large extent these various emphases reflect differences in the bureaucratic culture of intervention, as well as differences in the broad political consensus within this area of state involvement.

2.3.1 Place Prosperity vs People Prosperity

The choice between place prosperity and people prosperity (which is a generalisation of the choice between moving jobs to people and moving people to jobs) is one that most nations have not pondered carefully enough (Winnick 1966). As a broad generalisation we may say that the place-prosperity (or the-jobs-to-people) emphasis tends to be very strong in the nations of Western Europe, while the people-prosperity (or people-to-jobs) emphasis tends to be more common in North America, although there are exceptions to this generalisation in both cases (Hoover 1971). Also, occasions exist when the two emphases amount to the same thing (Richardson 1978). In a situation of highly localised unemployment, for example, measures designed to assist place prosperity inevitably have the effect of assisting people prosperity. It is worth considering briefly the *pros* and *cons* of both types of assistance. Place-prosperity measures have the real advantage of relieving unemployment, supporting ailing economies, preserving the social fabric of communities, and making a conscious effort to modify economic structures. On the other hand, place-prosperity measures frequently delay the process of migration that would have otherwise occurred, encourage higher participation rates, lead to return migration (because of the availability of new economic opportunities), and are to the advantage of many interests or groups that are not in need of assistance. People-prosperity measures, by contrast, aim at those groups which require to be helped and, through programmes to enhance skills and/or assist mobility, enable individuals/households to have a greater range of choice, and help them adjust more easily to the sometimes harsh realities of economic life. Against these advantages must be weighed the criticisms that such measures often raise expectations unreasonably, may be socially disruptive, and merely have the effect of redistributing poverty more evenly.

To argue that there should be a judicious blend of the two emphases is to make a rather weak statement. Yet such a viewpoint does draw attention to the need to avoid reliance on a single emphasis, which can seldom be justified. The fundamental drawback of place-prosperity measures is that these beg the following question: what is the place to be assisted - the region, the sub-region/district or the locality? Advocates of place-prosperity approaches invariably remain silent on this point. By contrast, the real weakness of people-prosperity measures is that these only appear to work in an efficient and very flexible economy, which is underlain by high levels of mobility and access to information.

2.3.2 Instruments of Policy

A very similar reliance on a single emphasis occurs with respect to the instruments of regional economic policy. In Germany, for example, there has always been the view that if only a community/region can be endowed with enough infrastructure facilities, this will set in train mechanisms for ending any structural weakness. In the US also, remedying deficiencies in the infrastructure has been seen as the key to economic success (the system of congressional appropriations has tended to encourage this process). In France, by contrast, the large show-piece project (an automobile assembly plant, a petrochemical complex and so on) has represented the typical emphasis, while in the UK there has until very recently been considerable reliance placed on the locational (inter-regional) manipulation of manufacturing activity by means of grants, loans and even prohibitions (from 1947 to 1980). Thus the development of a new industry in a prosperous region was automatically looked upon as the means by which a problem region could be assisted, if only adequate incentives were made available in the latter region. The question as to why this new industry had not developed there in the first place was seldom seriously considered.

Such preoccupations in the implementation of regional economic policy can lead to serious distortions. Infrastructure investment, except when it is a recognisably missing ingredient in a region with an otherwise strong potential, can quickly come to resemble the cargo cult of Papua-New Guinea in the years following World War II. By contrast, the emphasis on show-piece projects leads to highly localised development, which may subsequently become no more than 'cathedrals in the desert'. In the case of the locational manipulation of economic activity the fact that only manufacturing activity was considered in this connection was a definite weakness and one which is difficult to comprehend. Such locational manipulation also had a distorting effect on the problem region by creating an economy based on plants which were largely unrelated to the regional economy in terms other than labour inputs, and did little for the region. More important perhaps was the tendency to disregard the fact that the transplanted manufacturing activity might require a considerable infrastructure to support it, not simply involving the standard elements of infrastructure (including the supply of public utilities), but a technological and commercial infrastructure, customarily considered in terms of agglomeration economies.

2.3.3 Spatial and Sectoral Emphases

A further onesidedness in regional economic policy has concerned the dominance of spatial strategies over sectional strategies or *vice versa,* by which one set of strategies was pursued to the virtual exclusion of the other. In the regions of Western Europe (and less commonly North America) it was the case that a strategy was conceived in spatial terms, with sectoral considerations being made subservient to these or not considered at all. On other occasions, though less frequently perhaps, the strategy was designed in largely sectoral terms, with little or no regard for the spatial implications. Once again, this tendency for exclusiveness was misplaced, and sometimes led to unsatisfactory results and wasted resources.

In one rather obvious sense spatial considerations must be of central concern. The very notion of regional policy implies a focus on space: for policies undertaken at the national level, this involves multi-regional or inter-regional space, while for policies pursued by regional authorities, the concern is with intra-regional space. In both cases the focus on space is most apparent where policies are organised around place prosperity, and where the concerns are centred on some localised problem. The spatial issue sometimes leads to a serious dilemma, and we may consider this in the case of a problem region. Assuming that the region is to be assisted through a given level of investment, what is going to be the spatial priority? Should the worst parts of the region be assisted first (on the grounds of equity), or should the most promising parts of the region be selected (on the grounds that such a pattern will best help the region as a whole over the long run), or should the allocation be on a proportionate or fair-share basis (which will have the effect of perpetuating the existing spatial structure)? Two points are germane here. First, there are likely to be conduits by which growth spills over from one part of the nation (region) to another, and these need to be considered very carefully from the outset (this important issue will be discussed in Section 2.4). Second, for whatever spatial selection is made, it will be important to examine the sectoral implications in terms of the kinds of economic activity that can be expected to survive under such a spatial emphasis. Much of this argument underlies the spectacular failure of growth-pole strategies, in which sectoral considerations were usually of secondary importance.

Parallel problems arise when strategies are designed with a sectoral emphasis. As used to be asserted by central planners in the former USSR, 'every investment has an address'. Going beyond this aphorism, it is not difficult to appreciate that a given set of investments will have an identifiable and sometimes pronounced spatial outcome, which need not be unique. This may be consistent with national (regional) objectives, but it may well lead to outcomes that result in large parts of a nation (region) or to substantial portions of the population being unaffected or adversely affected. Much of the recent work on cluster-based development (with its obvious sectoral emphasis) has failed to examine the spatial implications of the proposals. Such is the case with a number of papers in the worthwhile volume recently assembled by Steiner (1998). In fact, strategies based on the development of clusters may well meet with the same lack of success and eventual disenchantment that was the fate of the growth-pole strategies (Parr 1999a, 1999b).

But what is the way out of this difficulty? Given a set of consistent and attainable goals (and this is often an heroic assumption), it seems logical to design a strategy in spatial *and* sectoral terms. Sometimes spatial imperatives will have to take precedence over sectoral ones, and sometimes the reverse will be true. In either case a certain measure of welfare may have to be foregone, but at least this will be known in advance, and taken into account in the eventual decision. The task of the policy maker would be made much easier in this connection, if there existed a conceptual framework which focused on the subtle and continuing inter-relationship between spatial structure and sectoral structure (Parr 1979). Elements of such a framework are available, but a complete framework is at present lacking. This surely represents one of the most important items on the research agenda of applied regional science.

2.3.4 The Tendency to Imitate

The final preoccupation in regional economic planning concerns the policy maker's sources of inspiration. There is a worrying tendency for policy makers from a problem region to look at some favourable feature of economic reality elsewhere, and then to assume that this can be replicated, so as to become the keystone of a strategy for economic revival or adjustment in their own region. To elaborate the argument, the policy maker observes various phenomena which represent beacons of economic success: the efficient agro-industry in particular regions of Denmark and the Netherlands; a spontaneous growth pole of medium size, which is helping to transform the problem region in which it is located; a knowledge-intensive cluster of economic activity such as Cambridge (UK) or Lyon (France); an interacting set of firms based on a network of centres, forming an industrial district specialising in quality textiles or clothing, such as in Emilia-Romagna (Italy). The common reaction of the policy maker to these observed successes is as follows: 'Now, I wish we had one of those' or, worse, 'We could do that' or, even worse, 'Let's develop one of those in our region'.

There is, of course, nothing wrong with looking at real-world successes: what is dangerous is the presumption that these can be replicated, if only there is enough vision and commitment of resources. Invariably, the successes of the type referred to are achieved within some form of market framework, and policy makers (by virtue of their background and disposition) are generally not able to appreciate the subtleties of the market. Equally importantly, the structures on which the successes are based tended to emerge over a very long period and often grew out of particular economic traditions, distinct social systems, supportive institutional environments and specific levels of occupational and geographic mobility. Even if their importance is recognised, none of these factors is readily amenable to policy manipulation, and certainly not in the short run. Thus, strategies which simply strive to reproduce these economic successes within the environment of a problem region frequently become exercises in wishful thinking. No more need be said.

2.4 NEGLECTED ISSUES IN REGIONAL ECONOMIC PLANNING

Regrettably, the catalogue of neglected issues in regional economic planning is large. Policy makers have often lacked the time (and on occasions the imagination) to think carefully about the complexities of the regional problem, and have been content to fall back on the comfortable certainties of conventional wisdom. And lest it be thought that radical or revolutionary approaches are being proposed, it is emphasised that the focus here is simply on approaches which are known about but which (for whatever reason) have not been exploited. Three such neglected issues, among the many, are singled out for consideration. One is technical, while another concerns the form of regional economic planning, and a third is concerned with its design.

2.4.1 Transmission Mechanisms

The spatial structure of a nation can be viewed as an elaborate set of linkages (both inter-regional and inter-sectoral). These relate to trade flows involving goods and services, flows of government funds, capital flows (and the associated reverse flows of property payments). Such an intricate spatial structure implies interconnectedness, so that an investment or some other autonomous shock within one region is likely to have repercussions (favourable and unfavourable) in terms of income, employment or activity levels in the other regions of a nation. Similar repercussions can be expected with respect to the sub-regions/districts of a region in response to a more contained shock at the regional scale. We may also consider the phenomenon in terms of an urban system, an appropriate focus in relatively urbanised economies. For example, if growth occurs within an urban centre at one level of the urban system there will be growth and/or decline at other centres of higher and lower levels, as well as within a rural supply area. For all three spatial scales we may speak of the transmission of growth, and multiplier effects are an obvious mechanism for this. We may also distinguish between inter-regional transmission (involving mainly trade flows, flows of government funds and capital flows) and intra-regional transmission (involving mainly trade and commuting flows), as well as inter-level transmission within the urban system (involving all types of flows).

The neglect here involves the lack of detailed knowledge about these transmission mechanisms. If policy makers were better informed about such mechanisms, it would be possible to say more about the overall spatial impacts of a given investment, in much the same way that input-output analysis can trace through the effects of the growth in one sector on the growth of other sectors. Sometimes this lack of information on transmission mechanisms can be the cause of unanticipated outcomes. What we do know is rather fragmented and highly generalised. Investment in poor regions (particularly peripheral regions) tends to involve spillovers to more prosperous regions (particularly core regions); figuratively speaking, potential income leaks out of the poor region. By contrast, the impact of investment in a core region tends to be confined there to a much greater extent, though by the Hirschman (1958) argument the demand for raw materials, goods (foodstuffs) and services produced in the peripheral regions may be increased, but even here the impact may be highly dispersed so as to leave a typical locality unaffected. The problem is very similar at the regional scale. The income-generation effects of investment in poor districts are generally not diffused outward but tend to be felt at a dominant regional centre, while the impact of investment at such a regional centre is generally not felt in nearby areas (except in the case of commuting) but is confined to the centre itself, or is felt in other regions. And if we consider the question in terms of the urban system, we find the overwhelming tendency for growth at one level of centre to be transmitted upwards to higher levels (and for the impact of growth at very high levels to be retained there) rather than to be transmitted downwards to lower level centres and to rural areas: such is the spatial structure of many urban systems (Parr 1999b).

Unfortunately, all this runs counter to the wishes of the policy maker, for whom life would be so much easier if the transmission was outwards or downwards rather than inwards or upwards. Nevertheless, knowledge of the reality of transmission of growth would be very helpful in deciding where to place investments within a nation (or within a region) or, if 'the where' had been decided in advance, what type of economic activity to place at 'the where'. Regarding the obvious question as to whether the transmission mechanisms can be retracked or redirected, so as to run along preferred channels, the answer must be in the negative. It is only over the long run (and with a careful spatial selection of investment) that the pattern of transmission mechanisms can be altered. Although the policy maker is obliged to work within the existing framework, knowledge of this framework will at least avoid the waste of resources and the build-up of unrealistic expectations.

2.4.2 Transfer Payments and Preferential Expenditures

The concern here is with two different (though related) aspects of regional economic planning that have probably not received the attention that these deserve. Consideration is given initially to the question of transfer payments, which seem to be better understood in federal systems, although the question does not turn on constitutional arrangements. A central government collects taxes and makes expenditures across the regions of a nation. Now if the taxation is progressive and if the expenditure patterns are based on need or on a common standard, the process is inherently redistributive in favour of the problem/poorer regions. An obvious example is the case of unemployment compensation, an important automatic stabiliser within many nations. If we add up all these transfer payments, including grants-in-aid to regional and local authorities, the equalising impact across regions becomes significant.

What we have here is 'invisible regional policy' or 'non-regional regional policy'. This involves policies which are not generally thought of (nor designed) in terms of regions, but which nevertheless have very important inter-regional implications. In fact, it has been estimated that for the countries of the European Union the impact of transfer payments in terms of income generation is about five times the impact of conventional (direct) regional policy (Wilson 1979). This is not, of course, an argument in favour of high state intervention, but it does suggest the existence of a powerful instrument of regional policy that might have been exploited to a greater extent. It is sometimes the case (for example in Germany, Australia and more recently in the UK, though only with respect to Scotland, Wales and Northern Ireland) that certain transfers take place directly from the centre, that is taxes are collected centrally, and then distributed as a lump sum to a regional government, on the basis of a predetermined formula, usually based on per capita income and/or need.

This leads us on to another facet of state expenditure, namely, central government purchases, as opposed to transfer payments. The central government tends to be a very large purchaser of items as different as defence equipment, motor vehicles, office machinery and supplies and so on. But from whom do governments buy these goods? In the case of defence equipment the purchases tend to be imported, but in most other cases the supplier is a domestic company, the process generally involving some form of competitive bidding. The government is therefore in a strong position to allocate expenditure among regions on a preferential basis, stipulating that a given percentage of expenditures must occur in problem regions, for example.

The private sector has an incentive to respond (particularly if granted a subsidy) by locating at least some of production facilities in preferred regions, the more so if the government uses the threat of procurement from overseas sources. There are certain additional costs associated with such a discriminatory programme of procurement, although these may turn out to be no higher than expenditures associated with other regional-development programmes. In the US the southern states have been particularly skilful in making use of the system of Senate seniority to secure a healthy share of defence-spending appropriations. Broadly similar arguments apply to the siting of central government offices, higher education facilities and specialised installations in the problem regions of a nation. This has been undertaken in a number of nations, though in most cases the approach has not reached anywhere near its full potential.

2.4.3 Compensation Mechanisms

A third neglected issue, also relating to the design of regional policy, is of major relevance in the case of policy directed at a particular region. It is often the case that a regional development programme may create considerable benefits to a region as a whole, but at the same time it may bring in its wake a number of backwash (Myrdal 1957) or polarisation (Hirschman 1958) effects. As a consequence some parts of a region remain unaffected and other parts may even be adversely affected. Confronted with such a mixed blessing, what is the response of the policy maker? If the programme is persevered with, awkward intra-regional equity issues are likely to emerge, to say nothing of fierce opposition from particular groups. If the programme is discarded, a valuable stream of net benefits will have been lost to the region, these perhaps being considerably greater than those offered by the next-best programme, although this might at least have the advantage of securing more equitable results. While the situation described is hypothetical, it is by no means atypical of the problems facing the policy maker in developed nations.

A third option is possible, but is seldom employed, partly because of its complexity. It involves proceeding with the programme, but with certain embellishments. These are collectively termed 'compensation mechanisms', which enable the parts of the region unaffected or adversely affected by the programme to share more equitably in its overall benefits. Such compensation mechanisms can be realised by a range of devices, including the following: deliberate efforts to help the problem areas by means of better accessibility to the favoured areas, thus widening the scope for commuting and improving the availability of consumer services and business services throughout the region; guaranteeing that away from the favoured areas a certain range of public services is available at some minimum standard, perhaps with a significant element of subsidy (as a counter to the possible centralisation of privately provided services); an easing of the impediments to migration by means of assistance for relocation and housing at the favoured areas; the establishment of more efficient banking systems, enabling earnings to be remitted from the favoured areas; the creation of a system of differential taxation which benefits those unaffected or adversely affected elements of the regional population (to the extent that this is within the scope of the prevailing system of public finance).

Incorporating the notion of compensation does not necessarily represent a serious dilution of the programme nor, therefore, a violation of its logic. Rather, it represents a means by which the (possibly considerable) net benefits of the programme can be realised without unacceptable outcomes and without, therefore, major political opposition. The cost of these compensation mechanisms is viewed as part of the cost of proceeding with the programme, and counted along with the other costs. Either the cost of the programme is increased or, if the regional policy budget is fixed, a certain measure of net benefits is deliberately sacrificed. It must be admitted, of course, that unless the introduction of such compensation mechanisms is undertaken very carefully, the programme will become significantly distorted, with the accompanying loss of net benefits. It is nevertheless a matter of some surprise that the possibility of using compensation mechanisms for large-scale projects has not been more widely entertained.

2.5 A CLOSING COMMENT

It will be apparent that there are many problem areas in regional economic planning that have not been touched upon, and it must be stressed that some of the issues mentioned do not constitute serious problems in every nation. The sub-title of this chapter ('Learning from Past Experience') raises the rather obvious question as to who should be doing the learning. Since the bulk of the preceding argument has concerned the developed world, this would suggest that it is the relevant regional-planning practitioners and analysts within developed nations who have the most to learn. It would be disappointing, to say the least, if shortcomings of the past were not recognised and responded to in current planning practice.

There is another arena in which the comments of this chapter might also have a resonance (if not now, then certainly in the future), and this concerns the developing world. Clearly, the issues considered above have a generality which extends beyond the developed world. Yet in the area of regional economic planning old habits die hard, and the continuing influence of developed-world practice is not to be underestimated. Moreover, policy makers in developing nations are probably just as susceptible to the tendency to imitate (discussed in Section 2.3) as their counterparts in developed nations. As a consequence there exists an in-built danger of repeating in the developing world the past mistakes of the developed world. What appears to be lacking in developing nations is a good model of regional economic planning, from which a good copy could be fashioned. What always exists, however, is the possibility of creating a good copy of a bad model, or at least a model that has been shown to be defective.

REFERENCES

Boudeville, J.R. (1966), *Problems of Regional Economic Planning*, Edinburgh: Edinburgh University Press.

Dickinson, R.E. (1947), *City, Region, and Regionalism*, London: Routledge and Kegan Paul.

Friedmann, J. (1956), 'The concept of a planning region', *Land Economics*, **32**, pp. 1-13.

Hirschman, A.O. (1958), *The Strategy of Economic Development*, New Haven, Conn.: Yale University Press.

Hoover, E.M. (1971), *An Introduction to Regional Economics*, New York: Alfred A. Knopf.

Hoover, E.M. and J.L. Fisher (1949), 'Research in regional economic growth', in *Problems in the Study of Economic Growth*, New York: Universities-National Bureau Committee on Economic Research.

Leven, C.L. (1964), 'Establishing goals for regional economic development', *Journal of American Institute of Planners*, **30**, pp. 100-110.

McKenzie, R.D. (1933), *The Metropolitan Community*, New York: McGraw-Hill.

Myrdal, G. (1957), *Economic Theory and Under-Developed Regions*, London: Duckworth.

North, D.C. (1955), 'Location theory and regional economic growth', *Journal of Political Economy*, **63**, pp. 243-58.

Parr, J.B. (1979), 'Regional economic change and regional spatial structure: some interrelationships', *Environment and Planning A*, **11**, pp. 825-37.

Parr, J.B. (1999a), 'Growth-pole strategies in regional economic planning: a retrospective view' (Part 1. Origins and advocacy)', *Urban Studies*, **36**, pp. 1195-215.

Parr, J.B. (1999b), 'Growth-pole strategies in regional economic planning: a retrospective view (Part 2. Implementation and outcome)', *Urban Studies*, **36**, pp. 1247-68.

Richardson, H.W. (1978), *Regional and Urban Economics*, Harmondsworth: Penguin.

Steiner, M. (ed.) (1998), *Clusters and Regional Specialisation* (European Research in Regional Science, Vol. 8), London: Pion.

Wilson, T. (1979), 'Regional policy and the national interest', in D. Maclennan and J.B. Parr (eds), *Regional Policy: Past Experience and New Directions*, Oxford: Martin Robertson.

Winnick, L. (1966), 'Place prosperity vs. people prosperity: welfare considerations in the geographical distribution of economic activity', in *Essays in Urban Land Economics*, Los Angeles: Real Estate Program, UCLA.

3. Dynamic Extended Input-Output Models: Some Initial Thoughts

Peter Batey, Fatemeh Bazzazan and Moss Madden

3.1 INTRODUCTION

In the last twenty years, one of the most important areas of development in the field of input-output analysis has been the modelling of the linkage between industrial and household activity, especially at the regional level. The linkages between them are usually modelled in an input-output framework by treating the household sector as an ordinary industry, which produces labour and consumes industrial products and is included in the transactions matrix. Extended versions of the input-output model have been introduced by adding further rows and columns to the inter-industry flow matrix. A number of different approaches have been taken to the design of extended input-output models. Some of this work has been based upon the pioneering efforts of Miernyk et al. (1967), who explored the effects of a rapidly expanding local economy in Boulder, Colorado. It includes research reported by Batey, Madden and Weeks (1987), Blackwell (1977), Sadler et al. (1973), and Tiebout (1969). The most interesting of these approaches are those which concentrate on the economic and demographic status of the household. The work of Schinnar (1976), Stone (1981), Batey and Madden (1981, 1983), Madden and Batey (1980) and Van Dijk and Oosterhaven (1986) in particular, have been important in demonstrating the value of input-output analysis as a framework for studying the interrelationships between demographic and economic variables.

The aim of the current chapter is to present some initial thoughts on a dynamic version of the extended model. The starting point is a simple static model in which household consumption is treated as a component of final demand and household income as a part of value added. This basic form of model is elaborated upon in a sequence of stages until a comprehensive version of the extended model is obtained. To a large degree the extended model conforms to the same principles as apply to a Leontief input-output system, the only differences concerning the presence of positive coefficients in some of the off-diagonal cells of the matrix of coefficients (Miller and Blair 1985). The review covers four general types of model, including the basic form, although attention is focused on two of these models and their equation systems, as these are later re-presented in dynamic form. In the following section, the basic elements and assumptions of the dynamic model are introduced. These are then applied to two dynamic extended models, one of which takes account of different household income groups, and the other distinguishes between employed and unemployed workers.

3.2 STATIC EXTENDED MODELS

Extensions to input-output models have a long history (see, for example, Leontief 1941). There has been increasing awareness of the need to improve the specification of the household sector in such models (for a comprehensive review, see Batey 1985). A variety of different approaches have been developed to household disaggregation and to the incorporation within an extended modelling framework of population-related variables, including household income, household consumption, income distribution, labour force participation, migration, employment and unemployment, in addition to industrial output. Going back further to the earliest work on the concept by Leontief in the simplest input-output model, final demand is exogenous and includes consumption purchases by households, as well as investment, government spending and exports. In the case of households, they earn incomes in payment for their labour input in the production process and as consumers they buy goods for final consumption. This simple model, in which households are treated exogenously, is characterised as a Type I Leontief model (Leontief 1941). It is given by:

$$x = (I - A)^{-1} \cdot f \qquad (3.1)$$

where x is a column vector of gross output,
   A is a technical coefficients matrix, and
   f is a column vector of final demand.

In a Type I model, the impact of household consumption of industrial output may be assessed, but the effect that a change in industrial output might have upon household income and expenditure is ignored. In other words, the consequences of direct and indirect household income change are modelled, but the induced effects of the presence of households in the economy are not captured.

The first, and most straightforward, extension involves the closure of the model with respect to households. To make the household sector endogenous, it is transferred from the final demand column to the inter-industry transactions table. The household sector is therefore assumed to behave like any other industrial sector. In this case the output is labour and the input is consumption. The household sector is assumed to behave like other industrial sectors with a linear and homogeneous consumption function.

Numerous attempts have been made to disaggregate households. Three important varieties of disaggregation can be identified, namely Types II, III and IV. The model developed by Miyazawa (1976) to disaggregate households into a number of income groups under the assumption of consumption homogeneity, may be regarded as a Type II extended input-output model. Equations and variables are as follows:

$$\begin{pmatrix} I-A & -h_c \\ -h_r & 1 \end{pmatrix} \begin{pmatrix} x_1 \\ x_h \end{pmatrix} = \begin{pmatrix} d_1 \\ d_h \end{pmatrix} \tag{3.2}$$

h_c is a column vector of household consumption,
h_r is a row vector of income from employment coefficients,
x_1 is a column vector of industrial gross output,
x_h is household income,
d_1 is a column vector of industrial final demand, and
d_h is exogenous household income, that is income received by residents living in the study area from sources outside the area,
and the equations are:

$$(I-A)x_1 - h_c(x_h) = d_1$$
$$-h_r(x_1) + x_h = d_h$$

Several criticisms can be made of this form of extended model.

The first criticism arises from the assumption of a linear and homogeneous consumption function. As households are confined to a single row and column in the model, that is one pattern of household consumption is represented, all households are assumed to have the same wage rate and consumption propensities. This is clearly an unrealistic assumption since any study area can be expected to contain a mixed assembly of households exhibiting widely differing consumption patterns (Batey and Madden 1983). Any changes in household income and consumption are regarded as being immediately related to each other, whereas in reality it is clear that decreases in wages to labour do not mean identical decreases in household consumption. As household income falls, or is removed completely by redundancy, households do not necessarily spend correspondingly less, or disappear altogether from the system, and in practice social security or unemployment benefits partly take the place of income from employment (Batey and Madden 1981).

Second, migrant flows are important elements in the economic system, introducing new consumers into regional economies or removing existing consumers, and so the explicit treatment of migration in an extended input-output model is essential. In a Type II model this is ignored.

Third, consumption propensities are implicitly assumed to apply exclusively to employed households. The consumption of unemployed households is treated exogenously, as a part of final demand, and so is not influenced by the consumption of employed households.

Fourth, in this model it is not clear what the source is of newly employed workers - are they from the local labour force or migrants? The impact of their existence before taking up employment has been ignored (Batey 1985; Batey and Weeks 1989; Batey 1990).

It was in an effort to overcome these problems that Miernyk and his colleagues developed a new form of input-output model for their study of the impact of the space programme on Boulder, Colorado (Miernyk et al. 1967). To circumvent the problem of linearity of the consumption function, Miernyk and his colleagues sub-divided existing workers into a number of income groups, each with different propensity to consume within the local economy. They furthermore assumed that changes in household income in a region could be divided into two types: extensive and intensive. Extensive growth was defined as an increase in output and employment without any increase in per capita income. Intensive growth is assumed to occur as a result of increases in productivity. Miernyk and his colleagues assumed that in-migrants receive the same wage rates as indigenous workers (extensive income), and they identified the difference between this and total income growth as intensive income, reflecting increases in productivity among the indigenous workforce (Batey and Weeks 1989). This form of extended model was labelled a Type III model by Miernyk and his colleagues. Although in its original form the model used an iterative solution method, Batey, Madden and Weeks (1987) have shown that it may be represented as a system of simultaneous equations or an activity-commodity framework. Slight variant household disaggregations have been developed based on the Miernyk model, including a model of Cork, Ireland, which specifies the previous residence of workers (Blackwell 1977).

A series of extended input-output models, under the general description of Type IV, have been developed in recent years. The most important characteristics of this work, which distinguish it from other studies, are as follows:

- The two main linkages in the relationship between economic and demographic variables have been specified as the economic-demographic and demographic-economic interfaces. The first of these represents the effects of the economic change on population and the second the effect that demographic factors have on an economy (Madden and Batey 1980).
- Identification of a particular inconsistency, which arises in the household-endogenous model Type II, concerning the calculation of the unemployment rate (Batey and Madden 1983).
- The finding that there are two approaches to the solution of the problem of demographic-economic change and its consequences, one based upon an iterative technique and the other using a simultaneous method offered by activity analysis, and establishing that these two approaches yield identical results (Batey and Madden 1983).
- Recognition of the importance of modelling the social security payments received by unemployed persons and by old age pensioners (Batey and Madden 1983). In more recent work, Madden and Trigg paid greater attention to migration and unemployment in the extended input-output model and developed a model which included only one group of migrants and unemployed (Madden and Trigg 1990). To achieve this they introduced a new column in the coefficients matrix to represent the consumption propensities of unemployed migrants (in most cases the same as those for indigenous persons) in one- and two-region formulations. Elsewhere Madden (1993) proposed a number of developments to the models of Madden and Trigg that are intended to remedy that failure, including introducing two levels of unemployment benefits - indigenous and in-migrant (Madden 1993).
- More attention was paid to the design, construction, application and sensitivity testing of the model, based on the principles of extended input-output analysis, at the metropolitan area level by developing a sub-regional input-output model. For this purpose the workforce was divided into three subgroups, namely employed, short-term unemployed and long-term unemployed or economically inactive workers. This enables the income received by workers from employment, welfare payments made to the short-term unemployment and those made to the long-term unemployed or economically inactive to be separately represented (Batey, Madden and Scholefield 1993).
- Madden (1993) introduced the government sector explicitly within the modelling framework as a (quasi-) economic sector with different rates of taxation on expenditure. He assumed three different categories of consumers reflecting the interrelationships of different income levels.

A simple extended Type IV input-output model, which has been formulated by Batey, Madden and Scholefield (1993), is given by:

$$
\begin{pmatrix}
I - A & -h_c^e & -h_c^a \\
-h^a & 1 & 0 \\
s \cdot l & 0 & 1
\end{pmatrix}
\begin{pmatrix}
x_1 \\
x_h \\
s \cdot u
\end{pmatrix}
=
\begin{pmatrix}
d_1 \\
d_h \\
s \cdot p
\end{pmatrix}
\tag{3.3}
$$

where;

x_1 is industrial gross output,

x_h is total income of employed workers,

h_c^e is the consumption propensity vector of employed workers,

h_c^u is the consumption propensity vector of unemployed workers,

h^a is the income coefficient vector of employer workers,

l is the vector of labour demand coefficients,

p is the total number of workers,

s is the welfare benefit payable to a single unemployed worker,

u is the number of unemployed workers.

The equations here are:

$$
(I - A)x_1 - h_c^e \cdot x_h - h_c^u \cdot s \cdot u = d_1
$$
$$
-h^a x_1 + x_h = d_h
$$
$$
l \cdot x_1 + u = p
$$

In a Type IV model employed and unemployed workers can be divided into subgroups with different propensities to consume, for migrants and indigenous workers, or those in receipt of welfare benefits. For simplicity they have been considered as a group. The model can be used to calculate income multipliers, production multipliers and employment multipliers representing the effects of explicitly modelled demographic-economic interaction (Madden and Batey 1983).

3.3 DYNAMIC EXTENDED INPUT-OUTPUT MODELS

This section begins by considering the dynamic extended model, which was first formulated by Madden and Batey (1983). Secondly, the assumptions that underlie such dynamic models are discussed, and finally three dynamic extended input-output models are presented.

Madden and Batey developed a (quasi-) dynamic extended input-output model in the following form:

$$(I - A - B)x_{it} + B x_{it-1} - h_c x_{ht} = d_t$$

where,

B is a matrix of capital coefficients, representing stocks of industries used per unit of output of industry,

t is a time subscript,

h_c is a vector of consumption propensities, and

x_h is the total household income.

Matrix B is introduced as part of the modelling system, but there is no discussion of it, apart from an outline of the problems in dealing with a dynamic model at the regional level such as: the lack of availability of data on capital stock measures, relationships of capacity to output, the definition of capacity, and so on. They also emphasise that changes in demographic variables will have to be obtained by estimation.

3.3.1 Assumptions of the Dynamic Extended Model

Despite the efforts to make static extended models more realistic a number of problems remain, some of which are best dealt with by dynamising the extended model.

First, in the static extended input-output model it is implicitly assumed that households consume all of their income, or it is assumed that households consume a proportion (average or marginal propensity to consume) of their income. The rest of what they earn is not modelled, in particular savings. An exception to this is the model developed by Stone and Weale (1986) who have described a model with saving and investment but these are considered as exogenous variables. In the model which is presented next, saving is modelled as an endogenous variable.

Second, households are assumed not only to buy ordinary goods but also durable goods, with much longer life.

Third, each industry is assumed to sell all of its products with nothing remaining. Clearly a producer needs to have raw materials and intermediate goods at least a few months before they would be used in the production process. Of course not all of an industry's production is being sold immediately, so some of the finished goods, intermediate goods and raw materials remain for the next period of the production process. If the stock of industries is assumed to be included in the capital formation, should the changes in stock be treated as endogenous or exogenous? If it is exogenous it should be seen as a part of final demand, although this depends on the output level which means it could be endogenous.

Fourth, in the static extended input-output model investment is exogenous, is a part of final demand and is regarded as capital formation. From an economic point of view investment is a function of the output, and so it could be introduced as an endogenous variable in the dynamic extended input-output model.

Two types of dynamic extended model will now be introduced, corresponding to two of the static models presented in Section 3.2. A number of assumptions are associated with these models. It is assumed that households do not spend their incomes completely, but save part of it in interest-bearing savings accounts or invest in industries by purchasing shares or bonds. So their income includes wages or salaries from employment and income from investment, both of which have been modelled. Income from employment is represented inside the transaction matrix and their investment income could be incorporated within the intersectoral capital coefficients matrix which forms part of the dynamic input-output model. This means that the transactions matrix and the capital coefficients matrix will need to have the same dimensions. Household capital formation has therefore been excluded from final demand and transferred into the intersectoral capital coefficient matrix. The first of the two dynamic extended models corresponds to the Type II static model:

$$\begin{pmatrix} I - A & -h_c \\ -h_r & 1 \end{pmatrix}\begin{pmatrix} x_1 \\ x_h \end{pmatrix} - \begin{pmatrix} B & h_d \\ 0 & r\,h_s \end{pmatrix}\begin{pmatrix} \Delta x_1 \\ \Delta x_h \end{pmatrix} = \begin{pmatrix} d_1 \\ d_h \end{pmatrix} \qquad (3.4)$$

where,

B is the inter-sectoral capital coefficients matrix in the conventional dynamic input-output model,

h_d is a column vector of savings output ratio (propensity to save) or $(1 - h_c)$,

rh_s is a row vector of profit to output ratios (profit from saving),

Δx_1 is a column vector of output growth,

Δx_h is a scalar of income growth,

d_1 is a column vector of final demand,

d_h is exogenous income received by workers.

The equations here are:

$$(I - A)x_1 - h_c x_h - B\Delta x_1 - h_d \Delta x_h = d_1$$
$$-h_r x_1 + x_h - r\,h_s \Delta x_h = d_h$$

The first of these equations is the usual Leontief formulation with

$h_c x_h$ household consumption,

$B\Delta x_1$ industrial investment, and

$h_d \Delta x_h$ household investment.

The second equation sets the income level,

$h_r \, x_1$ income from employment, and

$rh_s \, \Delta x_h$ income received by workers from investments.

More disaggregation can be provided in relation to household savings by distinguishing between indigenous household, in-migrant household and unemployment household savings. The second dynamic extended model, corresponding to the Type IV static model with two household groups, that is employment and unemployment groups, provides a suitable vehicle for incorporating these features:

$$\begin{pmatrix} I-A & -h_c^e & -h_c^u \\ -h^a & 1 & 0 \\ -sl & 0 & 1 \end{pmatrix}\begin{pmatrix} x_1 \\ x_h \\ su \end{pmatrix} - \begin{pmatrix} B & h_d^e & h_d^u \\ 0 & r\,h_s^e & 0 \\ 0 & 0 & r\,h_s^u \end{pmatrix}\begin{pmatrix} \Delta x_1 \\ \Delta x_h \\ \Delta s \cdot u \end{pmatrix} = \begin{pmatrix} d_1 \\ d_h \\ s \cdot p \end{pmatrix} \quad (3.5)$$

where

h_d^e is a column vector of savings output ratios for employed households,

h_d^u is a column vector of savings output ratios for unemployed households,

r is the interest rate or profit rate on household investment,

$\Delta s \cdot u$ in the short-term can be zero because the level of benefit is set by the policy makers but in the long-term could be different.

In this case the equations are:

$$(I-A)x_1 - h_c^e \cdot x_h - h_c^u \cdot s \cdot u - B\Delta x_1 - h_d^e \Delta x_h - h_d^u \Delta s \cdot u = d_1$$
$$-h^a x_1 + x_h - r\,h_s^e \Delta x_h = d_h$$
$$l \cdot x_1 + u = p$$

where

$h_c^e \, x_h$ is employed household consumption,

$h_c^u \cdot s \cdot u$ is unemployed household consumption,

$B\Delta x_1$ is investment by industries,

$h_d^e \Delta x_h$ is investment by employed households,

$h_d^u \Delta s \cdot u$ is investment by unemployed households,

$r\,h_s^e \Delta x_h$ investment income received by employed households.

Model (3.5) can be extended further by disaggregating employed households into income groups, and unemployed workers into short-term and long-term unemployed workers

3.4 CONCLUSIONS

Static extended input-output models are notably broader in scope than conventional input-output models, and typically include the study of household income and consumption and the interactions among a number of variables: income distribution, migration, labour force participation, employment and unemployment, and industrial output. Dynamic extended input-output models are also wider in scope than conventional dynamic input-output models, since they include the study of household saving, profit and industrial investment.

Dynamic extended input-output analysis has many benefits. One of its principal advantages lies apparently in relation to more realistic impact multipliers and forecasts. A wide variety of economic and demographic-economic multipliers may be derived. With regard to the dynamic extended model, it would be interesting to compare the multipliers with their equivalents derived from static model. Some evidence of how multipliers derived from a dynamic model compare with those from a static model is provided by Gowdy and Miller (1994). Unfortunately we do not yet have any experience of the new dynamic model, but in theory we know that when a new endogenous variable is incorporated in the model, the changes in multipliers are broadly predictable, although the precise magnitude of the changes will depend on the nature of the variable. In the new model, industrial investment has positive effects on the size of the multipliers but household saving represents the opposite of consumption and has negative effects. We can speculate about the relative size of multipliers, drawing upon earlier empirical work which compared static extended models. Batey and Weeks (1989), using an extended model of the Greater Cork region, observed the relationship between the size of employment obtained from Type I, Type II and Type IV models. We can expand the comparison to include the dynamic versions of the extended model, taking into account the nature of the changes that have been made, particularly in relation to the B matrix. The results of these intuitive approaches are shown in Figure 3.1.

Here it can be seen that the multipliers of the dynamic model for Types I, II and IV are larger than corresponding static models. It is predictable that although the differences between multipliers of dynamic extended Type I and Type II will be remarkable but between Types II and IV will be very small and, in the special case of a fixed policy on unemployment payments, no differences might be seen.

	Type I	Type II	Type IV
Static	smallest	largest	within limits set by Types I and II
Dynamic	second smallest	second largest	within limits set by Types I and II
Relative size of static and dynamic multipliers	dynamic > static	dynamic > static	dynamic > static

Figure 3.1   Static and dynamic multipliers compared

One the most useful applications of the input-output model is in forecasting and planning. The new models enable us to estimate the industrial investment and household saving resulting from the adoption of different economic policies in the short term and alternative economic development plans in the long term. These models also have potential applications at the national and regional levels of the economy, although data availability at regional level regarding the different types of goods (durable and non-durable) on industrial or sectoral household consumption may limit the scope for model building. However, the usual obstacles associated with dynamic Leontief analysis, that is singularity of the capital coefficients matrix, instability and causal determinism, remain to be investigated.

REFERENCES

Batey P.W.J. (1985), 'Input-output models for regional demographic-economic analysis: some structural comparisons', *Environment and Planning A*, **17**, pp. 73-99.

Batey P.W.J. (1990), 'Demographic-economic impact multipliers for Greater Manchester and Merseyside', Department of Civic Design, University of Liverpool, URPERRL, *Working Paper 8*.

Batey P.W.J. and M. Madden (1981), 'Demographic-economic forecasting within an activity-commodity framework: some theoretical considerations and empirical results', *Environment and Planning A*, **13** (9), pp. 1067-83.

Batey P.W.J. and M. Madden (1983), 'The modelling of demographic-economic change within the context of regional decline: analytical procedures and empirical results', *Socio-Economic Planning Sciences*, **17** (5), pp. 315-28.

Batey P.W.J. and A.Z. Rose (1990), 'Extended input-output models: progress and potential', *International Regional Science Review*, **13** (1&2), pp. 27-49.

Batey P.W.J. and M. Weeks (1989), 'The effect of household disaggregation in extended input-output models', in R.E. Miller, K.R. Polenske and A.Z. Rose (eds), *Frontiers of Input-Output Analysis*, New York: Oxford University Press.

Batey P.W.J., M. Madden and G. Scholefield (1993), 'Socio-economic impact assessment of large-scale projects using input-output analysis: a case study of an airport', *Regional Studies*, **27** (3), pp. 179-91.

Batey P.W.J., M. Madden and M. Weeks (1987), 'Household income and expenditure in extended input-output models: a comparative theoretical and empirical analysis', *Journal of Regional Science*, **27** (3), pp. 341-56.

Blackwell J. (1977), 'Disaggregation of the household sector in regional input-output analysis: some models specifying previous residence of worker', *Regional Studies* **12**, pp. 367-77.

Gowdy, J.M. and J.L. Miller (1994), 'Impact of capital formation on input-output multipliers', *Socio-Economic Planning Sciences*, **28** (4), pp. 211-17.

Leontief W. (1941), 'The structure of the American economy: 1919-1929', New York: Oxford University Press.

Madden M. (1993), 'Welfare payments and migration in a non-linear, extended input-output model with an application to Scotland', *Papers in Regional Science*, **72** (2), pp. 177-9.

Madden, M. and P.W.J. Batey (1980), 'Achieving consistency in demographic economic forecasting', *Papers of the Regional Science Association*, **44**, pp. 91-106.

Madden, M. and P.W.J. Batey (1983), 'Linked population and economic models: some methodological issues in forecasting, analysis and policy optimisation', *Journal of Regional Science*, **23** (1), pp. 141-64.

Madden M. and A.B. Trigg (1990), 'Interregional migration in an extended input-output model', *International Regional Science Review*, **13** (1&2), pp. 65-85.

Miernyk W.H., E.R. Bonner, J.H. Chapman and K. Shehammer (1967), *Impact of the Space Program on a Local Economy: An Input-Output Analysis*, Morgantown: West Virginia University Library.

Miller R.E. and P.D. Blair (1985), *Input-Output Analysis: Foundations and Extensions*, New Jersey: Prentice-Hall.

Miyazawa K. (1976), *Input-Output analysis and the Structure of Income Distribution*, Berlin: Springer Verlag.

Sadler P., B. Archer and C. Owen (1973), 'Regional income multipliers: the Anglesey study', *Bangor Occasional Papers in Economics* No. 1, University of Wales Press.

Schinnar A.P. (1976), 'A multi-dimensional accounting model for demographic and economic planning interaction', *Environment and Planning A*, **8**, pp. 455-75.

Stone J.R.N. and M.R. Weale (1986), 'Two populations and their economies', in P.W.J. Batey and M. Madden (eds), *Integrated Analysis of Regional Systems*, London Papers in Regional Science 15, London: Pion, pp. 74-89.

Stone R. (1981), 'The relationships of demographic accounts to national income and product accounts', in F.T. Juster and K.C. (eds), *Land Social Accounting Systems: Essay on the State of the Art*, New York: Academic Press, pp. 307-76.

Tiebout C.M. (posthumously) (1969), 'An empirical regional input-output projection model: the state of Washington, 1980', *Review of Economics and Statistics*, **51**, pp. 334-340.

Van Dijk J. and J. Oosterhaven (1986), 'Regional impacts of migrants' expenditures: an input-output vacancy chain approach', in P.W.J. Batey and M. Madden (eds), *Integrated Analysis of Regional Systems*, London Papers in Regional Science 15, London: Pion, pp. 122-47.

4. An Expanded Miyazawa Framework: Labour and Capital Income, Savings, Consumption and Investment Links

Michael Sonis and Geoffrey J.D. Hewings

4.1 INTRODUCTION

In two seminal publications of Miyazawa (1960, 1968), summarised in the Miyazawa book (1976), the author developed the generalisation of the Keynesian income multiplier in the form of matrix inter-relational income multiplier.

The matrix Miyazawa model has a form:

$$\begin{pmatrix} x \\ Y \end{pmatrix} = \begin{pmatrix} A & C \\ V & 0 \end{pmatrix} \begin{pmatrix} x \\ Y \end{pmatrix} + \begin{pmatrix} f \\ g \end{pmatrix} \tag{4.1}$$

Here A is a matrix of direct input coefficients; vector x is gross output, vector f is final demand, the vector Y represents the total income,[1] the matrix V represents the value-added ratios of households; vector g represents exogenous income; the matrix C represents consumption expenditures.

The following analysis holds (see Hewings et al. 1999): Miyazawa considers the following 2×2 block-matrix

$$M = \begin{pmatrix} A & C \\ V & 0 \end{pmatrix} \tag{4.2}$$

The Leontief inverse for the Miyazawa matrix (4.2) has a form:

$$B(M) = (I \quad M)^{-1}$$

$$= \begin{pmatrix} I & BC \\ 0 & I \end{pmatrix} \begin{pmatrix} I & 0 \\ 0 & K \end{pmatrix} \begin{pmatrix} B & 0 \\ VB & I \end{pmatrix} = \begin{pmatrix} B + BCKVB & BCK \\ KVB & K \end{pmatrix} \qquad (4.3)$$

$$= \begin{pmatrix} I & 0 \\ V & I \end{pmatrix} \begin{pmatrix} \Delta & 0 \\ 0 & I \end{pmatrix} \begin{pmatrix} I & C \\ 0 & I \end{pmatrix} = \begin{pmatrix} \Delta & \Delta C \\ VB & I + V\Delta C \end{pmatrix}$$

where $B = (I - A)^{-1}$ is the Leontief inter-industrial inverse matrix, $L = VBC$ is the matrix of inter-income group coefficients,

$$K = (I - L)^{-1} = (I - VBC)^{-1} = I + V\Delta C \qquad (4.4)$$

is the Miyazawa capital inter-relational income multiplier or generalised Keynesian multiplier,

$$\Delta = (I - A - CV)^{-1} = B + BCKVB \qquad (4.5)$$

is an enlarged Leontief inverse.

Also, the Miyazawa fundamental equations of income formation from capital hold:

$$\begin{cases} V\Delta = KVB \\ \Delta C = BCK \end{cases} \qquad (4.6)$$

In this chapter we extend the Miyazawa scheme of matrix inter-relational income multiplier by incorporating within it labour and capital income, savings, consumption and investments. Applications to the construction of Sraffa-Leontief-Miyazawa model and to the Pyatt-Round Social Accounting Model are considered in detail.

4.2 AN EXTENSION CONSIDERING WAGES, SAVINGS, CONSUMPTION AND INVESTMENT

The concept of extension presented in this chapter is stimulated by the matrix presentation of Sonis and Hewings (1988) of what may be referred to as an 'onion-skin' approach to demographic-economic impact analysis (see Stone 1981; Batey and Madden 1983; Batey 1985 and, especially, Batey and Weeks

1989, where the phrase 'onion skins' was introduced). Such an extension can be achieved by consideration of the block-matrices

$$V = \begin{pmatrix} W \\ S \end{pmatrix} \text{ and } C = \begin{pmatrix} \tilde{C} & \tilde{I} \end{pmatrix}$$

where the matrix W is a matrix of wages, the matrix S is a matrix of the savings coefficients, the matrix $\tilde{C}$ is a matrix of households consumption and the matrix $\tilde{I}$ is a matrix of investment coefficients.

In this case the Miyazawa block-matrix (4.2) takes the form of a 3 × 3 block-matrix:

$$M = \begin{pmatrix} A & \tilde{C} & \tilde{I} \\ W & 0 & 0 \\ S & 0 & 0 \end{pmatrix} \tag{4.7}$$

The formulae (4.3)-(4.6), thus, imply that the Miyazawa matrix of inter-income group coefficients multiplier takes the form:

$$L = \begin{pmatrix} W \\ S \end{pmatrix} B \begin{pmatrix} \tilde{C} & \tilde{I} \end{pmatrix} = \begin{pmatrix} WB\tilde{C} & WB\tilde{I} \\ SB\tilde{C} & SB\tilde{I} \end{pmatrix} \tag{4.8}$$

the Miyazawa inter-relational income multiplier or generalised Keynesian multiplier is (see Sonis and Hewings 2000a):

$$K = (I - L)^{-1} = \left(I - \begin{pmatrix} W \\ S \end{pmatrix} B \begin{pmatrix} \tilde{C} & \tilde{I} \end{pmatrix} \right)^{-1} \tag{4.9}$$

$$= I + \begin{pmatrix} W \\ S \end{pmatrix} \Delta \begin{pmatrix} \tilde{C} & \tilde{I} \end{pmatrix} = \begin{pmatrix} I + W\Delta\tilde{C} & W\Delta\tilde{I} \\ S\Delta\tilde{C} & S\Delta\tilde{I} \end{pmatrix}$$

and the enlarged Leontief inverse is:

$$\Delta = \left(I - A - \begin{pmatrix} \tilde{C} & \tilde{I} \end{pmatrix} \begin{pmatrix} W \\ S \end{pmatrix} \right) = (I - A - \tilde{C}W - \tilde{I}S)^{-1} \tag{4.10}$$

$$= B + B \begin{pmatrix} \tilde{C} & \tilde{I} \end{pmatrix} K \begin{pmatrix} W \\ S \end{pmatrix} B$$

Also the Miyazawa fundamental equations of income formation hold:

$$\begin{cases} \begin{pmatrix} W \\ S \end{pmatrix} \Delta = K \begin{pmatrix} W \\ S \end{pmatrix} B \\ \Delta \begin{pmatrix} \tilde{C} & \tilde{I} \end{pmatrix} = B \begin{pmatrix} \tilde{C} & \tilde{I} \end{pmatrix} K \end{cases} \tag{4.11}$$

4.3 AN EXTENSION LINKING CAPITAL AND LABOUR

Here we introduce the division of total income Y into income from employment and profits of capital with the help of a series of block-column and block-row vectors. The first block-column vector

$$Y = \begin{pmatrix} y_K \\ y_L \end{pmatrix}$$

represents the total income, the second,

$$V = \begin{pmatrix} V_K \\ V_L \end{pmatrix}$$

with the components V_K, V_L represents the income from capital profits and employment, the block-column vector

$$g = \begin{pmatrix} g_K \\ g_L \end{pmatrix}$$

represents the exogenous income from capital and labour, and the block-row vector $C = (C_K \quad C_L)$ represents consumption expenditures from income from employment and profits.

We obtain from Miyazawa scheme (4.1)-(4.2) the following model (Kimura et al. 2000):

$$\begin{pmatrix} x \\ y_K \\ y_L \end{pmatrix} = \begin{pmatrix} A & C_K & C_L \\ V_K & 0 & 0 \\ V_L & 0 & 0 \end{pmatrix} \begin{pmatrix} x \\ y_K \\ y_L \end{pmatrix} + \begin{pmatrix} f \\ g_K \\ g_L \end{pmatrix} \tag{4.12}$$

The model (4.12) includes two building blocks representing separately the income generation from capital and labour:

$$\begin{pmatrix} x \\ y_K \end{pmatrix} = \begin{pmatrix} A & C_K \\ V_K & 0 \end{pmatrix} \begin{pmatrix} x \\ y_K \end{pmatrix} + \begin{pmatrix} f \\ g_K \end{pmatrix} \tag{4.13}$$

$$\begin{pmatrix} x \\ y_L \end{pmatrix} = \begin{pmatrix} A & C_K \\ V_L & 0 \end{pmatrix} \begin{pmatrix} x \\ y_L \end{pmatrix} + \begin{pmatrix} f \\ g_L \end{pmatrix} \qquad (4.14)$$

These building blocks have the original Miyazawa form of income generation. Therefore, the following analysis holds (see Hewings et al. 1999).

Consider first the Miyazawa model (4.13) for income generation connected with capital. Miyazawa considers the following block matrix

$$M_K = \begin{pmatrix} A & C_K \\ V & 0 \end{pmatrix} \qquad (4.15)$$

The Leontief inverse for the Miyazawa matrix (4.15) has the form:

$$B(M_K) = (I - M_K)^{-1} =$$

$$= \begin{pmatrix} I & BC_K \\ 0 & I \end{pmatrix} \begin{pmatrix} I & 0 \\ 0 & K_K \end{pmatrix} \begin{pmatrix} B & 0 \\ V_K B & I \end{pmatrix} = \begin{pmatrix} B + BC_K K_K V_K B & BC_K K_K \\ K_K V_K B & K_K \end{pmatrix}$$

$$= \begin{pmatrix} I & 0 \\ V_K & I \end{pmatrix} \begin{pmatrix} \Delta_K & 0 \\ 0 & I \end{pmatrix} \begin{pmatrix} I & C_K \\ 0 & I \end{pmatrix} = \begin{pmatrix} \Delta_K & \Delta_K C_K \\ V_K B & I + V_K \Delta_K C_K \end{pmatrix} \qquad (4.16)$$

where $B = (I - A)^{-1}$ is the Leontief inter-industrial inverse matrix,

$$K_K = (I - V_K BC_K)^{-1} = I + V_K \Delta_K C_K \qquad (4.17)$$

is the Miyazawa capital inter-relational income multiplier or generalised Keynesian multiplier,

$$\Delta_K = (I - A - C_K V_K)^{-1} = B + BC_K K_K V_K B \qquad (4.18)$$

is an enlarged Leontief inverse.

Also the Miyazawa fundamental equations of income formation from capital hold:

$$\begin{cases} V_K \Delta_K = K_K V_K B \\ \Delta_K C_K = BC_K K_K \end{cases} \qquad (4.19)$$

Analogously, it is possible to obtain the similar results for the Miyazawa model (4.14) for income generation connected with labour, replacing the index K by the index L in formulae (4.16)-(4.19).

Returning to the Miyazawa model (4.12) we will present the results of analysis using the substitutions into (4.15)-(4.19) of block vector

$$V = \begin{pmatrix} V_K \\ V_L \end{pmatrix}$$

and $C = (C_K \quad C_L)$ instead of V_K, C_K (see Hewings et al. 1999): for the Miyazawa matrix

$$M = \begin{pmatrix} A & C_K & C_L \\ V_K & 0 & 0 \\ V_L & 0 & 0 \end{pmatrix} \tag{4.20}$$

the Leontief inverse

$$B(M) = (I - M)^{-1} =$$
$$= \begin{pmatrix} I & 0 & 0 \\ V_K & I & 0 \\ V_L & 0 & I \end{pmatrix} \begin{pmatrix} \Delta & 0 & 0 \\ 0 & I & 0 \\ 0 & 0 & I \end{pmatrix} \begin{pmatrix} I & C_K & C_L \\ 0 & I & 0 \\ 0 & 0 & I \end{pmatrix}$$
$$= \begin{pmatrix} \Delta & \Delta C_K & \Delta C_L \\ V_K \Delta & I + V_K \Delta C_K & V_K \Delta C_L \\ V_L \Delta & V_L \Delta C_K & I + V_L \Delta C_L \end{pmatrix} \tag{4.21}$$

where

$$\Delta = (I - A - CV)^{-1} = \left(I \quad A - (C_K \quad C_L) \begin{pmatrix} V_K \\ V_L \end{pmatrix} \right)^{-1}$$
$$= (I \quad A \quad C_K V_K \quad C_L V_L)^{-1} \tag{4.22}$$

is the enlarged Leontief inverse for the model (4.12), and

$$
K = (I - VBC)^{-1} = \left(I - \binom{V_K}{V_L} B \begin{pmatrix} C_K & C_L \end{pmatrix} \right)^{-1}
$$

$$
= \left(I - \begin{pmatrix} V_K BC_K & V_K BC_L \\ V_L BC_K & V_L BC_L \end{pmatrix} \right)^{-1} \tag{4.23}
$$

$$
= I + V\Delta C = \begin{pmatrix} I + V_K \Delta C_K & V_K \Delta C_L \\ V_L \Delta C_K & I + V_L \Delta C_L \end{pmatrix}
$$

is the Miyazawa labour-capital inter-relational income multiplier or generalised Keynesian multiplier for labour-capital.

The fine structure of the Miyazawa labour-capital inter-relational income multiplier K can be presented with the help of the interlaced inter-relational income multipliers

$$
\Delta_{KLK} = (I - V_K \Delta_L C_K)^{-1} = I + V_K \Delta_L C_K;
$$
$$
\Delta_{LKL} = (I - V_L \Delta K C_L)^{-1} = I + V_L \Delta_K C_L \tag{4.24}
$$

This fine structure of the Miyazawa labour-capital inter-relational income multiplier K has the following form:

$$
K = \begin{pmatrix} \Delta_{KLK} & K_K V_K BC_L \Delta_{LKL} \\ K_L V_L BC_K \Delta_{KLK} & \Delta_{LKL} \end{pmatrix} \tag{4.25}
$$

where the Miyazawa fundamental equations of income formation have the form:

$$
\Delta C_K = \Delta_L C_K \Delta_{KLK}; \quad V_K \Delta = \Delta_{KLK} C_K K_K;
$$
$$
\Delta C_L = \Delta_K C_L \Delta_{LKL}; \quad V_L \Delta = \Delta_{LKL} C_L K_L \tag{4.26}
$$

So the Leontief inverse (4.20) can be presented in the form:

$$
B(M) = \begin{pmatrix} \Delta & \Delta_L C_K \Delta_{KLK} & \Delta_K C_L \Delta_{LKL} \\ \Delta_{KLK} V_K \Delta_K & \Delta_{KLK} & K_K V_K BC_L \Delta_{LKL} \\ \Delta_{LKL} V_L \Delta_L & K_L V_L BC_K \Delta_{KLK} & \Delta_{LKL} \end{pmatrix} \tag{4.27}
$$

4.4 THE SRAFFA-LEONTIEF-MIYAZAWA INCOME DISTRIBUTION MODEL

The Sraffa-Leontief income distribution model can be presented in the following form (Sonis and Hewings 2000b):

$$px = (1+r)pAx + w^* p(I-A)x \qquad (4.28)$$

where x is a vector of gross output, p is a vector of prices, A is a matrix of direct input coefficients, f is a vector of final demand, r is a uniform rate of capital profits and w^* is a wage rate of labour. Sraffa found the linear trade of relation between the rate of profits r and the wage rate w^* (see Sraffa 1960, and also Pasinetti 1977):

$$r = (1-w^*)\frac{1-\mu}{\mu} \qquad (4.29)$$

where μ is the Perronean maximal simple eigenvalue ($0<\mu<1$) corresponding to the left hand p and right hand x eigenvectors of positive matrix A:

$$pA = \mu p; \quad Ax = \mu x \qquad (4.30)$$

Therefore, the capital income

$$V_K = rpA = r\mu p \qquad (4.31)$$

and the labour income

$$V_L = w^* p(I-A) = w^*(1-\mu)p \qquad (4.32)$$

generate the block-matrix of income

$$V = \begin{pmatrix} V_K \\ V_L \end{pmatrix} = \begin{pmatrix} r\mu p \\ w^*(1-\mu)p \end{pmatrix} = (1-\mu)\begin{pmatrix} 1-w^* \\ w^* \end{pmatrix}p \qquad (4.33)$$

Next let us introduce the block-matrix of consumption $C = (C_K \quad C_L)$ whose components are the capital and labour consumption. With such specifications of block-matrices V and C, the Miyazawa model (4.12) with a matrix (4.20) represents the Sraffa-Leontief-Miyazawa income generation model and formulae (4.21)-(4.27) represent its analysis.

4.5 THE INTERCONNECTION BETWEEN THE MIYAZAWA 3 × 3 BLOCK-MATRIX MODEL OF INCOME PROPAGATION AND THE PYATT-ROUND SOCIAL ACCOUNTING MODEL

It is possible to prove the following

Statement 1: The 3 × 3 block Pyatt-Round Social Accounting model SAM, (see details and references in Pyatt and Round 1985)

$$
\begin{pmatrix} y_1 \\ y_2 \\ y_3 \end{pmatrix} = \begin{pmatrix} A_{11} & 0 & A_{13} \\ A_{21} & 0 & 0 \\ 0 & A_{32} & A_{33} \end{pmatrix} \begin{pmatrix} y_1 \\ y_2 \\ y_3 \end{pmatrix} + \begin{pmatrix} x_1 \\ x_2 \\ x_3 \end{pmatrix}
\tag{4.34}
$$

is equivalent to a 3 × 3 block Miyazawa model

$$
\begin{pmatrix} y_1 \\ y_2 \\ y_3 \end{pmatrix} = \begin{pmatrix} A_{11} & 0 & A_{13} \\ A_{21} & 0 & 0 \\ B_3 A_{32} A_{21} & 0 & 0 \end{pmatrix} \begin{pmatrix} y_1 \\ y_2 \\ y_3 \end{pmatrix} + \begin{pmatrix} x_1 \\ x_2 \\ x_\beta \end{pmatrix}
\tag{4.35}
$$

where

$$
B_3 = (I - A_{33})^{-1}; \quad x_\beta = B_3 A_{32} x_2 + B_3 x_3
\tag{4.36}
$$

The structure of the Pyatt-Round accounting multiplier M_1 for the system (4.34) and the structure of the Miyazawa multiplier M_2 for the system (4.35) can be ascertained with the help of an analytical technique developed for $n \times n$ block Leontief multipliers in subsection 3 of Sonis and Hewings (1988):

$$
M_1 = \begin{pmatrix} I - A_{11} & 0 & -A_{13} \\ -A_{12} & I & 0 \\ 0 & -A_{32} & I - A_{33} \end{pmatrix}^{-1}
$$

$$
= \begin{pmatrix} B_{11} & B_{11} A_{13} B_3 A_{32} & B_{11} A_{13} B_3 \\ B_{22} A_{21} B_1 & B_{22} & B_{22} A_{21} B_1 A_{13} B_3 \\ B_3 A_{32} A_{21} B_{11} & B_3 A_{32} B_{22} & B_{33} \end{pmatrix}
\tag{4.37}
$$

$$M_2 = \begin{pmatrix} I - A_{11} & 0 & -A_{13} \\ -A_{21} & I & 0 \\ -B_3 A_{32} A_{21} & 0 & I \end{pmatrix}^{-1} = \begin{pmatrix} B_{11} & 0 & B_{11} A_{13} \\ B_{22} A_{21} B_1 & I & B_{22} A_{21} B_1 A_{13} B_3 \\ B_3 A_{32} A_{21} B_{11} & 0 & B_{33}^L \end{pmatrix} \quad (4.38)$$

where

$$\begin{aligned}
B_1 &= (I - A_{11})^{-1}; \\
B_{11} &= (I - A_{11} - A_{13} B_3 A_{32} A_{21})^{-1}; \\
B_{22} &= (I - A_{21} B_1 A_{13} B_3 A_{32})^{-1}; \\
B_{33}^L &= (I - B_3 A_{32} A_{21} B_1 A_{13})^{-1}; \\
B_{33} &= (I - A_{33} - A_{32} A_{21} B_1 A_{13})^{-1} = B_{33}^L B_3
\end{aligned} \quad (4.39)$$

Further, it is possible to compare the SAM with the original 2×2 Miyazawa system. First of all, we consider a statement, which is implicitly made in Pyatt (1998).

Statement 2: The 3×3 block SAM model (4.34) is equivalent to the pair of 2×2 block Miyazawa models (α), (β):

$$\begin{pmatrix} y_1 \\ y_2 \end{pmatrix} = \begin{pmatrix} A_{11} & A_{13} B_3 A_{32} \\ A_{21} & 0 \end{pmatrix} \begin{pmatrix} y_1 \\ y_2 \end{pmatrix} + \begin{pmatrix} x_\alpha \\ x_2 \end{pmatrix} \quad (\alpha)$$

where $x_\alpha = x_1 + A_{13} B_3 x_3$ and

$$\begin{pmatrix} y_1 \\ y_3 \end{pmatrix} = \begin{pmatrix} A_{11} & A_{13} \\ B_3 A_{32} A_{21} & 0 \end{pmatrix} \begin{pmatrix} y_1 \\ y_3 \end{pmatrix} + \begin{pmatrix} x_1 \\ x_\beta \end{pmatrix} \quad (\beta)$$

where $x_\beta = B_3 A_{32} x_2 + B_3 x_3$

The Miyazawa multipliers for the systems (α), (β) are:

$$M_\alpha = \begin{pmatrix} I - A_{11} & -A_{13} B_3 A_{32} \\ -A_{21} & I \end{pmatrix}^{-1} = \begin{pmatrix} B_{11} & B_{11} A_{13} B_3 A_{32} \\ B_{22} A_{21} B_1 & B_{22} \end{pmatrix} \quad (4.40)$$

$$M_\beta = \begin{pmatrix} I - A_{11} & -A_{13} \\ -B_3 A_{32} A_{21} & I \end{pmatrix}^{-1} = \begin{pmatrix} B_{11} & B_{11} A_{13} \\ B_3 A_{32} A_{21} B_1 & B_{33}^L \end{pmatrix} \quad (4.41)$$

The statement can be formulated:

Statement 3: The 3×3 block SAM model (4.34) is equivalent to the pair of 2×2 block models $(\gamma), (\delta)$:

$$\begin{pmatrix} y_1 \\ y_3 \end{pmatrix} = \begin{pmatrix} A_{11} & A_{13} \\ A_{32} A_{21} & A_{33} \end{pmatrix} \begin{pmatrix} y_1 \\ y_3 \end{pmatrix} + \begin{pmatrix} x_1 \\ x_\gamma \end{pmatrix} \quad (\gamma)$$

where $x_\gamma = A_{32} x_2 + x_3$ and

$$\begin{pmatrix} y_2 \\ y_3 \end{pmatrix} = \begin{pmatrix} 0 & A_{21} B_1 A_{13} \\ A_{32} & A_{33} \end{pmatrix} \begin{pmatrix} y_2 \\ y_3 \end{pmatrix} + \begin{pmatrix} x_\delta \\ x_3 \end{pmatrix} \quad (\delta)$$

where $x_\delta = A_{21} B_1 x_1 + x_2$

The Schur-Miyazawa multipliers for the systems $(\gamma), (\delta)$ are (compare subsection 2, Sonis and Hewings 1988):

$$M_\gamma = \begin{pmatrix} I - A_{11} & -A_{13} \\ -A_{32} A_{21} & I - A_{33} \end{pmatrix}^{-1} = \begin{pmatrix} B_{11} & B_{11} A_{13} B_3 \\ B_{33} A_{32} A_{21} B_1 & B_{33} \end{pmatrix} \quad (4.42)$$

$$M_\delta = \begin{pmatrix} I & -A_{21} B_1 A_{13} \\ -A_{32} & I - A_{33} \end{pmatrix}^{-1} = \begin{pmatrix} B_{22} & B_{22} A_{21} B_1 A_{13} B_3 \\ B_3 A_{32} B_{22} & B_{33} \end{pmatrix} (4.43)$$

Statements 1, 2 and 3 enable interpretations to be made that are compatible with conventional economic reasoning. Moreover, the important fact is that the exclusion of the first column and row from the Pyatt-Round accounting multiplier M_1 (see (4.37)) gives the Schur-Miyazawa multiplier M_δ; the exclusion of the second column and row gives the Schur-Miyazawa multiplier M_γ; and the exclusion of the third column and row gives the Miyazawa multiplier M_α.

Furthermore, the extensions of the SAM model by introducing the different assets (including human capital) that provide factor services and including different types of institutions lead to an $n \times n$ SAM model, whose accounting multiplier can be constructed by the analytical technique used for $n \times n$ Block Input-Output analysis in Sonis and Hewings (1988), see also Appendix.

4.6 EXPANSION TO INCLUDE LAYERS OF WAGES, PROFITS, SAVINGS, CONSUMPTION AND INVESTMENT BY LABOUR AND CAPITAL

Such an extension can be achieved by the consideration of following block-matrices:

$$V = \begin{pmatrix} W_L \\ S_L \\ P_K \\ S_K \end{pmatrix}; \quad C = \begin{pmatrix} C_L & I_L & C_K & I_K \end{pmatrix} \tag{4.44}$$

where W_L, S_L, C_L, I_L are the wages, savings, consumption and investments from labour, P_K, S_K, C_K, I_K are the profits, savings, consumption and investments from capital. So, the Miyazawa matrix has the form:

$$M = \begin{pmatrix} A & C_L & I_L & C_K & I_K \\ W_L & 0 & 0 & 0 & 0 \\ S_L & 0 & 0 & 0 & 0 \\ P_K & 0 & 0 & 0 & 0 \\ S_K & 0 & 0 & 0 & 0 \end{pmatrix} \tag{4.45}$$

The Miyazawa matrix of inter-income group coefficients multiplier has a form:

$$L = \begin{pmatrix} W_L \\ S_L \\ P_K \\ S_K \end{pmatrix} B \begin{pmatrix} C_L & I_L & C_K & I_K \end{pmatrix} = \begin{pmatrix} W_L BC_L & W_L BI_L & W_L BC_K & W_L BI_K \\ S_L BC_L & S_L BI_L & S_L BC_K & S_L BI_K \\ P_K BC_L & P_K BI_L & P_K BC_K & P_K BI_K \\ S_K BC_L & S_K BI_L & S_K BC_K & S_K BI_K \end{pmatrix}$$

$$\tag{4.46}$$

and the Miyazawa inter-relational income multiplier or generalized Keynesian multiplier is:

$$K = (I - L)^{-1} = I + \begin{pmatrix} W_L \\ S_L \\ P_K \\ S_K \end{pmatrix} \Delta (C_L \quad I_L \quad C_K \quad I_K)$$

(4.47)

$$= \begin{pmatrix} I + W_L \Delta C_L & W_L \Delta I_L & W_L \Delta C_K & W_L \Delta I_K \\ S_L \Delta C_L & I + S_L \Delta I_L & S_L \Delta C_K & S_L \Delta I_K \\ P_K \Delta C_L & P_K \Delta I_L & I + P_K \Delta C_K & P_K \Delta I_K \\ S_K \Delta C_L & S_K \Delta I_L & S_K \Delta C_K & I + S_K \Delta I_K \end{pmatrix}$$

with the enlarged Leontief inverse:

$$\Delta = \left(I - A - (C_L \quad I_L \quad C_K \quad I_K) \begin{pmatrix} W_L \\ S_L \\ P_K \\ S_K \end{pmatrix} \right)^{-1}$$

(4.48)

$$= (I - A - C_L W_L - I_L S_L - C_K P_K - I_K S_K)$$

Also the Miyazawa fundamental equations of income formation hold:

$$\begin{cases} \begin{pmatrix} W_L \\ S_L \\ P_K \\ S_K \end{pmatrix} \Delta = K \begin{pmatrix} W_L \\ S_L \\ P_K \\ S_K \end{pmatrix} \\ \\ \Delta (C_L \quad I_L \quad C_K \quad I_K) = B (C_L \quad I_L \quad C_K \quad I_K) \end{cases}$$

(4.49)

The components of formulae (4.45)-(4.49) represents the different layers of the income formation and expenditure and savings and investment in the extended Miyazawa model.

4.7 CONCLUSION

This paper explores the possibility of enlarging the original Miyazawa 2×2-block income generation scheme to the case of many layers of labour and capital income, savings, consumption and investments. This 'onion-skin' approach allows us to include the Miyazawa income generation and propagation mechanism in the Sraffa-Leontief model and to explain the conceptual and structural interconnection of Miyazawa's ideas with the ideas of the independently elaborated Pyatt-Round Social Accounting scheme.

REFERENCES

Batey, P.W.J. (1985), 'Input-output models for regional demographic-economic analysis: some structural comparisons', *Environment and Planning A*, **13**, pp. 73-9.

Batey, P.W.J. and M. Madden (1983), 'The modelling of demographic-economic change within the context of regional decline: analytical procedures and empirical results', *Socio-Economic Planning Sciences*, **17**, pp. 315-28.

Batey, P.W.J. and M.J. Weeks (1989), 'The effect of household disaggregation in extended input-output models', in R.E. Miller, K. Polenske and A.Z. Rose (eds), *Frontiers of Input-Output Analysis*, New York, Oxford: Oxford University Press, pp. 119-33.

Hewings, G.J.D., M. Sonis, M. Madden and Y. Kimura (eds) (1999), *Understanding and Interpreting Economic Structure: Essays in Honor of Ken'ichi Miyazawa*, Advances in Spatial Sciences, New York: Springer Verlag.

Kimura, Y., G.J.D. Hewings and M. Sonis (2000), 'Sraffa-Leontief-Miyazawa model' (unpublished manuscript).

Miyazawa, K. (1960), 'Foreign trade multiplier, input-output analysis and the consumption function', *Quarterly Journal of Economics*, **74**, pp. 53-64.

Miyazawa, K. (1968), 'Input-output analysis and interrelational multiplier as a matrix', *Hitotsubashi Journal of Economics*, **7**, pp. 39-58.

Miyazawa, K. (1976), *Input-Output Analysis and the Structure of Income Distribution*, New York: Springer Verlag.

Pasinetti, L.L. (1977), *Lectures on Theory of Production*, New York: Columbia University Press.

Pyatt, G. and J.I. Round (eds) (1985), *Social Accounting Matrices: a basis for planning*, Washington, DC: The World Bank.

Pyatt, G. (1998), 'Some early multiplier models of the relationship between income distribution and production structure', Paper presented at XII International Conference on Input/Output Techniques, New York, 18-22 May 1998.

Sonis, M. and G.J.D. Hewings (1988), 'Superposition and decomposition principles in hierarchical social accounting and input-output analyses', in F. Harrigan and P.G. McGregor (eds), *Recent Advances in Regional Economic Modeling*, London: Pion.

Sonis, M. and G.J.D. Hewings (2000a), 'LDU-factorization of the Leontief inverse, Miyazawa income multipliers for multiregional systems and extended multiregional Demo-Economic analysis', *The Annals of Regional Science*, (forthcoming).

Sonis, M. and G.J.D. Hewings (2000b), 'On the Sraffa-Leontief Model', Paper presented at XIII International Conference on Input/Output Techniques, Italy, Macerata, August 21-25, 2000.

Stone, R. (1981), 'The relationship of demographical accounts to national income and product accounts', in F.T. Juster and K.C. Land (eds), *Social Accounting Systems: Essays on the State of the Art*, New York: Academic Press.

Sraffa, P. (1960), *Production of Commodities by Means of Commodities*, Cambridge: Cambridge University Press.

NOTES

1. In Pyatt (1998), discussion is raised of the distinction between factor income (Miyazawa) and institutional income (social accounting models) in more extensive input-output/social accounting systems. It is not clear in the Miyazawa system what types of other income are included in g in equation (4.1), referred to as exogenous income. In all probability, it will be less inclusive than the institutional income found in the social accounting system.

PART TWO

Innovation and Knowledge Creation

Introduction to Part Two

Technology and knowledge are increasingly recognized as key endogenous factors in regional economic growth. In most advanced economies, public investment in innovation and technological development attempts to influence the rate and direction of technological change and in addition, sometimes tries to steer this growth into particular places. This part looks at the way in which innovative activity impacts on regional growth and examines the efficacy of the public policy instruments that have been used. A mixture of case-study and aggregate evidence is presented calling particularly on the experiences of regional growth in small, fast-growth economies such as Ireland and Israel.

Knowledge is the building-block for any regional change and in Chapter 5 Peter Maskell addresses the way in which it is produced and transmitted, arguing that spatial proximity is a key element in this process. He describes how firms organize in network-type organizational structures in order exploit the existence of increasing returns and reduced transaction costs and how proximity is an important (but insufficient) condition for network formation. For the emergence of clusters, however, spatial proximity would seem to be a crucial condition. This is because the key feature of the cluster is the accumulation of social capital off which it feeds. It is this repository of non-market interactions that gives a region a competitive edge. Further rounds of investment are attracted and a growth dynamic is set in motion grounded in increasing returns in which growth is 'locked-in' to one region and simultaneously 'locked-out' of others.

Public policy to promote innovation is examined in Chapter 6. Here, Stephen Roper compares national innovation systems in three countries and the extent to which public assistance translates into success across three indicators of innovation: patent registrations, product innovation and world market shares in electronic products. The findings indicate that while Israel's national innovation system seems to be producing results in patenting and market shares, in terms of product innovation the situation is rather different. Israeli firms introduce new products at a similar rate to UK and Irish firms in high technology sectors but in low technology sectors they trail far behind. This implies that the public benefits of national investment in innovation have not been fully realized. While public investment in innovation in Israel has attempted to 'jump-start' the growth process, this evidence may suggest that innovative capabilities sometimes run ahead of national capacity to absorb and commercialise the fruits of that innovation.

In Chapter 7, David Jacobson, Kevin Heanue and Ziene Mottiar further pursue the notion of targeted public policy, this time focussing on a traditional sector that has been the subject of much public activity. They present a case study of the Irish furniture industry. This study emphasises the way in which two networks have developed in this sector: one based on spatial proximity (the County Monaghan industrial district) and the other lacking any spatial basis (the Dublin-Wicklow-Cork network). These networks also reflect the different thrusts of industrial policy in Ireland. Public investment mediated through individual firms (grant aid, subsidised loans and so on) has indirectly given rise to a network grounded in spatial proximity. On the other hand, direct attempts at network formation have resulted in a non-spatial network where a common institutional environment substitutes for geographic contiguity.

Finally, the determinants of innovation are examined in Chapter 8, on the basis of a survey of a sample of high technology plants in Israel and Ireland. In this chapter, Daniel Shefer, Amnon Frenkel and Stephen Roper use a logit model to test the for the effects of location, plant attributes and technological capability on the probability of innovating. They find that while high technology plants in both countries are generally young and export-oriented, Israeli plants are generally smaller, more R&D-based and funded by local investment. They also find a significant effect for R&D investment on the likelihood of innovating. This suggests a role for R&D incentives in promoting innovation. However, coupling R&D policy with regional policy (for example increased R&D assistance to firms in peripheral regions) is likely to prove ineffective. This is because of the tendency for innovative activity to locate in select metropolitan agglomerations and the 'shadow effect' that is cast by these concentrations on all other regions.

5. Knowledge Creation and Diffusion in Geographic Clusters: Regional Development Implications

Peter Maskell

5.1 INTRODUCTION

This chapter looks at the role of regions in the knowledge-based economy. It does so by discussing how knowledge is created, dispersed and reassembled in different organisational structures: within networks of interdependent firms in different regions (and perhaps even in different countries), and within geographical clusters of firms in a single sub-national region. The main argument is that proximity might be helpful when transmitting certain kinds of knowledge between and among firms as it reduces the investments needed prior to the exchange.

The chapter is structured along the following lines. The next section focuses on the consequences of the dispersion of knowledge for further knowledge generation within firms. In Section 5.3, the building of networks among firms is considered as a means to reassemble useful knowledge residing in independent firms. Section 5.4 highlights the special case of knowledge creation and diffusion in geographical clusters with accumulated social capital. Finally, some crude policy recommendations are forwarded in Section 5.5 and conclusions presented in Section 5.6.

5.2 KNOWLEDGE CREATION IN FIRMS

Knowledge becomes distributed or dispersed as an unavoidable consequence of the way by which it is produced. Individuals have different perceptive powers, divergent insights and unlike attitudes. They face disparate problems in diverse circumstances of time and place. Consequently, they develop a variety of solutions as an intricate part of the ongoing process of learning-by-doing. The resulting variation in outcomes are important as a source of further learning, as Marshall once pointed out: 'The tendency to variation is the chief cause of progress' (Marshall (1890) 1920, p. 355).

Firms learn by employing knowledgeable individuals or by the learning conducted by individuals already employed (Simon 1991). The vision, routines and organisational structure of a firm form a common interpretative context which helps to ensure that what each employee learns is somehow connected to what the other employees might know or learn. However, what individuals learn when sharing a mutual experience is never exactly identical and initial differences multiply over time as knowledge is in itself an important source for further knowledge creation. The particular circumstances of place and time in which such knowledge is created and stored gives it a particular applicability in contrast to the general applicability of scientific knowledge. However, the enhanced knowledge creation stemming from the division of labour applies to both. Individuals and firms specialising in performing certain tasks are motivated to find solutions and notice peculiarities otherwise overlooked, giving rise to the suspicion that the process of innovation and learning is fuelled by the development of distinct bodies of knowledge developed in independent organisations pursuing objectives of competitiveness (Loasby 2000).[1] The boundaries of the firm thus impact directly on the (possible) level of learning in the economy.

Each body of knowledge that a firm possesses is linked to distinct technologies and associated with the performance of certain tasks that may require a particular set of criteria for decision-making and a specific style of management. An attempt to hold many bodies of knowledge within a single firm may therefore result in divergent objectives, conflicting norms, or deviating visions that hamper rather than facilitate the prospects of the firm. The co-existence of many bodies of knowledge within the same firm might also have negative effects on the firm's general learning abilities, as recently pointed out by Brian Loasby:

> There is no general purpose algorithm which can be applied to all fields of knowledge; each has its own connecting principles ... and the principles which give coherence to one body of knowledge often seem to impede rather than assist the comprehension of knowledge which is differently organised. (Loasby 2000, p. 6)

When knowledge creation and the use of new knowledge become increasingly important for maintaining and improving a firm's competitiveness, markets tend to favour specialised firms with a coherent body of knowledge. The market process thus leads to a dispersion of knowledge among individual firms. But in order to be useful for developing new tangible or intangible products or processes firms need to supplement the relevant parts of their own knowledge base with knowledge residing in other firms.[2]

Any dispersion of knowledge increases the cognitive distance that firms have to cover when becoming engaged in inter-firm product development projects. Inter-firm knowledge creation is thus subject to thresholds, before the knowledge bases of separate firms have grown sufficiently apart for interacting to imply learning, as well as ceilings, after which the cognitive distance becomes too great for firms to bridge, and where inter-firm learning will, consequentially, cease.

Firms build external relationships when struggling to obtain a profitable balance. Two distinct strategies can be identified. One consists of the deliberate building of dynamic networks of relations to possessors of valuable knowledge. The other is based on employing the norms and shared beliefs residing in a geographical cluster by becoming a part of that community.

5.3 NETWORK FORMATION

In order to overcome the common market failures for the exchange of knowledge between firms, open market relations must be supplemented with or superseded by stable and reciprocal exchange arrangements. Pure market interactions have generally proved incapable of transmitting the qualitative information needed. It takes time as well as considerable managerial effort to undertake the three stages needed to build relationships capable of transmitting complex knowledge.

In the first stage, the transfer of knowledge usually involves the employment of a very old-fashioned, pre-capitalist exchange mechanism: barter. Knowledge is here exchanged directly, without the use of money, between partners who both suspect that they might benefit from obtaining some knowledge that the other possesses. Such pair-wise exchange arrangements limit the firm's possible loss of competitive advantage when making knowledge available to others, though it does not completely eliminate the risk. Barter implies that each party needs to produce new knowledge in order to get access to new knowledge produced elsewhere. Though the use of this old mechanism is not uncommon for exchanging knowledge - for instance within and between academic research groups - it is often very costly and inefficient to use. It is costly in both money and search time because the seller will have to identify a potential buyer, who at the same time wants to exchange knowledge that might be useful; and it is inefficient as many potentially beneficial exchanges will not take place simply because buyers and sellers do not find each other.

In the second stage a more efficient arrangement has evolved as the partners in previous transactions save some or all of the search costs by keeping in contact with each other, thus initiating a 'dyadic', semi-stable relation. Former misunderstandings and suspicions are gradually eliminated, and the exchange can encompass a still wider range of subtle pieces of knowledge. By repetition of knowledge exchanges, both parties thus benefit from a decrease in cost and an increase in quality of the knowledge transmitted. Each new link created, each new experience with the partner's peculiar ways, and each adaptation and modification accomplished in order to facilitate future exchange represent the sinking of costs in building the routines and conventions that reduce the friction of interaction. Gradually, the cognitive distance is overcome so that knowledge can be exchanged with some portion still tacit. As the deepening of the relationship continues, the perceptions of both parties become intensified and the received tacit knowledge better understood. Both parties benefit from the somewhat idiosyncratic investment of learning to work together.

In the third stage, the dyadic partnerships interconnect in building network relations through which each participant might access knowledge bases still further afield while benefiting from the trust-enhancing investments made by the initial sinking of costs in one or a few relationships: 'your friend is my friend'. Any infringement of trust by firms in such closely knitted business networks is so severely penalised that in effect malfeasance becomes a non-option.[3] Cheaters are selected to make a convincing reparative gesture for any first-time misdeed however small. The collective awareness of this mechanism makes it possible to exchange knowledge even between competitors within a network, to an extent that no outsider can aspire to achieve.

When the majority believe that opportunism is penalised, firms act as if they trust each other. It is then possible to go further in the division of labour than if trust was absent. Network arrangements reduce inter-firm transaction costs, that is, search and information costs, bargaining and decision costs, and policing and enforcement costs (Dahlman 1979). Lower search and information costs improve the efficiency of resource allocation and help to overcome the adverse effects of the innate asymmetrical distribution of knowledge between the partners regarding the main characteristics of what is exchanged. Reduced costs for bargaining and decision making facilitate the coordination of diverse activities between firms and enable an even further division of labour (Richardson 1953, 1972). Diminishing costs of policing and enforcement free up resources to be used in ways that are more productive. What market relations are unable to accomplish, inter-firm networks can. Arrangements made stable by sunk costs provide mechanisms for anticipating how local adjustments might affect the whole and for disseminating ideas and visions that help to guide and coordinate the actions of the participants.

The explicit and tacit knowledge needed to uphold a continuous stream of innovations can thus be exchanged through networks of long-term inter-firm relations secured by relation-specific sunk costs under the assumption that any present imbalance in the exchange-related benefits will be equalised in the long run. In the quaint terminology of economic parlance, trust will thus characterise a relation between firms when each is confident that the other's present value of all foreseeable future exchanges exceeds the possible benefits of breaking the relation. The larger the cost sunk into building an inter-firm relationship, the greater the confidence and the trust.

The members of a network are often concentrated in space but some networks obtain returns to scale by including actors around the globe. The nuclear power plant industry benefits, for instance, from the continuous interaction among a highly specialised community of professionals. When the innovation rate increases such arm-length network relations rarely suffice. Physical distance easily occasions cognitive filters that hinder the transmitting of tacit knowledge crucial for interactive innovative activities. Hence, the emerging Israeli electronics industry and the huge, front edge Taiwanese information technology industry are, for instance, based on individuals with working experiences in the Valley and whose close personal networks are maintained through frequent face-to-face interaction, forming a strong cross-border industrial community of core personnel (Saxenian 1999; Hsu and Saxenian, forthcoming).

5.4 GEOGRAPHIC CLUSTERS

The tendency for related firms to agglomerate in certain locations and for areas to specialise in producing certain products or services has been noticed and commented on by many scholars, most noticeable by Alfred Marshall who specified how:

> an established centre of specialized skill ... is generally in a position to turn to account quickly any new departure affecting its work; and if the change comes gradually, there is no particular time at which strong incitement is offered to open up the industry elsewhere ... history shows that a strong centre of specialized

industry often attracts much new shrewd energy to supplement that of native origin, and is thus able to expand and maintain its lead. (Marshall, (1919) 1927, p. 287).

Three factors - all relating directly to the division of labour - are of particular significance for the development of 'specialised skill' in a geographical cluster. When firms hold uncertain and divergent beliefs about their chances of success if using one of several possible approaches when facing similar problems, they will display a variety in the solutions they choose. Firms in geographical clusters are by their co-location placed in a situation where the difference in solutions chosen is clear to be seen for anyone who cares to notice. Usually the firms in the cluster care intensively because it is by watching, discussing and comparing dissimilar solutions that they become engaged in the process of continuous improvements on which their survival depends. The variation between and among firms doing similar things in a geographical cluster promotes the generation of ideas and guides interpretations without imposing uniformity.

The second factor of particular importance for the survival and success of the firms in a geographical cluster is the role of social capital[4] when coordinating and reassembling dispersed knowledge needed for the production of new tangibles or intangibles. Knowledge can more easily be transferred and utilised within a community made up of firms who understand the language and share norms and codes. The mere location of firms in a geographical cluster represents an irreversible investment that provides them with an arsenal of instruments to obtain and understand the most subtle, elusive and complex information of possible relevance.

In a knowledge-based economy, the benefits of a geographical cluster of related firms spring from the need to access knowledge that cannot easily be acquired on the market.[5] The benefits of proximity are related to the time geography of individuals. As long as it includes at least some element of face-to-face contacts, interactive collaboration will be easier the shorter the distance between the participants. The benefits of proximity can thus be translated into a force of agglomeration in relation to firms engaged in interactive learning processes. When codified knowledge is globally disseminated faster than ever before, tacit and spatially more 'sticky' forms of knowledge are becoming increasingly important as a basis for sustained competitive advantage. The more tacit the knowledge involved, the more important is spatial proximity between the actors taking part in the exchange (Maskell and Malmberg 1999).

The third factor is perhaps the most important for the enhanced level of incremental innovations and improvements often found in geographical clusters. Because of the local variance and the ease of reassembling dispersed knowledge within the cluster, the division of labour can be deepened. The deepened division of labour within, compared to outside a geographical cluster, will in turn enhance the level of knowledge creation.

Beside the three characteristics influencing the geographical cluster's innovative performance, firms often compete while at the same time helping each other in overcoming technical problems by lending materials and swapping surplus capacity or by exchanging information. Location in clusters allows 'cognitive repertoires, including knowledge both of how to do things and of how to get things done by other people' (Loasby 2000, p. 12). Lawyers or written contracts are rarely used and the costs of using the internal market diminish to a point where a configuration of mostly smaller firms can become more efficient than a configuration with larger firms, burdened with the cost of internal control and measures against shirking (Alchian and Demsetz 1972).

Given that firms embedded in the right kind of milieu will tend to learn faster and become more competitive, one should expect a general drive towards agglomeration in such milieus when knowledge creation becomes increasingly important for firm competitiveness. The relatively few published empirical investigations (Krugman 1991; Enright 1993, 1998; Ellison and Glaeser 1994; Herrigel 1993; Brusco 1999) provide empirical support for the view that a strong geographical agglomeration characterises a broad spectrum of industries. Detailed analyses of the development in the locational pattern of manufacturing industry in the Nordic Countries through the last 20 years reveals that although manufacturing industry as a whole has been continually decentralising (Malmberg et al. 1996; Malmberg 1996) there is simultaneously a general process of geographical concentration taking place within almost all sectors of industry (Malmberg and Maskell 1997).

The 'transmission mechanism' (Nelson and Winter 1982) contains two self-reinforcing elements whereby even genuinely new firms reproduce and reinforce the agglomerative locational pattern. First, theory predicts and empirical investigations support[6] the notion that entrepreneurs within a given business sector will concentrate in areas where this sector is already strongly represented. Here, the potential entrepreneur has learnt the necessary trade-specific qualifications and gained the needed experience. In addition, during this period of learning he or she has established personal contacts and has become familiar with the local institutions, both of which are prerequisites for opening a new business.

Second, a geographical agglomeration of firms within a given business sector in a region will make the region especially suited to meet the specific location requirements of the firms within the sector. Even assuming that a new firm or an incumbent is completely free in its choice of location, the optimal location would usually be a region with a long track record of servicing firms in just that sector: only such a region has had the opportunity to develop the desired locational capabilities. The differences in capabilities between regions will (by definition) be revealed in discrepancies in the competitiveness of firms located there, with long-term consequences for their survival rate. This is also why many of the most talented individuals within the film industry tend to end up in Hollywood and many of the best ICT-specialists are drawn to Silicon Valley. In this sense the agglomeration gives rise to increasing returns (Young 1928) thus making it difficult - and often even impossible - for latecomers to catch up or out-compete a geographical cluster once established.

When geographical clusters disappear - and they sometimes do - the reason is mainly to be found internally, in the inability to adjust to changing circumstances in demand or technology. The inability is often linked to the existing formerly beneficial institutions because a geographical cluster sometimes produces results that are surprisingly successful even to those directly involved in the process. Such results tend to beget routines of extraordinary durability. Success creates internal bonds and firm-specific commitments that can make routines more durable than needed: they are retained and sometimes even aggressively defended long after changes in the external conditions of the geographical cluster have made them redundant (Demsetz 1988). It is difficult to *unlearn* successful habits of the past, also in cases where it is obvious to everyone concerned that they hinder future success (Imai et al. 1986).

In geographical clusters, as elsewhere in the economy, wanting to unlearn might go hand in hand with an increasing resistance towards new ideas, a growing bureaucratic inertia and a general organisational degeneration, especially when the firms are operating in generous markets (Eliasson 1996). Experienced success results in a flatter forgetting curve, and accepted best practices assume a life of their own (Hamel and Prahalad 1994). It is an established fact of life that it is a lot easier to challenge the orthodoxy of others compared with one's own, and firms - sometimes whole geographical clusters - are sometimes led by their former success into trajectory-specific lock-ins (David 1985; Arthur 1989).[7]

5.5 CLUSTER POLICIES

The so-called cluster policies, which recently have gained popularity in certain quarters, do not always take existing clusters as their point of departure but consider ways to emulate the economic success of Italian districts or other spatial agglomerations of highly specialised related activities. Theoretically such 'green-field' cluster policies are based on the linkage between proximity and enhanced learning. Empirically the regional and national interest in cluster policies is based on the recognition that the specific path of specialisation or the industry towards which the specialisation converges is of considerably less importance for economic performance than the specialisation itself:

> [E]ach country has developed a distinct model of specialization, concentrating its efforts in particular fields where world class capacities have often been developed ... There seems to be a specific advantage in a higher degree of specialization in technological fields, associated with the economics of scale and scope made possible at the national level. This advantage emerges regardless of the particular sector in which individual countries concentrate their efforts; in other words, for advanced countries being specialised appears to be even more important than choosing the 'right' field. (Archibugi and Pianta 1992, pp. 148 and 150)

However, these findings only hold in a market economy where the pattern of sustained specialisation is the outcome of a stream of investment decisions made by rent-seeking firms usually over a considerable number of years. If during the process it turned out that the path taken gave steadily decreasing returns firms would rethink their strategies or die. The outcome of such adaptation and selection processes taking place on the market would be a change in the avenue of specialisation guided by what the firms perceive as better investment opportunities.

For the indigenous clusters the initial impetus to what later becomes a highly competitive pattern of territorial market-led specialisation might be a deliberate decision by an investor or entrepreneur or certain basically arbitrary factors might have played the major role. However, while success or failure can easily be determined *ex post*, even the most sagacious find it extremely difficult to assess *ex ante* the possible long-term results of being the first to do something. The typical long response time when specifying and adjusting public policies and the reluctance to implement unpopular decisions swiftly when justified by events make public authorities and agencies less suited for picking and developing future clusters with any chance of commercial success. Even more important are the absence of incentives available to rent-seeking firms and the lack of perceptiveness to crucial information transmitted through marked relations which ensure a discouraging trade-off between money spent and results obtained of public 'green-field' cluster policies.

In a similar vein the OECD has recently summarised the evaluations and assessments of the outcome of a large and diverse set of cluster policies applied in a number of different countries:

- 'The creation of clusters should not be government-driven but rather should result from market-induced and market-led initiatives.
- Government policy should not be strongly oriented to directly subsidising industries and firms or to limiting rivalry in the marketplace.
- Government policy should shift away from direct intervention towards indirect inducement. Public interference in the marketplace only can be justified in the presence of a clear market or systemic failure. Even if clear market and systemic imperfections exist, it cannot necessarily be concluded that government intervention will improve the situation.
- Government should not try to take the direct lead or ownership in cluster initiatives, but should work as a catalyst and broker, bringing actors together and supplying support structures and incentives to facilitate the clustering and innovation process.
- Cluster policy should not ignore small and emerging clusters; nor should it focus only on 'classic', existing clusters.
- Clusters should not be created from 'scratch'. The cluster notion has sometimes been appropriated by (industrial) policy makers and used as an excuse to continue more or less traditional ways of defensive industrial policy making.' (OECD 1999, pp. 420-21)

The likelihood of success is, the OECD argues, perhaps larger if a nucleus of valuable capabilities is already in place, and where the public sector might sometimes help in improving the 'receiving system' when helping firms identify and utilise international technological innovations and other scarce information faster than would otherwise be the case. Deficiencies in the receiving system can be surprisingly stable and long-lasting, making firms in a newly formed cluster unable to take full advantage of improvements otherwise available.

5.6 CONCLUSIONS'

The overriding theme in this chapter is associated with learning; that is with improving the innovative capacity of firms in research intensive as well as research extensive sectors. The way in which learning takes place and the means applied might differ across space but the general recommendations offered to managers and policy makers will to a large extend be identical when emphasising the need to conceive strategies and policies that enhance learning.

However, if managers with a long established feel of the market, with all the signals of the market available to them, and with unrestricted access to the firm's market and technological knowledge base, still sometime fail to make the right decisions regarding what *specific* learning trajectory to follow, what are then the chances that regional or national policy makers, with generally substantially lesser information and a blunter sensory apparatus, can do it better?

The conclusion is that when the process of globalisation push national economies into a world of learning and innovation regional policy makers must take a step back from direct interfering with markets and firms and confine themselves to the equally important task of securing the institutional framework for market exchange that favours knowledge exchange.

The final conclusion regarding the preconditions for regional development policies aiming at economic development is therefore simple but clear:

- Good regional policy is *context-specific*, taking into account the peculiarities of the regions economic structure and non-market institutions.
- Good regional policy is *market-led*, supporting activities already selected by the market.
- Good regional policy respond to the process of globalisation by *focusing on learning*, concentrating their efforts on helping firms bridging the cognitive distance to valuable knowledge bases outside their present reach, and helping accumulating and protecting social capital needed for inter-firm co-operation and exchange of partly tacit knowledge.

ACKNOWLEDGEMENT

This chapter is part of the output from a project on Competitiveness, Localized Learning and Regional Development Policies, generously supported by The Nordic Centre for Spatial Development (NORDREGIO), Stockholm, Sweden. I am grateful to the other members of the project: Anders Malmberg, Mark Lorenzen and Staffan Larsson and to the editors of this volume for comments on an earlier version.

REFERENCES

Afuah, A. (2000), 'How much do your competitors' capabilities matter in the face of technological change?', *Strategic Management Journal*, **21** (3), pp. 387-404.

Alchian, A.A. and H. Demsetz (1972), 'Production, information costs, and economic organisation', *American Economic Review*, **62**, pp. 777-95.

Ahuja, G. (2000), 'The duality of collaboration: inducements and opportunities in the formation of interfirm linkages', *Strategic Management Journal*, **21** (3), pp. 317-43.

Archibugi, D. and M. Pianta (1992), *The Technological Specialization of Advanced Countries*, Dordrecht: Kluwer.

Arthur, W.B. (1989), 'Competing technologies, increasing returns, and lock-ins by historical events', *Economic Journal*, **99**, pp. 116-31.

Bellandi, M. (1996), 'Innovation and change in the Marshallian industrial district', *European Planning Studies*, **4** (3), pp. 357-68.

Bourdieu, P. (1980), 'Le capital social: notes provisoires', *Actes de la Recherche en Sciences Sociales*, **31** (Janvier), pp. 2-3.

Brusco, S. (1999), 'The rules of the game in industrial districts', in A. Grandori (ed.), *Interfirm Networks. Organization and Industrial Competitiveness*, London & New York: Routledge, pp. 17-40.

Burt, R.S. (1992), *Structural Holes. The Social Structure of Competition*, Cambridge, Mass.: Harvard University Press.

Coleman, J.S. (1988), 'Social capital in the creation of human capital', *American Journal of Sociology*, **94** (Supplement), pp. S95-S120.

Dahlman, C.J. (1979), 'The problem of externality', *Journal of Law and Economics*, **22** (1), pp. 141-62.

David, P.A. (1985), 'Clio and the economics of QWERTY', *American Economic Review*, **75**, pp. 332-7.

Demsetz, H. (1988), 'The theory of the firm revisited', *Journal of Law, Economics and Organization*, **4** (1), pp. 141-61.

Doz, Y.L., P.M. Olk and P.S. Ring (2000), 'Formation processes of R&D consortia: which path to take? Where does it lead?', *Strategic Management Journal*, **21** (3), pp. 239-66.

Eliasson, G. (1996), *Firm Objectives, Controls and Organization. The Use of Information and the Transfer of Knowledge within the Firm*, Dordrecht: Kluwer Academic Publishers.

Ellison, G. and E.L. Glaeser (1994), Geographical Concentration in the US Manufacturing Industries. A Dartboard Approach, Working Paper no. 4840, Cambridge, Mass: National Bureau of Economic Research (NBER).

Enright, M.J. (1993), 'The determinants of geographic concentration in industry', Working Paper no. 952, Boston Harvard Business School.

Enright, M.J. (1998), 'Regional Clusters and Firm Strategy', in A.D. Chandler, P. Hagström and Ö. Sölvell (eds), *The Dynamic Firm*, Oxford: Oxford University Press, pp. 315-342.

Freeman, C. (1982), *The Economics of Industrial Innovation*, London: Pinter Publishers.

Freeman, C. (1991), 'Networks of innovators: a synthesis of research issues', *Research Policy*, **20** (5), pp. 499-514.

Fukuyama, F. (1995), *Trust. The social virtue and the creation of prosperity*, London: Hamish Hamilton.

Glaeser, E.L., C.L. Laibson, J.A. Scheinkman and C.L. Soutter (1999), 'What is social capital? The determinants of trust and trustworthiness', Working paper no. 7216, Cambridge, Mass.: NBER.

Hagedoorn, J. and J. Schakenraad (1992), 'Leading companies and networks of strategic alliances in information technologies', *Research Policy*, **21**, pp. 163-81.

Håkansson, H. (1989), *Corporate Technological Behaviour: Co-operation and Networks*, London: Routledge.

Hamel, G. and C.K. Prahalad (1994), *Competing for the Future*, Boston: Harvard Business School Press.

Hatzichronoglou, T. (1996), 'Globalisation and competitiveness: relevant indicators', Working Papers no. 16 (IV), Paris: The Organisation for Economic Co-Operation and Development (OECD), Directorate for Science, Technology and Industry.

Herrigel, G. (1993), 'Power and the redefinition of industrial districts - the case of Baden-Württemberg', in G. Grabher (ed.), *The Embedded Firm - on the Socioeconomics of Industrial Networks*, London: Routledge, pp. 227-51.

Hsu, J.-Y. and A. Saxenian (forthcoming), 'The limits of Guanxi capitalism: transnational collaboration between Taiwan and the US', *Environment and Planning A*.

Imai, K., N. Ikujiro and T. Hirotaka (1986), 'Managing the new product development process: Companies learn and unlearn', in K.B. Clark, R.H. Hayes and C. Lorenz (eds), *The Uneasy Alliance. Managing the Productivity-Technology Dilemma*, Boston: Harvard Business School Press.

Johnson, B. (1992), 'Institutional learning', in B.-Å. Lundvall (ed.), *National Systems of Innovation*, London: Pinter.

Kale, P., H. Singh and H. Perlmutter (2000), 'Learning and protection of propretary assets in strategic alliencies: building relational capital', *Strategic Management Journal*, **21** (3), pp. 217-37.

Kline, S.J. and N. Rosenberg (1986), 'An overview of innovation', in R. Landau and N. Rosenberg (eds), *The Positive Sum Game*, Washington D.C.: National Academy Press.

Kogut, B. (2000), 'The network as knowledge: generative rules and the emergence of structure', *Strategic Management Journal*, **21** (3), pp. 405-25.

Krugman, P.R. (1991), 'Increasing returns and economic geography', *Journal of Political Economy*, **99** (3), pp. 483-99.

Loasby, B.J. (2000), 'Organisations as interpretative systems', Paper presented at the DRUID summer conference (www.business.auc.dk/druid).

Lundvall, B.-Å. and P. Maskell (2000), 'Nation states and economic development - From national systems of production to national systems of knowledge creation and learning', in G.L. Clark, M.P. Feldmann and M.S. Gertler (eds), *Handbook of Economic Geography*, Oxford: Oxford University Press, pp. 353-72.

Malmberg, A. (1996), 'Industrial geography. Agglomerations and local milieu', *Progress in Human Geography*, **20** (3), pp. 392-403.

Malmberg, A., Ö. Sölvell and I. Zander (1996), 'Spatial clustering, local accumulation of knowledge and firm competitiveness', *Geografiska Annaler*, **78B**, pp. 85-97.

Malmberg, A. and P. Maskell (1997), 'Towards an explanation of industry agglomeration and regional specialization', *European Planning Studies*, **5** (1), pp. 25-41.

Markusen, A., P. Hall and A.K. Glasmeier (1986), *High Tech America*, Boston: Allen and Unwin.

Marshall, A. (1890/1920), *Principles of Economics*, London: MacMillan, 8th edition printed 1920.

Marshall, A. (1919/1927), *Industry and Trade. A Study of Industrial Technique and Business Organization, and of their Influences on the Condition of Various Classes and Nations*, London. Reprinted 1927.

Maskell, P. (1992/1994), *Nyetableringer i industrien og industristrukturens udvikling (New Firm Formation and the Industrial Restructuring)*, Copenhagen: Copenhagen Business School Press. Reprinted 1994 and published by Nyt Nordisk Forlag/Arnold Busk.

Maskell, P. (2000), 'Social capital and competitiveness', in J. Field, T. Schuller and S. Baron (eds), *Social Capital Collection*, Oxford: Oxford University Press, pp. 111-23.

Maskell, P., H. Eskelinen, I. Hannibalsson, A. Malmberg and E. Vatne (1998), *Competitiveness, Localised Learning and Regional Development. Specialisation and Prosperity in Small Open Economies*, London: Routledge.

Maskell, P. and A. Malmberg (1999), 'Localised learning and industrial competitiveness', *Cambridge Journal of Economics*, **23** (2), pp. 167-86.

Nelson, R.R. and S.G. Winter (1982), *An Evolutionary Theory of Economic Change*, Cambridge Mass.: The Belknap Press of Harvard University Press.

OECD (1992), *Industrial Policy in the OECD countries*, Annual Review, Paris: The Organisation for Economic Co-Operation and Development.

OECD (1999), *Boosting Innovation: The Cluster Approach*, OECD Proceedings, Paris: The Organisation for Economic Co-Operation and Development.

Putnam, R.D. (1993), *Making Democracy Work. Civic Traditions in Modern Italy*, Princeton, New Jersey: Princeton University Press.

Putnam, R.D. (1995), 'Tuning in, tuning out: the strange disappearance of social capital in America, *PS: Political Science and Politics*, **28** (4), pp. 664-83.

Richardson, G.B. (1953), 'Imperfect knowledge and economic efficiency, *Oxford Economic Papers*, **5** (2), pp. 136-56.

Richardson, G.B. (1972), 'The organisation of industry', *Economic Journal*, **82**, pp. 883-96.

Rosenberg, N. (1972), *Technology and American Economic Growth*, White Plains, N.Y.: Sharpe.

Saxenian, A. (1999), *Silicon Valley's New Immigrant Entrepreneurs*, San Francisco, CA: Public Policy Institute of California.

Simon, H.A. (1991), 'Bounded rationality and organizational learning', *Organization Science*, **2**, pp. 125-34.

Woolcock, M. (1998), 'Social capital and economic development: toward a theoretical synthesis and policy framework', *Theory and Society*, **27**, pp. 151-208.

Young, A. (1928), 'Increasing returns and economic progress', *Economic Journal*, **38**, pp. 527-42.

NOTES

1. Competitiveness means 'the ability of companies, industries, regions, nations or supernational areas to generate, while being and remaining exposed to international competition, relatively high factor income and factor employment levels on a sustainable basis' (Hatzichronoglou 1996).

2. The belief that innovation is usually an interactive process emanate from recent innovation studies, but has been around for quite some time. See for instance: Freeman (1982, 1991); Rosenberg (1972); Håkansson (1989); Kline and Rosenberg (1986); Hagedoorn and Schakenraad (1992); OECD (1992); while Kale et al. (2000), Doz et al. (2000), Ahuja (2000), Afuah (2000) and Kogut (2000) add new empirical evidence and new insight on the coordination mechanisms at play within a knowledge creating and sharing network of firms. Theories on national and regional innovation systems use the interactive nature of innovations as its basic building block (Lundvall and Maskell 2000).

3. Following Glaeser et al. (1999) trust might be defined as the commitment of resources to an activity where the outcome depends upon the cooperative behaviour of others. Without trusting that the business partner will eventually pay for valuable knowledge transferred, no knowledge will be forthcoming and the innovative capability of both partners will be hampered. Trust is thus an excellent mechanism to overcome intricate market failures (Maskell et al. 1998).

4. The term 'Social capital' has been forwarded by a diverse group of current scholars (Bourdieu 1980; Coleman 1988; Burt 1992; Putnam 1993, 1995; Fukuyama 1995; Woolcock 1998; Maskell 2000) when referring to the values and beliefs that citizens share in their everyday dealings and which give meaning and provide design for all sorts of rules.

5. The tendency to emphasise the learning aspect of clustering - rather than cost-minimisation - is also reflected in the most recent works on the Italian industrial districts (Bellandi 1996) and on American high-technology industries (Markusen et al. 1986).

6. The phenomenon can be illustrated with data on new firm formation in Denmark (Maskell 1994). Consider a matrix, where all the 208 sectors in manufacturing industry are placed on one axis and the twelve Danish counties on the other. Though the majority of the cells of the matrix were empty, 87 percent of the new firms established between 1972-92 were found in 'occupied cells', for example in the same sector and region as at least one incumbent firm.

7. Imai et al. (1986) attribute an important part of Japan's economic success to the ability to unlearn former organisational or institutional rigidities through the acceptance of managerial declarations of a state of emergency or crisis, which make radical changes easier to swallow. Johnson (1992) makes a distinction between 'just forgetting' and 'creative forgetting' thus emphasising the role of unlearning as part of the knowledge-creating process.

6. Innovation Policy in Israel, Ireland and the UK: Evolution and Success

Stephen Roper

6.1 INTRODUCTION

Advances in endogenous growth theory have highlighted the central role of innovation to promoting economic growth. This appreciation of the importance of innovation has been matched in Israel, Ireland and the UK by a long-standing belief that the level of innovative activity is too low.[1] Although it is argued that high quality basic or scientific research is being conducted in each country, there are thought to be weaknesses in the capability or willingness of industry to exploit this research. This has induced governments in each of the three countries to introduce policy initiatives to increase firms' innovation capacity and to raise the level of innovative activity. The success of these measures can, however, only be understood in the context of their specific environments, that is in the context of the National System of Innovation (NSI), and the wider economic, cultural and historical conditions, in which they have developed (Metcalfe 1997). In Section 6.2 we therefore give an overview of the development of the NSI in the UK, Israel and Ireland focusing on the extent of public commitment to scientific and technological development and the relationship between technology and industrial policy. Section 6.3 then reviews the evidence on firms' innovation capability in the three countries using data on patent applications and product innovations. Section 6.4 summarises the main characteristics of innovation policy in each country and highlights the key policy lessons.

6.2 DEVELOPMENT OF NATIONAL SYSTEMS OF INNOVATION

The structures of the NSIs of Israel, Ireland and the UK have their roots in the very different historical, cultural and industrial traditions of the three countries (Metcalfe 1997).[2] Perhaps the most striking distinction of the post-war period, however, is the contrast in governments' commitment to the development of the NSI between Israel on the one hand and the UK and Ireland on the other (Teubal 1993; Walker 1993; Yearly 1995). In Israel, the long-standing belief that science provides the basis for a strong nation in both economic and military terms has been reflected in a consistent development of the nation's institutional and technological infrastructure.[3] By contrast in the UK, apart from a short spell in the 1960s, the development of the NSI has been a consistently low policy priority. Writing in 1993, for example, Walker notes:

> The first thing to emphasise about Britain's contemporary innovation system is that its development, whether by the industry or the state has become a relatively low priority. This may be the natural economic behaviour of a country that now has relatively low income levels and needs to catch up with international best practice, and whose manufacturing companies no longer match the scale or sophistication of their main foreign rivals. But it is also a consequence of the greater dynamism in Britain of services and other activities, and of a prevailing economic culture, even ideology, which has come to place quick gains before the patient long-term development of industrial capabilities. (p.160)

Similar sentiments are found elsewhere. Williams (1988) summarises the situation by saying:

> The university, industrial and governmental sectors were going their separate ways to an inevitable perdition. University research was little influenced by the country's R&D needs, only a few companies were enlightened enough to provide themselves with a comprehensive R&D capability, and government when it was not lavishing its resources on defence was often embarking on costly civil R&D of doubtful commercial promise, as in the case of Concorde and the Advanced Gas Cooled Reactor. (Williams, 1988, p. 139)

In Ireland too, albeit for different reasons, little priority was given to the integration of scientific and technological research and industrial development until the 1980s. Yearly (1995) argues that, historically, this failure to integrate technology and industrial policy stems back to the pre-partition period when science was '*primarily practised as a form of high culture*' (p. 173). Following Irish partition in 1921, and the creation of the modern Irish state, this tendency was, if anything, exacerbated by the desire to distance the country from the British legacy and a concentration of public and academic resources on cultural and linguistic rather than scientific development (Lee 1989).

One consequence of this lack of applied scientific research in Ireland was a relatively low level of innovative activity among indigenous Irish companies which persisted into the 1970s. Although this was masked to some extent by significant flows of inward investment, particularly from the US (for example O'Riain 1997), it contributed to the development of a dual economy in Ireland: a technologically advanced externally-owned sector based largely on R&D conducted elsewhere and a technologically weaker indigenously-owned sector (Wrynn 1997). As a result, neither the externally-owned sector nor the weaker indigenously-owned manufacturing sector demanded or contributed much to the development of the Irish NSI (OECD 1974). This situation persisted until the mid-1980s when difficult macro-economic conditions highlighted the lack of competitiveness of much indigenously-owned industry in Ireland and the vulnerability of the Irish economy to external circumstances. A re-orientation of Irish industrial policy towards a more balanced strategy followed, involving the development of the export capacity of indigenous industry alongside continued attempts to attract high-technology inward investment (National Board for Science and Technology 1983). Implicit in the policy shift was the recognition, perhaps for the first time, that the international competitiveness of indigenous Irish industry depended on its technological development, a move strongly supported by the EU through both the Structural Funds and the Framework programmes (see, for example, STIAC 1995, vol. 3, pp. A42-43).

Ireland's technological dependency is not, however, limited to technology policy. Large scale inward investment since the late 1950s has meant that 44.1 percent of manufacturing employment, 68.4 percent of net output and 87.7 percent of manufacturing exports are now accounted for by foreign-owned enterprises (Ruane and Gorg 1997). Moreover, only two Irish-owned firms appear in the list of Ireland's top 20 electronics companies (Roper and Frenkel 2000, Table 5), and only 2 percent of patent applications made in Ireland are now made by Irish residents.[4]

Ireland's willingness to accept this degree of external control, and the implied degree of technological and strategic dependency, contrasts sharply with Israel's efforts to achieve economic and military independence. During the 1950s and 1960s, in particular, Israel maintained a strong protectionist stance as it sought to develop its physical, industrial and institutional infrastructure (Plessner 1994). At the same time the Israeli government - dominated for most of this period by the interventionist Labour party - adopted a strong strategic role in both the military and economic spheres.[5] In military terms, expansion during the 1960s was based largely on the licensed production of some weapon systems based on partnerships between foreign firms and Israeli public sector organisations.[6] This collaboration came to an abrupt end, however, with the French embargo on defence sales to Israel following the Six Day War of 1967, stimulating a massive expansion in the indigenous Israeli defence industry. The growth of the Israeli military complex did not take place in isolation, however, with both production and managerial techniques and military technologies quickly transferred to the civil sector.[7]

Alongside its lead role in the development of the military complex, the Israeli government also adopted a strong strategic role in the development of the nation's civilian industrial, scientific and technological infrastructure. Towards the end of the 1960s in particular, development policy shifted away from the promotion of basic industries towards more export-oriented, capital-intensive and eventually high-technology sectors. The main form of assistance for Israeli private sector companies over this period was capital grants which had been available since the 1950s (Lavy 1994). As early as the 1960s, however, the Israeli government - through the Ministry of Industry and Trade - also supported the development of Science Parks at the universities (for example the Kiryat Weizmann Science Park in 1967; Felsenstein 1994). Also during the 1960s, the Israeli government began to give R&D grants to individual firms, a development that Teubal (1993) suggests might be the first instance of this type of policy intervention.[8] During the 1970s, Israel became more open to trade and foreign investment. A Free Trade Agreement was negotiated with the EU in 1975 and bi-national R&D funds were established with the US (that is BIRD) and Germany (that is the German-Israel Foundation or GIF). Relatively unsuccessful attempts were also made during this period to attract more inward investment, particularly to more peripheral areas (Shefer and Bar-El 1993).[9] Despite this, rapid structural change was taking place in the indigenously-owned sector as the military build-up continued and the related civil electronics and aircraft industries expanded. From 1968 to 1983, for example, high-technology industry in Israel increased its share of output from 6 to 24 percent and its share of exports from 5 to 28 percent (Teubal 1993).

Israel's subsequent macro-economic crisis had little lasting effect on the NSI. More important perhaps were the cancellation in 1987 of the Lavi fighter project, the end of the Cold War and the easing of the geo-political situation in the Middle East which reduced both export and domestic demand for military hardware. These demand reductions released substantial amounts of highly skilled labour into the Israeli labour market and there is anecdotal evidence that this stimulated high-technology entrepreneurship in Israel.[10] Despite this, and the fact that since 1994 there has been a marked increase of FDI, high-technology industry in Israel continues to be dominated by indigenously-owned firms supported by high levels of R&D grant support (Trajtenberg 2000).

In terms of its effect on the Israeli NSI, flows of human capital, particularly the large-scale immigration to Israel from the former Soviet Union (FSU), have been more important than inward investment over the last decade. Simmons (1993), for example, notes that from 1989 to 1992, there were some 450,000 immigrants to Israel from the FSU (equivalent to 10 percent of the 1989 Israeli population) of whom 40 percent were university graduates compared to 10 percent of the established workforce. Israel's windfall gain of human capital from the FSU comes on top of the benefits from a higher level of public investment in education (as percentage of GDP) than that in the UK. Israel's universities also produce a higher proportion of first-degree graduates with engineering and medical and health related degrees than in either the UK or Ireland. Moreover, a higher proportion of Israeli graduates (45.9 percent) go on to do higher or research degrees than in either the UK (30 percent) or Ireland (41.1 percent). Higher staying-on rates in Israel reflect two major institutional differences between the Israeli and Irish and UK NSI. First, levels of civil R&D spending in Israel have been consistently higher than those in the UK and Ireland, and a much greater proportion of all Israeli civil R&D is undertaken by the higher education sector. For example, in 1994/95 civil R&D spending by the Israeli higher education sector was 0.83 percent of GDP compared to 0.27 percent in Ireland and 0.39 percent in the UK.[11] Secondly, external research grants and international funds contribute substantially to higher education in Israel, particularly in the natural sciences and medicine (Frucht-Eren 1996). The high proportion of Israeli science graduates who undertake higher degrees, and immigration from the FSU, means that Israel now has a higher proportion of engineers and scientists in the labour force than any other country in the world - 133 for every 10,000 citizens (Frucht-Eren 1996). The influx of scientists and technicians from the FSU into Israel has prompted a number of important developments in both the academic and commercial sectors. One of the most significant of these has been the technology incubators programme which was introduced in 1991 (Goldberg and Lavi-Steiner 1996; Modena and Shefer 1998; Roper 1999). Other important developments in Israeli technology policy during the 1990s have included the extension of the range of bilateral and international co-operation agreements with Israel participating, for example, in the EU 4th and 5th Framework Programmes. In addition, since 1994, there have been attempts to introduce a more strategic element to Israeli R&D with the Ministry of Industry setting national priorities for R&D support.

In Israel, as in Ireland, central government plays an important role by providing substantial financial support for all types of R&D from basic research in universities through to near-market product and process development. In Israel in particular this support remain substantial, although as Trajtenberg (2000) indicates an increasing proportion of Israeli government support for industrial R&D is self-financing because of payback provisions.[12] By contrast, in the UK over the last two decades, government has sought to withdraw from supporting near-market R&D, concentrating instead on supporting basic or pre-competitive research (Ashcroft et al. 1995). The origin of this policy can be traced to the 1972 Rothschild Committee that advocated the adoption of distinct policy approaches for basic and applied R&D. For applied research, the Rothschild committee advocated a customer-contractor principle in which mission-oriented government departments, acting as customers, commissioned research from outside organisations. Basic research on the other hand was to be funded by what was then called the Department of Education and Science through the Research Councils.

The election of the Conservative government in the UK in 1979, with its emphasis on the restoration of a free market economy, reinforced this distinction as the government sought to reduce public spending and the level of intervention in the economy. Even in terms of basic research, however, levels of support were low by international standards and by 1987 had fallen well below that in France and Germany on a per capita basis (Walker 1993). This decline in public support even for basic research typifies one of the major criticisms made by Walker (1993) of UK innovation policy during the 1980s and early 1990s, namely the unwillingness of government to invest in developing the UK's technological capability. Moreover, there were few signs over this period that the UK private sector was either willing or capable of filling the vacuum. Despite productivity and profits growth during the 1980s there was slower growth in private R&D investment and capital investment (Walker 1993). More recently, Van Reenen (1997) points out that, even standardising for differences in industrial structure, UK firms have been slower to increase their R&D intensity than those in other major OECD economies. By 1994/95, UK business R&D as a percentage of GDP had fallen below the OECD average although remaining above that in Ireland and above the level of (civil) R&D spending in Israel.

As in Ireland, the withdrawal of UK central government from supporting industrial R&D over the last decade has been offset by the increased importance of EU initiatives such as the 5th Framework Programme. Regional initiatives have also flourished in the UK with the development agencies in Scotland, Wales and Northern Ireland developing their own support measures to promote technological development by supporting innovation and attracting inward investment (Ashcroft et al. 1995; Roper and Thanki 1995; Roper 2001; Morgan 1997). Local Enterprise Agencies and Science Parks established by the universities and local government have also sought to attract and develop high-technology businesses, some with considerable success (see, for example, Massey et al. 1992; Enterprise Panel 1996). More generally, however, the effect of this uncoordinated decentralisation of technology and innovation policy has been to exacerbate the lack of co-ordination within the UK's NSI highlighted by Walker (1993). Other continuing weaknesses cited by Walker relate to the lack of intermediate technology transfer institutions (for example the German Fraunhofer Institutes), the weakness of the UK skills base and the distortionary effect of defence related R&D.

Recent developments in Ireland and Israel have been more positive. In Israel, the government's attempts during the early 1990s to pump-prime the venture capital funds through the Yozma Venture Capital fund proved hugely successful, reinforced by an increasingly wide international appreciation of the quality of many Israeli high-technology companies. Subsequent flotations by Israeli high-technology businesses on the NASDAQ and investments by major multi-nationals in the Israeli high-technology sector have secured Israel's reputation as a global centre for high-technology industry. Both developments have brought much needed private capital into Israeli industry reducing to some extent the pressure on state R&D support (Trajtenberg 2000). In Ireland, a significant expansion has also taken place in the availability of venture capital but perhaps more important have been recent announcements of a sharp expansion of public support for R&D in indigenous firms. In particular, in March 2000 a £560m Technology Foresight fund was announced to promote technology support in niche areas of information technologies and biotechnology.

In terms of any overall assessment of the effectiveness of policy measures designed to increase the level of innovative activity by businesses, the central question is whether the Israeli, Irish or UK NSI provides a more conducive environment for innovation. The availability of high quality, research-trained personnel stemming from high levels of investment in R&D in higher education and immigration from the FSU, for example, would seem to give companies in Israel a decided advantage. Whether the Israeli advantage extends to other occupational groups that might be involved in the adoption and production of new or improved products or processes is less clear, however. In institutional terms, the size of the UK confers some advantages in terms its ability to sustain specialist research and support institutions. The unwillingness of successive UK governments to focus resources on the development of the NSI, EU framework programmes to encourage international collaboration, and aggressive programmes of institutional development in Israel (and to a lesser extent Ireland) have all served to weaken this historical advantage. Most notable among these developments have been the Israeli government's attempts to establish bilateral and multilateral R&D agreements. Similar tendencies can be identified in terms of the availability of venture capital funding in the three countries. Ten years ago this too would have been an area in which UK-based companies would have had a marked advantage; recent developments in both Israel and Ireland have done much to 'level the playing field'.

6.3 MEASURING SUCCESS: INNOVATION AND TECHNOLOGICAL DEVELOPMENT DURING THE 1990S

In this section we consider three indicators of the extent to which these developments in the NSIs of the three countries have been successful in promoting innovation activity. Patents applications data are used first to given an indication of the overall level of technological activity in each of the three countries. Patents data are limited, however, in that they provide little insight into the importance or commercial impact of the technologies developed. To offset these problems we also examine evidence derived from surveys of firms' innovative activity and on the commercial application of new technologies.

6.3.1 Patent Applications

Standardised figures for patent applications are regularly published by the OECD and summary statistics for patent applications in Israel are published in the Statistical Abstract for Israel. In each case, patent applications by residents and non-residents are given separately and can be used to define three diagnostic ratios (Table 6.1). In terms of the Inventiveness Coefficient, which measures domestic patent applications by residents relative to population, Israel (2.6) is just ahead of Ireland (2.3) but below the UK (3.2). That is, more patent applications were made per resident of the UK than in either Israel or Ireland. The Auto-sufficiency Ratio also suggests that over a quarter of all patent applications in Israel were made by residents compared to 20 percent in the UK and 2 percent in Ireland. Essentially the same point is reflected in the Dependency Ratio; Israel has a higher degree of technological self-sufficiency than either the UK or Ireland, at least as measured by patent applications. This is consistent with the largely insular development of the Israeli NSI and may also reflect the country's high level of R&D investment.

Table 6.1 Patenting ratios for Israel, Ireland and the UK: 1994

	Inventiveness Coefficient	Auto-sufficiency Ratio	Dependency Ratio
Israel	2.60	0.286	2.49
Ireland	2.30	0.020	49.61
UK	3.20	0.200	4.03

Notes: Dependency ratio (non-resident/resident patent applications); Auto-sufficiency ratio (resident/national patent applications); Inventiveness coefficient (resident patent applications/10,000 population).

Sources: Israel, *Statistical Abstract of Israel*; OECD *Main Science and Technology Indicators*.

This result may also reflect the nature of the home markets of the three countries rather than reflecting any underlying differences in the process or effectiveness of knowledge creation. For example, companies may choose not to patent products in Israel because of a lack of local competitors or because they do not intend to sell in the Israeli market. One way round this potential problem is to examine the patents registered by nationals of each country in a neutral market. Maital et al. (1993), for example, looked at patents registered by Israel and the EU countries at the US patent office between 1984 and 1986. At that time, Israel's patent performance at the USPTO was in line with that in the EU generally.[13] Table 6.2 updates the basic data reported by Maital et al. (1993) to cover the period up to 1996 for the EU15 and Israel. Part A of the table reports an Inventiveness Coefficient defined as the number of US patent applications by national residents per 10,000 of population. Over the whole period since 1977, Israel and the UK have very similar Inventiveness Coefficients to the EU15, with Ireland around a quarter of the average EU level. These averages, however, hide the sharp increase in the number of patent applications by Israel in the US, particularly since 1983, while the UK and Ireland have more closely tracked the EU average. Measuring US patent applications relative to national GDP, suggests a similar picture with Israel having a consistently higher number of patents applications per unit of GDP than either Ireland or the UK (Table 6.2).

Table 6.2 US patent applications by Israel, Ireland and the UK

	1977-1980	1981-1985	1986-1990	1991-1993	1994-1996	1977-1996
A. US Patents per 10,000 Population						
Ireland	0.05	0.07	0.14	0.17	0.18	0.12
UK	0.45	0.43	0.51	0.47	0.45	0.46
Israel	0.26	0.34	0.60	0.66	0.80	0.51
EU15	0.38	0.40	0.51	0.50	0.48	0.45
B. US Patents Per GDP ($1996bn)						
Ireland	0.60	0.78	1.17	1.14	1.02	1.05
UK	3.02	2.91	2.89	2.63	2.32	2.69
Israel	2.43	3.30	4.46	4.50	5.15	4.38
EU 15	2.27	2.48	2.55	2.37	2.15	2.37

Sources: Patents: *Patent Counts by Country/State and Year, All Patents, All Types*, USPTO, August 1997. Population, GDP: *European Marketing Data and Statistics*, various, Euro-monitor. Israel: *Statistical Abstract of Israel.*

This evidence from the USPTO supports that from the OECD and points to Israel's disproportionately strong patent performance. Not only is this evident in terms of a greater degree of technological self-sufficiency in the Israeli market but also in terms of the increasingly strong Israeli presence in US patent applications. This latter point is also evident if we compare the number of patent applications registered domestically and in the US by Israeli, UK and Irish nationals. In 1994, the number of patent applications made by Israelis in the US was 27.3 percent of the number of applications registered domestically (by Israelis); in the UK and Ireland corresponding figures were 13.1 and 6.5 percent respectively.

6.3.2 Innovation Survey Comparisons

Although no national survey of innovation activity by Israeli businesses currently exists there is some survey evidence from the electronics, plastics and metals sectors in Northern Israel (for example Frenkel and Shefer 1996). For Ireland and the UK, comparable evidence is available from the Product Development Survey (Roper et al. 1996). Table 6.3 gives the proportion of manufacturing businesses in different parts of the UK, Northern Israel and Ireland introducing any new or improved products over the 1991-93 period (1992-94 for Israel).

Table 6.3 Percentage of businesses introducing new or improved products

	Electronics, Electrical Engineering, Optic etc.	Metals, Rubber and Plastics
Northern Israel	74.4	36.5
UK	73.2	56.9
Ireland	73.3	65.4

Sources: See Frenkel and Shefer (1996); Roper et al. (1996).

Little difference exists between the proportion of electronics companies introducing new or improved products between the different areas. In the more traditional industries, however, the proportion of innovating plants in Northern Israel is notably lower than that in the UK and Ireland (Table 6.3). This suggests, in broad terms, that product innovation in Israel in electronics and related sectors is broadly on a par with that in the UK and Ireland, with more traditional sectors in Israel lagging somewhat. In terms of Israel's relatively high levels of R&D and patenting activity this is suggestive of the type of weakness in the commercialisation of new technologies suggested by Maital et al. (1993).

6.3.3 World Market Shares

Other potentially valuable indicators of innovation success are world market shares for high-technology products. Table 6.4, for example, gives the world export shares of a tightly defined group of domestic, commercial and industrial electronic products. In 1996, Israel had an average world market share of around 0.5 percent, compared to 2.0 percent in Ireland and 6.7 percent in the UK. Israel's share of world exports was notably higher, however, in the most research-intensive sectors, that is telecommunications and medical diagnostic equipment. Ireland, by contrast, largely as a result of US inward investment, had above average world market shares in the manufacture of computer equipment, parts and accessories. The position of the UK was more mixed with above average market shares in the export of computer equipment, office machinery, TV receivers and telecommunications equipment. Again these trade patterns reflect the very different industrial and technological strategies of the three countries in recent decades. Israeli technological strengths in research-intensive sectors dominated by Israeli-owned businesses contrast markedly, for example, with the more mass-market production of computers and computer components by externally-owned businesses in Ireland.

Table 6.4 World export market shares for electronic products in 1996

	UK %	Ireland %	Israel %
Office Machines	8.7	0.2	0.0
Computer Equipment	9.4	4.9	0.5
Office Equipment Parts	7.1	4.8	0.3
Television Receivers	11.1	0.0	0.0
Radio Receivers	2.8	0.0	0.9
Sound/TV Recorders etc.	5.6	0.1	0.1
Telecommunications Equipment nes	7.9	0.9	1.5
Electricity Power Transmission Equipment	4.9	0.7	0.2
Electric Circuit Equipment	5.0	1.1	0.5
Electrical Distribution Equipment	4.8	1.3	0.2
Medical Electronic Diagnostic Equipment	3.5	0.1	1.7
Domestic Equipment	4.6	1.2	0.1
Valves, Transistors etc.	4.9	1.1	0.3
Electrical Equipment nes	7.5	0.6	0.4
Total	6.7	2.0	0.5

Source: International Trade Statistics Yearbooks, United Nations Statistical Office, New York.

6.4 CONCLUSIONS

The large relative size of the UK economy inevitably confers some potential advantage over Israel and Ireland in terms of the UK's ability to support diverse and specialised research and support institutions for innovation. The unwillingness of successive UK governments to devote resources to the development of the UK's National System of Innovation has, however, significantly offset any such advantage. EU Framework Programmes and other measures to encourage international collaboration, and consistent programmes of institutional development in Israel (and more recently Ireland) have also served to weaken the UK's historical advantage. Most notable among recent developments have been the Israeli government's support for bilateral and multilateral R&D agreements and attempts by both the Israeli and Irish governments to increase the availability of venture capital funding. Arguably, the Israeli NSI is also superior to that of the UK and Ireland in terms of the availability of high quality, research-trained personnel. In part this is due to high levels of Israeli investment in R&D in higher education but it also owes something to the massive immigration from the former Soviet Union since 1991.

Of the three countries, the internal dynamic for innovation is probably strongest in Israel. This dynamic has its roots in the flow of research trained manpower coming from the Israeli university network, from immigration and from R&D undertaken in Israeli higher education institutions and is sustained by high levels of public commitment to supporting commercial R&D and innovative activity. The results are evidenced both by high levels of patenting activity and by Israel's substantial world market share in research-intensive sectors such as electronic medical diagnostic equipment. Innovation survey data paints a less comforting picture, however, with the proportion of Israeli firms introducing new products on a par with the UK and Ireland in high-technology sectors but trailing somewhat in more traditional industries. The suggestion is that in these sectors at least Israel still has some way to go in maximising the commercial benefit of its R&D outputs and inventive activity. For the UK and Ireland the success of Israel in building up its NSI over the last three decades and developing strong indigenous technological capabilities is a valuable example of what is possible. A renewed public and policy commitment to promoting innovation, investment in higher education and substantial support for private sector R&D activity and high-technology start-ups will, however, be essential if the UK and Ireland are to maintain their position in global high-technology markets.

ACKNOWLEDGEMENTS

Much of the material for this chapter was collected while I was visiting the S. Neaman Institute for Advanced Studies in Science and Technology, Technion, Haifa in summer 1998. I am grateful for financial support to the Ministry of Science and the Arts, the British Council in Israel and the Northern Ireland Departments of Economic Development and Finance and

Personnel. I am also very grateful to Dr Amnon Frenkel without whose patience this chapter would not have been completed. The opinions and mistakes in the chapter are my own.

REFERENCES

Ashcroft, B., S. Dunlop and J.H. Love (1995), 'UK innovation policy; a critique', *Regional Studies*, **29**, pp. 307-11.

Cohen, J.S., A. Mintz, R. Stevenson and M.D. Ward (1996), 'Defence expenditures and economic growth in Israel - the indirect link', *Journal of Peace Research*, **33**, pp. 341-52.

De Rouen, K.R. (1995), 'Arab-Israeli defence spending and economic growth', *Conflict Management and Peace Science*, **14**, pp. 25-47.

DTI (1998), *Our Competitive Future - Building the Knowledge Driven Economy*, Cm 4176, London.

Enterprise Panel (1996), *Growing Success*, London: Enterprise Panel, Securities Institute.

Felsenstein, D. (1994), 'University related science parks - seedbeds or enclaves of innovation?', *Technovation*, **14**, pp. 93-110.

Frenkel, A. and D. Shefer (1996), 'Modelling regional innovativeness and innovation', *Annals of Regional Science*, **30**, pp. 31-54.

Frucht-Eren, E. (1996), *Israel: A Science Profile*, Tel Aviv: British Council - Department of Trade and Industry.

Goldberg, A.I. and O. Lavi-Steiner (1996), 'Developing an effective technological incubator - the experience of Israel', *Industry and Higher Education*, December, pp. 371-6.

Lavy, V. (1994), 'The effect of investment subsidies on the survival of firms in Israel', Discussion Paper 94.04, Jerusalem: The Maurice Falk Institute for Economic Research in Israel.

Lee, J.J. (1989), *Ireland 1912-85: Politics and Society*, Cambridge: Cambridge University Press.

Maital, S., A. Frenkel, H. Grupp and K. Koschatzky (1993), 'Exporting goods .., or know-how - an empirical comparison of the relationship between scientific and technological excellence and export performance for Israel and the European countries', Working Paper, Haifa: S. Neaman Institute, Technion.

Massey, D., P. Quintas and D. Wield (1992), *High Tech Fantasies: Science Parks in Society, Science and Space*, London: Routledge.

Metcalfe, S. (1997), 'Technology systems and technology policy in an evolutionary framework', in D. Archibugi and J. Michie (eds), *Technology, Globalisation and Economic Performance*, Cambridge: Cambridge University Press.

Modena, V. and D. Shefer (1998), 'Technological incubators as creators of new high technology firms in Israel', Paper presented at the 38th European Regional Science Association Congress, Vienna.

Morgan K. (1997), 'The learning region: institutions, innovation and regional renewal', *Regional Studies*, **31**, pp. 491-504.

National Board for Science and Technology (1983), *National Programme for Science and Technology*, Dublin.

O'Riain, S (1997), 'The birth of a celtic tiger', *Communications of the Association for Computing Machinery*, **40**, pp. 11-16.

OECD (1974), *Review of National Science Policy: Ireland*, Paris.

Plessner, Y (1994), *The political economy of Israel - from ideology to stagnation*, State University of New York Press.

Roper, S (1999), 'Israel's technology incubators - repeatable success or costly failure?', *Regional Studies*, **33**, pp. 175-80.

Roper, S. (2001), 'Innovation, networks and plant location: some evidence for Ireland', *Regional Studies*, **35** (3), pp. 215-28.

Roper, S. and A. Frenkel (2000), 'Different paths to success: electronics growth in Ireland and Israel', *Environment and Planning C*, **18**, pp. 651-65.

Roper, S. and N. Hewitt-Dundas (1998), *Innovation in Ireland: Lessons for Irish Companies*, Dublin: Oaktree Press.

Roper, S. and R. Thanki (1995), 'Innovation 2000: an ex ante assessment of northern Ireland's research and development strategy', *Regional Studies*, **29**, pp. 81-7.

Roper S., B. Ashcroft, J.H. Love, S. Dunlop, H. Hofmann and K. Vogler-Ludwig (1996), *Product Innovation and Development in UK, German and Irish Manufacturing*, Northern Ireland Economic Research Centre/Fraser of Allander Institute, University of Strathclyde.

Ruane, F. and H. Gorg (1997), 'Reflections on Irish industrial policy towards foreign direct investment', Trinity Economic Papers Series, 97/3, Dublin.

Shefer, D. and E. Bar-El (1993), 'High technology industries a vehicle for growth in Israel's peripheral regions', *Environment and Planning C*, **11**, pp. 245-61.

Simmons, D.K. (1993), 'An evaluation of current efforts to promote entrepreneurship in Israel', Unpublished Masters Thesis, Haifa: Faculty of Architecture and Town Planning, Technion.

STIAC (1995), *Making Knowledge Work for Us*, Report of the Science, Technology and Innovation Advisory Council, Dublin: The Stationary Office.

Steinberg, G. (1985), 'Technology, weapons and industrial development - the case of Israel', *Technology in Society*, **7**, pp. 387-98.

Teubal, M. (1993), 'The innovation system of Israel: description performance and outstanding issues', in R.R. Nelson (ed.), *National Innovation Systems: A Comparative Analysis*, Oxford: Oxford University Press.

Trajtenberg, M. (2000), 'R&D policy in Israel: an overview and re-assessment', NBER Working Paper 7930, October.

Van Reenen, J. (1997), 'Employment and technological innovation: evidence from U.K. manufacturing firms', *Journal of Labour Economics*, **15** (2), pp. 255-84.

Walker, W. (1993), 'National innovation systems: Britain', in R.R. Nelson (ed.), *National Innovation Systems: A Comparative Analysis*, Oxford: Oxford University Press.

Williams, R.J.N. (1988), 'UK science and technology policy - controversy and advice', *Political Quarterly*, **59**, pp. 132-44.

Wrynn, J. (1997), 'Foreign direct investment to a peripheral country - the case of Ireland', in B. Fynes and S. Ennis (eds), *Competing From the Periphery*, Dublin: Oaktree Press.

Yearly, S. (1995), 'From one dependency to another: the political economy of science policy in the Irish Republic in the second half of the twentieth century', *Science, Technology and Human Values*, **20**, pp. 171-96.

NOTES

1. In Ireland, for example, the recent STIAC report commented that 'despite our history of distinguished contributions to science, we have shown a remarkable capacity to allow much of this information ... to congeal and to preserve our continuing indifference to a visional and strategic response to world STI developments' (STIAC 1995, Vol. 2, p. 9). From a more academic standpoint Maital et al. (1993) commented: 'Israel has failed to fully convert its scientific achievements into export led growth. In proportion to its GDP, Israel outpaced European countries in patents publications and citations, yet lagged in R&D intensive exports' (p. 108). And, in the UK: 'We have a world class reputation in science and engineering ... Yet Britain suffers long-standing shortcomings which still hold us back. Too many British firms fail to match the performance of their overseas competitors, not just in terms of productivity but in innovation and quality' (DTI 1998, pp. 10-11).

2. They are also a reflection of the size and industrial structure of the three economies.

3. This tradition dates back to before the creation of the state of Israel and is reflected in the foundation of the Hebrew University (1925), the Technion (1924) and the Weizmann Institute (1934) and in particular the Jewish Agricultural Research Stations (now the Volcani Institute) also in the 1920s. Industrial research in Ersatz Israel was pioneered by the Palestine Potash Company which founded the Dead Sea Laboratories in 1930.

4. Source OECD, Main Science and Technology Indicators, 1998, Table 76. See Roper and Hewitt-Dundas, 1998, pp. 20-22 for a discussion.

5. See Plessner (1994) for an assessment of the impact on the Israeli economy of continued government intervention and particularly the continued public sector dominance of the capital market.

6. Israel Aircraft Industries (IAI), for example, began producing Fouga Magister jet trainers under French license and the defence electronics sector was established through Tadiran and Elbit (Steinberg 1985, pp. 390-91).

7. Steinberg (1985) highlights in particular the expansion of IAI into civilian aircraft production, the move by Tadiran and Elbit into civilian markets and the rapid growth of sub-contracting in the defence industries in the 1970s.

8. See Trajtenberg (2000) for a detailed discussion of Israeli R&D support.

9. One notable success, however, was the establishment by Intel in 1974 of a major research and development facility in Haifa. This recently expanded development was at the time Intel's only R&D facility outside the US (Frucht-Eren 1996).

10. Recent examples of this type of development are ECI Telecom, a producer of telecommunications systems for PTTs, which was founded by people who had previously served in the IDF communications units. Former IDF intelligence staff also founded NICE Systems, producers of digital recording systems (Source: *Financial Times*, July 15 1996, Survey of Israel - 'Swords into Ploughshares'). More formal statistical and econometric studies, however, provide little evidence that defence spin-offs have been significant at an economy-wide level. De Rouen (1995), for example, analyses the impact of military spending on GDP growth in Israel for the period up to 1988 and finds only weak evidence of positive spin-off effects. Similarly, Cohen et al. (1996) are able to identify no significant spin-off effect from Israeli defence spending on levels of labour productivity.

11. Sources: Main Science and Technology Indicators 1998, Table 6, OECD, Paris; Statistical Abstract of Israel 1997, Table 23.1.

12. More specifically Trajtenberg (2000) reports figures suggesting that R&D paybacks in Israel increased from 7 per cent of the total R&D support budget in 1988 to 32 per cent in the late 1990s.

13. Maital et al. (1993) also examined the relationship between patent activity and the share of manufacturing exports which were high-technology products. Their evidence suggested that, in comparison to the other EU countries, Israel had a lower proportion of high-technology exports than would be expected given the countries relatively high levels of R&D expenditure and patenting activity. This led Maital et al. (1993) to conclude that during this period Israel was better at generating scientific ideas than in translating these ideas into commercially acceptable products.

7. Industrial Districts and Networks: Different Modes of Development of the Furniture Industry in Ireland?

David Jacobson, Kevin Heanue and Ziene Mottiar

7.1 INTRODUCTION

The Irish economy has obtained in the last few years the title 'Celtic Tiger'. Not all experts agree with this. Sweeney (1999), among others, has argued in favour of the notion but O'Hearn (1998) is more sceptical of the appropriateness of the implied comparison with the East Asian tiger economies. There is general agreement that Ireland has successfully attracted foreign direct investment (FDI), particularly from the United States and particularly in industries like electronics (including computers), software and pharmaceuticals, all industries in which there are relatively high R&D expenditures. There is less agreement on such questions as how technologically advanced the activities of the multinational corporation (MNC) subsidiaries in Ireland are. It is also unclear as to how embedded they are into the Irish economy. These uncertainties exist, notwithstanding a great deal of attention to these issues in the popular press, among state institutions and in the academic journals (Barry and Bradley 1997).

Among the doubts about the Irish economy is the extent to which indigenous firms are capable of surviving in the increasingly open trading environment in Europe. Employment in Irish-owned manufacturing firms declined by 23 percent between 1973 and 1998 (while employment in foreign-owned manufacturing firms increased by 105 percent - see Table 7.2 below). The following table provides some clear evidence of this decline in one such industry. It also shows, on the other hand, what appears to be an arresting of this decline in the 1990s. The increase in 1991 is largely accounted for by the change in the NACE[1] category, plastic and metal furniture having been excluded from 'furniture' up to then and included from then on. But there is clear decline up to 1990 and increase from 1991 onwards.[2]

Table 7.1   Employment in the furniture industry in Ireland, selected years, 1982-98

	1982	1986	1990	1991	1994	1998
Employment	4,360	3,505	3,119	3,776	4,037	6,130
No. of Estabs./Units	403	253	212	245	269	315
Empl. per Estab./Unit	10.8	13.9	14.7	15.4	15.0	19.5

Note: NACE 467 from 1982 to 1990, NACE Rev.1 3611-5 from 1991 on. NACE Rev.1 3611-5 includes plastic and metal furniture.

Source: CSO, *Census of Industrial Production*, various years.

Given the relative paucity of work on 'traditional' sectors[3] we concentrate in this paper on an example of such a sector, namely the furniture industry. We begin with a brief outline of Irish industrial policy in general. Towards the end of this section we turn to a specific aspect of recent industrial policy, namely network policy. In the next section we briefly describe and compare two examples of the organisation of production in the furniture industry, the wooden furniture industrial district in County Monaghan and the TORC[4] network in Dublin, Wicklow and Cork. Finally, we consider the implications of these two developments for theory and policy in Ireland. The main aims of the chapter are to examine the development of the furniture industry in the context of policy changes, and to compare two different forms of industrial organisation in the furniture industry in Ireland.

The County Monaghan example is an industrial district while the TORC network is more widely dispersed. The theoretical context is therefore one resting on such issues as the spatial limits of agglomeration in a small economy, and the differences between agglomerations and networks. Implications for policy include support for networking in general, and not just among spatially proximate firms.

7.2 IRISH INDUSTRIAL POLICY

There have been three main broad development strategies adopted in Ireland over the period since independence in 1922. Each was closely related to the types of policies that were being adopted by other countries. Between independence and 1932 the policy was one of agriculture-led growth. This was basically a free trade policy. Opposition to this grew over the decade and, together with a shift to protectionism in the early 1930s in all Ireland's trading partners, led to a change in government and policy in 1932.

From 1932 until around 1958 Irish governments followed a policy of import-substituting industrialisation (ISI). Virtually anything that could be produced in Ireland was given protection, and industrial output and employment grew. This was true for most traditional industries like furniture, clothing and footwear, but also for relatively new industries like car assembly. Where there were significant increasing returns to scale either the government should have been more interventionist, and selected a small number of firms to support, or less interventionist, allowing efficient foreign firms access to the Irish market. Car assembly, for example, although assembling some 40 different models by the 1960s, ceased as soon as possible after the removal of protectionism.

During the 1950s protectionist policies reached their limit. With the exception of one or two larger companies, indigenous firms were in general producing only for the protected local market. Capital goods and manufactured sub-assemblies in virtually all sectors were imported. Industrial stagnation led to unemployment and emigration. However, the absence of strong, competitive firms in the traditional manufacturing industries - like furniture, and clothing and footwear - resulted in reluctance to open up the economy.

Eventually, responding both to the internal stagnation and to the external availability of mobile capital, new, outward-looking policies were introduced in 1958. A strategy of export-led growth (ELG) was adopted, based on encouraging foreign direct investment (FDI), gradually removing protectionism, and providing incentives for firms to export.

The ELG policies - particularly low corporate profit tax rates and capital grants - were generally successful, in that they attracted FDI, reduced unemployment, and arrested the deterioration in the balance of payments. They also paved the way first for entry into an Anglo-Irish Free Trade Agreement in 1966, and subsequently into the European Economic Community (EEC) in 1973. However, over the decade or so following entry into the EEC, it became clear that while employment in subsidiaries of MNCs was increasing, employment in indigenous firms was declining. (This trend has broadly continued since then - see Table 7.2.)

Table 7.2   Employment in manufacturing in Ireland, by ownership

	1973	1980	1998
Irish	166,000	161,000	128,000
Foreign	56,000	82,000	115,000
Total	222,000	243,000	243,000

Source: O'Malley (1985, Table 1.1); CSO, *Census of Industrial Production*, 1998.

The decade of the 1970s was marked globally by oil crises, but these were not identified as the cause of the problem. Both international consultants (Telesis 1982) and some local experts (for example O'Malley 1985) were convinced that what was required was a shift in industrial policy, to favour MNC subsidiaries less and indigenous firms more.

A White Paper on Industrial Policy in 1984 did indeed lead to change, though not as substantial a change as had been suggested. A National Linkage Programme - which had mixed results - and a Company Development Programme were introduced. Sector-specific policies began to be adopted, aimed at identifying already successful firms in each sector and assisting them, rather than providing blanket assistance at lower levels, for larger numbers of firms. These new policies were applied both to traditional sectors like furniture, and to advanced technology industries like electronics.

A second consultancy exercise to examine Irish industry and industrial policy was published in 1992. The Culliton Report's major recommendations included the reorganisation of the industrial development organisations into two main agencies, one of which should specifically address the development needs of indigenous, Irish-managed industry (Culliton 1992). The report also contained an innovative proposal, informed by the work of Porter (1990), to change the focus of industrial policy towards promoting the growth of industrial clusters around niches of national competitive advantage. These recommendations have to varying extents been adopted. Crucially, for our purposes, together with a new national focus on innovation systems and learning (STIAC 1995), they led to the adoption of a Pilot Inter-firm Co-operation Programme (the 'Pilot Network Programme') in 1996.[5]

The policy changes since the mid-1980s have had some impact. O'Malley (1998) argues that since 1987 the performance of Irish-owned firms has improved considerably, relative not only to Ireland's own historical experience but also compared to that of industrial countries in general.

(Others, including O'Hearn 1998, remain doubtful about whether there has been a fundamental change in the strength of the indigenous sector.)

In the next section of this chapter we examine the furniture industry, focusing in particular first on the wooden furniture industrial district in County Monaghan, and then on a small network, established in the Pilot Network Programme.

7.3 THE FURNITURE INDUSTRY IN IRELAND

Table 7.1 shows that there were in 1998 (the latest year for which data are available) 315 firms providing employment for 6,130 people. The Census is based on firms employing three or more people, so very small firms of two or less are excluded. The following map, Figure 7.1, shows the distribution of wooden furniture firms, including very small ones, by county. (The numbers are estimates, based on a database kept by the Furniture Technology Centre in Letterfrack, County Galway.) Dublin, in the middle of the eastern seaboard, is by far the largest population centre, and is also the location of the largest number of furniture firms (104). Other large population centres include County Cork (the southernmost county) and County Galway (in the middle of the western seaboard) which also, as expected, have relatively large numbers of furniture firms. The main surprise is County Monaghan, a border county with Northern Ireland. Ranking 21st in terms of population, County Monaghan ranks third after Dublin and Cork in terms of the number of furniture firms.

7.3.1 The Industrial District in County Monaghan[6]

There has been a concentration of wood-working in Monaghan for hundreds of years (Mottiar 1997). The current cluster of firms, mainly in or near Monaghan town and its northern hinterland, originate in large part from the firm John E. Coyle, established in 1936. A total of more than 75 percent of the furniture firms in the district are run by men who served apprenticeships in Coyles, or in firms set up by men who had served their apprenticeships in Coyles.

There are varying levels of co-operation among furniture firms in the district. The best known formal co-operation in the district occurs between McNally and Finlay, and Sherry Brothers, two of the larger firms. These firms jointly manufacture the Rossmore range of furniture. Their jointly employed designer designs products for each firm. Instead of specialising in particular products for the range, they each produce the same goods and then compete on the market. Thus they co-operate to have the products designed, sell under the same brand name and in Ireland use the same agents (in the UK they are more competitive and have different agents). This arrangement appears to be successful for both parties. Moreover, the difficulties of altering such a long-standing agreement would be complex and are likely to encourage continued compliance.

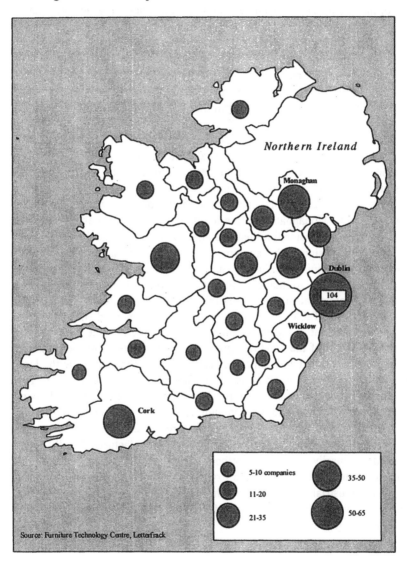

Figure 7.1 Distribution of furniture companies in Ireland, by county, 1997

Most of the smaller firms produce inputs for the two or three larger firms. In some cases this is based on a 'putting out' relationship, where the larger firm supplies the materials, and the subcontractor machines them into the required shape and size and returns them as completed components to the larger firm.

Informal co-operation includes lending machinery (particularly hand-tools) and sharing information about customers who have not paid their bills. In one case, where two firms both produce a similar product, they both refrain from poaching each other's customers.

Close proximity, competition as well as formal and informal co-operation,[7] close inter-firm relationships - both horizontal and vertical - and people having been trained in one firm then establishing their own firms, are all characteristics of the industrial districts of the 'Third Italy', about which so much has been written in the last 20 years (see Jacobson and Mottiar 1999, and references therein). These industrial districts are based on industrial agglomeration and are embedded in various institutional and commercial ways into their local environments. Jacobson and Mottiar (1999) have shown that while some of the normal characteristics of industrial districts are absent from the County Monaghan furniture industry, the elements described above, together with a professional milieu and an awareness of mutuality of interest, are sufficient to designate this agglomeration as an industrial district.

How did the furniture industry - and the Monaghan industrial district in particular - respond to the changes in industrial policy? Following two decades of protectionism, the furniture industry was virtually untraded by 1960 (see below, Table 7.3). In the new, more open market, some firms declined or went out of business, some start-ups came into the industry, and the more efficient of the old firms grew. By 1980 a quarter of the output of the Irish industry was being exported (Table 7.3). At the same time the local market became more import penetrated, following the shift to ELG. This intra-industry specialisation is typical of trade development following liberalisation (Jacobson and McDonough 1998). It is explained by the fact that certain types of furniture - not manufactured locally - are popular in the local market, and other types of furniture - manufactured locally - are marketed primarily in the Northern Irish and British markets. A disproportionately large part of the exports have been accounted for by the Monaghan industrial district, and this has been at least in part a consequence of the substantial grant aid received by the Monaghan firms from the development agencies.

Table 7.3   Performance of the furniture industry in Ireland, selected years
*   1960-96*

	Imports as % of furniture market	Exports as % of output	Exports/ Imports
1960	1.0	6.8	8.00
1973	23.0	8.0	0.29
1980	44.9	24.5	0.40
1985	48.4	31.7	0.50
1990	63.8	54.1	0.67
1996	41.3	35.3	0.77
1998	42.3	28.4	0.54

Sources: CSO, *Trade Statistics of Ireland*, Division 82; CSO, *Census of Industrial Production*, various years.

Grant aid to firms was, and still is, conditional upon those firms being exporters. The Monaghan companies - particularly the larger ones - being relatively successful, obtained state support and became the main sources of exports of furniture from Ireland. Enterprise Ireland (whose remit is to focus on the development of indigenous firms) has provided substantial grant aid, particularly to the largest of the Monaghan companies, John E. Coyle. The purpose of the most recent grant package was to assist the firm in developing new processes and products in the modular furniture area, particularly for the British market. These developments have, however, not yet had the expected results in that modular furniture by Coyles has not yet broken into the British market.

In relation to quality and design, it should be pointed out that the main Monaghan products are relatively low-priced reproduction furniture, based on panel material such as MDF (medium density fibreboard). Technology is advanced but not fully utilised due to skill shortages. Innovations are based primarily on small design changes - for example in the colour of the veneers.[8]

Among the important questions are whether there are limits to growth in the Monaghan industrial district, and what if any the relationship is between these limits and industrial agglomeration. In addition, are there opportunities for growth for the Irish furniture industry outside the Monaghan industrial district?

The most recent data suggest the timeliness of such questions. As Table 7.3 shows, in the late 1990s there has been a decline in the proportion of output exported (and in the export-to-import ratio) back to 1980s levels; at the same time, import penetration has remained relatively low. Given the continuing rapid growth of the Irish market it may be that the increase in demand is more than absorbing the local industry's capacity for expansion. Moreover, the Irish market is growing much more rapidly than the target markets abroad, so it would be surprising if there was not a decrease in the proportion of Irish output being exported.

Fundamental questions are timely because the policies appropriate under conditions of stagnation and unemployment may be different from those appropriate under conditions of rapid industrial growth. Just as stagnation shows weaknesses in industrial production systems, so may incapacity to respond rapidly and flexibly to growing markets.

7.3.2 The TORC Network[9]

A possible alternative (or addition) to the support for existing agglomerations and in particular the successful firms within those agglomerations, is to support firms to develop networks. As mentioned above, the Irish government - through the local development agency - introduced a Pilot Network Programme (PNP) in 1996. The PNP - involving 17 networks and a total of 31 SMEs (small and medium enterprises) - aimed to encourage small firms to co-operate in activities they were unable to undertake individually due to their small scale. The objective of the PNP was to put in place some of the resources needed to facilitate and establish formal networks of the 'Danish' type (Rosenfeld 1996), to help the networks devise joint solutions to common problems and to evaluate the results. The general principles guiding the Pilot phase of the programme were:

- Networks should consist of at least three firms (SMEs) and not more than eight. A network could include one multinational or large scale Irish firm, or one foreign firm or third level college.
- Networks could be developed on a sectoral basis, in customer/supplier chains, or in a technology or market sector.
- The objective of each network should be to create new business or to increase the competitiveness of the firms involved.
- Once established, the activities to be undertaken by the network would be a matter for agreement among participating firms.

Funding was provided to cover the costs of training network brokers, the participation of Danish experts in the formation of a network, network set-up costs, publicity and management of the programme. A manager and three network brokers were appointed within Enterprise Ireland to run the programme. SMEs were identified for potential inclusion in the programme using a number of sources. Although some of the SMEs had been involved previously in formal or informal co-operation arrangements, they were not selected on that basis.

There were few networks in Ireland prior to the introduction of the PNP and those few were characterised by low levels of interaction. The main benefit of the PNP for SMEs was that it enabled the companies to work together as a team on the strategic development of new business opportunities. Although a high proportion of SMEs are interested in participating in a network programme of longer duration, companies from the same industrial sector frequently have difficulty co-operating because of competitive rivalry between them. Notwithstanding this, and in spite of a weak history of inter-firm co-operation in Ireland, the PNP demonstrated that networking could be advanced by following the 'Danish' model. The use of trained network facilitators was found to be the most important feature of this method.

One network of furniture firms was included in the PNP. Having been set up under this programme, it now continues to grow. It consists of three firms: D.F. Caulfield in Dublin, Castlebrook Furniture and Design in Wicklow and O'Donnell Designs in Cork. Although Caulfields and Castlebrook are located only 20 miles from each other, they had not previously co-operated in any way and the owners did not know each other personally. In contrast, notwithstanding the 200 mile gap between O'Donnells and the other two companies, the owner of O'Donnells personally knew the owner of Caulfields, and had met the proprietor of Castlebrook on an international trade visit organised by the industrial support agencies. The network operates in the hotel bedroom furniture sub-sector.

All three firms were established in the 1970s or early 1980s, all are small, employing 14 (Caulfields), 25 (Castlebrook) and 30 (O'Donnells) people, and all have been producing hotel bedroom furniture in recent years. As independent entities, the three firms are heavily dependent on the Irish market. A small part of their output is exported primarily to the United Kingdom, with even smaller amounts to Germany, Russia and Estonia.

The network was initiated by Enterprise Ireland, the state agency responsible for indigenous industrial development. First O'Donnells and Caulfields were invited to become involved in the Pilot Network Programme. Following some discussion these two identified a third participant - Castlebrook - which joined the network. Both O'Donnells and Caulfields were aware of this company by reputation alone, particularly in relation to its professionalism and the quality of its work.

The three firms, after participating in the facilitation phase of the network programme, agreed to set up a product development and marketing company as a joint venture, which they registered under the trade name TORC. Following market research, three new hotel bedroom product ranges were designed and copyrighted, promotional material was developed and the products were launched at a London show in December 1998. A part-time manager for the network, who works two/three days a month was appointed and is paid for by the network. There is also a sales manager, who works as an agent and is paid on a commission basis. Each of the three companies has the capability to make the entire product range. As TORC is a product development and marketing firm rather than a production entity, an invitation to tender for business must be passed on to one of the three companies. Which particular company fulfils any particular order depends on availability although there is an understanding that the opportunity to fulfil an order will rotate among the three firms. Whichever particular firm is fulfilling a contract is the one that deals with the customer.

The network members suggested that there were three main reasons for joining the network.[10] First, the individual firms had already acknowledged that as separate entities they lacked the required critical mass and resources to enter the United Kingdom hotel furniture market in a significant way. Second, the firms felt that the three companies working together would be able to obtain assistance (grants for marketing, R&D, design and so on) from industrial support agencies that would be unavailable if they applied separately. This was particularly important for access to export markets. Third, there was a common perception among the companies that the recent expansion of the Irish contract furniture market, fuelled by the property boom of the past five years, was reaching its peak and therefore it was prudent to plan for market diversification.[11] O'Donnells had already begun an in-house programme to focus on the UK and had completed some contracts. Caulfields' experience outside Ireland was mostly in continental Europe and a particular concern of this company was in the development of marketing tools.

The members of the network meet face to face once a month to monitor progress and ascertain availability for work. One of the first items on the agenda for each meeting is what jobs should be priced, and who should price them. More frequent scheduled physical meetings only arise in exceptional circumstances. However, there is telephone, fax or email contact between the network members two to three times a week.

The network is so far successful, having obtained a number of contracts. The three partners have together developed a strategic plan, have submitted proposals to appropriate agencies for assistance - for example in training[12] - and have gained from each other's experience. The other two, for example, have gained from Castlebrook's experience in outsourcing components. Their activities within TORC represented an increase of 5.5 percent in the firms' total turnover.

All three companies - independently of the TORC network - have had and continue to have significant links with the relevant state and industry institutions. They have all received capital and/or employment grant assistance in the past from Enterprise Ireland or its predecessor. In addition, O'Donnells and Caulfields were involved - with three other Irish firms and a Danish design and marketing company - in a previous network project in the early 1980s. It failed primarily due to downturns in the target markets. All three proprietors have participated in trade visits abroad instigated by various industrial support agencies; most of these visits took place in the mid to late 1980s. The owners of O'Donnells and Caulfields have also participated in various ways in the development of training and education for the furniture industry.

The current relationships of the TORC network firms with Enterprise Ireland include Caulfields' and O'Donnells' involvement in Company Development projects, the latter having obtained approval for an R&D investment. In addition, O'Donnells is about to start a World-Class Business Cluster initiative with Enterprise Ireland, and Castlebrook has also applied to be involved in this initiative. All three firms are members of the National Furniture Manufacturers Association (NFMA). The proprietors of both O'Donnells and Castlebrook are participating in PLATO[13] - the Small Business Development network.

This multiplicity of contexts in which the activities of the TORC firms intersect, does not imply an absence of competition. They continue to regard each other as competitors on the Irish market (albeit in slightly different quality and quantity sub-sectors) though they have an informal agreement about the nature of competition. Although the firms' main market is in the same geographic area, they pursue non-aggressive practices towards each other and, for instance, pass on tender information if they feel it is more appropriate for one of the others. Outside Dublin and the east coast, each of the firms tends to focus on particular areas of the country.

In relation to subcontracting, Castlebrook has been most active. Up to 50 percent of its manufactured content is outsourced, though it controls the finishing process itself. At least two small furniture making enterprises in a 10 mile radius owe the majority of their turnover to component production for Castelbrook. O'Donnells also engages to some extent in subcontracting, obtaining veneered panels from a number of suppliers in different EU countries and semi-processed panels and turned components from two Irish companies, one in Tipperary and one in Wexford, neither spatially proximate as conventionally defined. In addition, the TORC firms have begun to subcontract within the network. O'Donnells has some experience subcontracting for Caulfields, and Castlebrook is doing work for O'Donnells.

Many of these elements of interaction among the three members of TORC suggest comparison with the Monaghan industrial district and industrial districts in general. There is both competition and co-operation, there is a range of organisational settings in which the proprietors of the network firms have interacted, and, not least, there is evidence of learning from each other. An aspect of industrial districts which is missing in the TORC network, but which is fundamental both in Marshall's (1890) original formulation and in the application to 'the Emilian model' (Brusco 1982) is close proximity.

7.4 THEORETICAL AND POLICY IMPLICATIONS

Industrial agglomeration is a process whereby firms cluster together spatially in order to derive certain benefits. These benefits are external economies - they arise from activities, relationships or developments outside the firm and outside the market (Jacobson et al. 2001). They are untraded benefits. In the case of the Monaghan industrial district, for example, the proximity of the many furniture firms in the area is a key factor in their survival, and additional firms have set up there because it is already a concentration of furniture manufacturers. Many of the firms are spin-offs from Coyles; this suggests an element of serendipity - they set up in that place because they already lived there. However, the presence of up- and downstream firms and the availability of an appropriate labour force, are among the factors generating economies of agglomeration. In recent years new firms have been set up in Monaghan by proprietors who have come from other places in Ireland.

Economies of agglomeration are present in the case of the Monaghan industrial district; other externalities - such as the process of learning from each other's differences - have arisen from the shared experiences of the TORC proprietors both within the network and in the state agency and educational organisation contexts. These other externalities are usually associated with industrial agglomeration. Can the firms in the TORC network, even if up to 200 miles apart, be considered to be deriving economies of agglomeration?[14] The spatial limits of economies of agglomeration depend to some extent on the size of the industry, its technology and the nature of the production system, the types of raw materials and sub-assemblies, and the nature of the transport system. It may be that as technologies - especially information and communication technologies - change and transport systems improve, the range within which economies of agglomeration can arise increases. On the other hand, such Marshallian notions as knowledge about an industry being 'in the air' and thus resulting in rapid diffusion of innovations, may require the tighter agglomeration of a concentrated and homogeneous labour force.

Arita and McCann (2000) provide some recent econometric evidence on the issue of the spatial limits of agglomeration. They suggest that economies of agglomeration consist of both formal and informal information flows. Based on an examination of industrial alliances in the US semiconductor industry, they provide evidence that the strength of formal information flows is less geographically constrained than may be expected. Specifically, in their study, the strength of formal inter-firm information exchanges does not differ statistically between situations in which the firms are in the same place, and those where they are within one day's return journey by air. This is not to say that there is no distance effect; beyond a one-day return journey by air, increasing geographical distance is indeed associated with a falling intensity in formal information exchanges.

There are important differences between this case and the TORC example. In Arita and McCann's (2000) study, the technology, production and transport systems are quite different to the furniture industry. However, the evidence of a distance effect beyond one day's return journey in the US semiconductor industry raises the possibility that there may be unexpected distance effects in other industries.

Ironically, this proposition is supported by a recent description of Italian industrial districts. Irrespective of the spatial limits of industrial districts, on which Lazerson and Lorenzoni (1999) are 'agnostic', they show that 'leading firms' in industrial districts forge relationships with other firms, both local and distant, and they suggest that this engenders increasing flexibility in the district's responsiveness to markets. They call for further 'research into the combined effects of geography and relationships on firms'. For our purposes, these arguments at least lend credence to the contention that the TORC network could be benefiting from economies of agglomeration.

Turning now to the implications for policy, the contrast is between first, the policy of assisting individual companies that have already shown evidence of success, and, second, the policy of encouraging networks. In the last few years the first has been applied in the case of Coyles, with mixed success; Coyles has not yet achieved the expected results. The second has generated the TORC network which, so far, is successful. From a cynical perspective it could be argued that the proprietors of the TORC network have simply behaved as rent seekers. Indeed, from this perspective the very formation of the TORC joint venture could be seen as a consequence of rent seeking. Even if this is the case, however, if the consequence is the development of a successful network that would not otherwise have arisen, then the policy may be justified.

7.5 CONCLUSION

In this chapter, we have examined the development of the furniture in the context of policy changes, and compared two different forms of industrial organisation in the furniture industry in Ireland. What emerges is that there appears to have been an element of cumulative causation in the relationship between state support and the Monaghan industrial district. As the furniture industry grew in the area, and industrial policy changed to focus to an increasing extent on firms that already had provided evidence of competitiveness - particularly in export markets - so the support for Monaghan firms grew. Other than the two-firm Rossmore example, however, there is no evidence of the type of inter-firm networking that has been the basis of the TORC joint venture. In addition, although individually many of the Monaghan firms have had dealings with the state agencies, TORC is a better example of firms being embedded in a rich institutional environment (Granovetter 1985; Grabher 1993). The TORC proprietors, as we have shown, have interacted - and, ultimately, co-operated - in such a wide range of organisational contexts that they have developed a shared perspective on strategy. They are, to use the language of networks, realising their complementarity potential by being compatible (see note 10).

While we are hesitant to generalise from the particular examples discussed here, it is at least appropriate to raise questions, such as whether support for individual companies within industrial agglomerations is a strategically correct policy. The organisational integration (Lazonick 1991; Lazonick and West 1995) expressed in the financial commitment of the three TORC companies to the network is not evident among the Monaghan firms. It may be a factor in the success of the network and may constitute a weakness in the Monaghan industrial district. We would agree with Lazerson and Lorenzoni's (1999) cautious conclusion: 'Although we have no evidence, it is very likely that an individual firm's survival is very much connected to the relationships it has forged with other firms'. This should, arguably, be recognised in all industrial policies.

REFERENCES

Arita, T. and P. McCann (2000), 'Industrial alliances and firm location behaviour: some evidence from the US semiconductor industry', *Applied Economics*, **32**, pp. 1391-403.

Barry, F. and J. Bradley (1997), 'FDI and trade: the Irish host-country experience', *Economic Journal*, **107**, pp. 1798-811.

Best, M.H. (1990), *The New Competition*, Cambridge: Polity Press.

Brusco, S. (1982), 'The Emilian model: productive decentralization and social integration', *Cambridge Journal of Economics*, 6, pp. 167-84.

Culliton, J. (1992), *A Time for Change: Industrial Policy for the 1990s*, Report of the industrial policy review group, Dublin: Stationery Office.

Economides, N. (1996), 'The Economics of Networks', *International Journal of Industrial Organization*, 14 (6), pp. 673-99.

Grabher, G. (ed.) (1993), *The Embedded Firm: On the Socioeconomics of Industrial Networks*, London: Routledge.

Granovetter, M. (1985), 'Economic action and social structure: the problem of embeddedness', *American Journal of Sociology*, 91 (3), pp. 481-510.

Jacobson, D. and T. McDonough (1998), 'International trade and European integration', in E. O'Shea and M. Keane (eds), *Core Issues in European Integration*, Dublin: Oak Tree Press.

Jacobson, D. and Z. Mottiar (1999), 'Globalization and modes of interaction in two sub-sectors in Ireland', *European Planning Studies*, 7 (4), pp. 229-45.

Jacobson, D. and D. O'Sullivan (1994), 'Analysing an industry in change: the Irish software manual printing industry', *New Technology, Work and Employment*, 9 (2), pp. 103-14.

Jacobson, D., K. Heanue and C. van Egeraat (2001), 'Industrial agglomeration', in W. Lazonick (ed.), *IEBM: Handbook of Economics*, London: Thomson.

Lazerson, M.H. and G. Lorenzoni (1999), 'The firms that feed industrial districts: a return to the Italian source', *Industrial and Corporate Change*, 8 (2), pp. 235-66.

Lazonick, W. (1991), *Business Organization and the Myth of the Market Economy*, Cambridge: CUP.

Lazonick, W. and J. West (1995), 'Organizational integration and competitive advantage: explaining strategy and performance in American industry', *Industrial and Corporate Change*, 4 (2), pp. 229-70.

Marshall, A. (1890), *Principles of Economics*, London: Macmillan.

Mottiar, Z. (1997), *Industrial Districts and Industrial Clusters Compared: Applications to Ireland*, Unpublished PhD thesis, Dublin City University.

O'Hearn, D. (1998), *Inside the Celtic Tiger*, London: Pluto Press.

O'Malley, E. (1985), 'The performance of Irish indigenous industry: some lessons for the 1980s', in J. Fitzpatrick and J. Kelly (eds), *Perspectives on Irish Industry*, Dublin: IMI.

O'Malley, E. (1998), 'The revival of Irish indigenous industry 1987-1997', Economic and Social Research Institute Seminar paper, Dublin.

Porter, M.E. (1990), *The Competitive Advantage of Nations*, London and Basingstoke: Macmillan.

Rosenfeld, S. (1996), 'Does cooperation enhance competitiveness? Assessing the impacts of inter-firm collaboration', *Research Policy*, 25, pp. 247-63.

Sweeney, P. (1999), *The Celtic Tiger: Ireland's Continuing Economic Miracle*, Dublin: Oak Tree Press.

STIAC (1995), *Making Knowledge Work for Us*, Report of the Science, Technology and Innovation Advisory Council, Dublin: Stationery Office.
Telesis (1982), *A Review of Industrial Policy*, NESC Report No. 64, Dublin: NESC.
White Paper on Industrial Policy (1984), Dublin: Stationery Office.

NOTES

1. NACE is the Eurostat 'activity nomenclature', or system for classifying industrial activity.
2. The increase after 1991 is based primarily on wooden furniture production; metal and plastics as a proportion of total furniture in fact declines from 25 per cent in 1995 to 21 per cent in 1998.
3. Jacobson and O'Sullivan (1994) on printing and Jacobson and Mottiar (1999) on furniture and printing are among the exceptions.
4. Torc is the Irish word for a twisted metal necklace or armband in Celtic design.
5. The Pilot Network Programme is discussed in detail in Section 7.3.2 below.
6. The material on the furniture industrial district is based on Mottiar (1997).
7. On the importance of the presence of both competition and co-operation see Best (1990).
8. There are also a small number of firms producing solid, hardwood products, including bar counters manufactured for Irish pubs all over the world.
9. The information in this section was obtained from interviews during July and October 1999 with the three furniture firms in the TORC network, the Manager of the Pilot Network Programme from Enterprise Ireland and the TORC network manager.
10. These reasons are all consistent with the idea in network theory (see Economides, 1996) that there is complementarity among the partners that generates externalities in production networks. For TORC to be a network, as defined in theory, there must be greater profit through working together than there would be if the three firms operated individually. However, to realise the externalities, the partners must also be compatible. The extent to which the partners in a network are compatible can often only be shown over time.
11. Note that the network was formed in 1997/8. The most recent information available on industry growth is presented in Tables 7.1 and 7.3 above. It is clear that the building boom continued beyond the TORC firms' expectations.
12. Under the government and EU-funded SKILLNETS programme
13. PLATO supports owner-managers of SMEs to develop their management skills facilitated by leading local companies. To date, approximately 980 small companies and over 90 of Ireland's leading firms are involved in PLATO networks across Ireland.
14. At the workshop in Jerusalem at which the first draft of this chapter was presented, an American participant considered 200 miles to be well within the range for industrial agglomeration while a British participant expressed the view that much smaller distances were required for industrial agglomeration.

8. Innovation and Plant Characteristics of High-Technology Firms in Israel and Ireland

Daniel Shefer, Amnon Frenkel and Stephen Roper

8.1 INTRODUCTION

The industrial sectors of Israel and Ireland have achieved impressive growth over the last decade, although that of the high-technology sectors is particularly striking. Between 1991 and 1998, for example, industrial high-technology production in Ireland and Israel grew at an annual average rate of 8.4 percent and 15.5 percent respectively. The average annual rate among countries of the EU stood at only 3.6 percent for those years. During the 1990s, the high-technology sectors also came to dominate the industrial sector in both countries. Thus, for example, the proportion of those employed in high-technology industries accounted for 17.5 percent of the total number of those employed in industry in Israel and 27.7 percent in Ireland in 1998. In both countries, the high-technology industry is also one of the principal exporting sectors. In 1998, exports from the high-technology sector accounted for 37.2 percent of Israel's total industrial exports, while in Ireland, they accounted for 37.3 percent. The importance of this export data is emphasised by the relatively small size of the Israeli and Irish home markets, and the consequent need for firms to develop export sales if they are to continue to grow.[1]

The impressive achievements of the high-technology sectors in Ireland and Israel maybe connected to policy programmes, which have created the basis for the growth. At the same time, each country has adopted a development strategy, which has led to very different types of high-technology development. While Ireland may be seen largely as a European production platform, characterised by large-scale production-only plants, Israel, has concentrated more on R&D-intensive activities. Thus, Israeli high-technology plants are relatively small and combine significant R&D with small- to medium-scale production activities (Roper and Frenkel 2000).

The objective of this study is to examine the similarities and differences in the spatial distribution and structure of the high-technology sector in Israel and Ireland in the context of their national success. The chapter examines both the structural and spatial characteristics of these industries and the impact of location choices on firms' ability to innovate. The comparison is based on data collected from a sample of high-technology plants in Ireland and Israel. This study adds to a growing literature which focuses on inter-state and inter-regional variations in the extent and determinants of innovation activity (for example Alderman and Fischer 1992; Suarez-Villa and Fischer 1995; Suarez-Villa and Han 1990, 1991; Suarez-Villa and Karlsson 1996; Suarez-Villa and Rama 1996; Nelson 1993; Kleinknecht 1996; Roper et al. 1996; Frenkel et al. 2001a).

The second section of this chapter provides a very brief overview of the high-technology industries in Israel and Ireland. The third section presents the methodological framework of the study, while the fourth contains a comparative statistical analysis of the characteristics of high-technology plants, at the national level. The fifth section analyses and measures the influence of selected variables on the extent of innovation in high-technology firms. Finally, the sixth section concludes the chapter.

8.2 THE HIGH-TECHNOLOGY INDUSTRIES IN ISRAEL AND IRELAND[2]

One possible explanation for the very different development paths of the high-technology sectors in Israel and Ireland are differences in science policy and tradition which characterise the two countries. While Israel is distinguished by a tradition of scientific research, which began long before the establishment of the State, in 1948, the emphasis in Ireland was mainly on academic research which did not contribute directly to industrial or commercial applications (Roper and Frenkel 2000).

The impressive development of the high-technology sector in Israel was given a particular boost in 1967. The government of Israel adopted a strategic policy aimed at developing a scientific and technological infrastructure that would promote civilian industrial development. This was also an era of industrial structural change with a shift in emphasis from traditional industries towards export-based industries. A swift structural change occurred in the local, high-technology sector as the civilian sector expanded along with the military one. In the 1970s, the focus was on the continued development of advanced industry and military technology, although these developments were undertaken in the context of increased openness to exports and foreign markets. Measures such as providing investment incentives were used, intentionally favouring the high-technology sector. The government of Israel even supported the establishment of science parks near academic institutions, such as the Weizman science park established in 1967 (Felsenstein 1994), and started providing R&D grants to individual firms (Teubal 1993), and tend to attract investment in peripheral areas. However, despite the generous grants policy, success in this direction was rather meagre (Shefer and Bar-El 1993).

The policy of incentives that provided fixed capital grants and R&D support also continued during the 1980s. R&D grants were institutionalised in 1984 with the Law Encouraging Industrial R&D, that provides fixed support of 50 percent of the expense of an approved R&D programme. The end of the Cold War and the geo-political changes in the Middle East resulted in a considerable reduction in military industries in Israel. Concomitantly, a mass migration from the former Soviet Union, many of whom were highly technologically trained and thus contributed to the already existing large pool of skilled labour, brought about the relocation of many employees with high levels of professional skill to the civilian labour market. This factor significantly influenced the growth in high-technology initiatives in Israel. From 1994, an impressive increase in the extent of foreign direct investment (FDI) in Israel was noted, and the electronics industry continued to be led by companies which located their headquarters in Israel.

In Ireland, the 1970s witnessed a change in industrial policy, manifested in a sharp move towards the development of high-technology industries, especially electronics and chemistry. This shift contributed to the development of a dual economy in Ireland: on the one hand, a sector with advanced technology, owned by foreign investors and based on R&D undertaken in other places abroad, and on the other hand, a traditional industrial sector employing unsophisticated, locally-owned technology (NESC 1982).

The external influence of the European Community in 1982 resulted in a significant change in the industrial incentives offered by the Irish government. The government was forced to make structural changes to their package of incentives to reduce any export bias. A policy of technological development was also introduced, based largely on finance provided by the European Union structural funds. The share of the foreign-owned industrial firms in Ireland grew along with the continued decline in the number of those employed in local firms. The growth of the externally-owned high-technology sector in Ireland, and its dispersal throughout the country, has had substantial impact on employment and economic development in more lagging regions (see, for example, McAleese and McDonald 1978; O'Farrell and O'Loughlin 1980, 1981).

8.3 FRAMEWORK OF THE STUDY

8.3.1 Methodology

This study intends to explore the differences in the spatial distribution and the structural characteristics of high-technology firms within and between the two countries, using data collected from a sample of plants. The purpose of the analysis is to examine to what extent the rate of innovation in the high-technology sector in the two countries is differed from each others.

8.3.2 Hypotheses

We assume that a supportive innovative environment encourages the innovation of firms located in that region. Infant firms, taking their first steps, are more dependent on existing markets and a large pool of highly skilled labour. They will choose to locate in metropolitan areas that provide support for young high-technology firms (Davelaar and Nijkamp 1988; Shefer and Frenkel 1998). Thus we hypothesised that plants located within metropolitan areas, are therefore expected to show a higher rate of innovation than plants located in the other areas, *ceteris paribus* (Ciccone and Hall 1996).

A firm's characteristics may influence its tendency to innovate. Young high-technology plants, in the first stages of their life cycle, may engage more in innovation. With age, and the shift from research and development to production, the plant expands and grows, tending to focus more on mass production and less on developing new products. Thus, we hypothesised that the size and age of the plant influence the rate of innovation.

In both Israel and Ireland a policy is applied, aimed at encouraging direct foreign investments in the high-technology sector. We hypothesised that ownership type could be a determinist factor that influence the firm's rate of innovation.

Finally, we hypothesised a direct influence of the plant's technological capability, as expressed by the allocation of capital and manpower to R&D, on its tendency to innovate. The decision to invest in R&D bears witness to the plant's technological capability (Rosenberg 1985; Nelson 1986; Dosi 1988; Roper 1996; Frenkel 1997). We also hypothesised that the plant's ability to engage in R&D activities is connected, on the one hand, to the availability and supply of a highly skilled labour force and, on the other hand, to the public support programmes of R&D. The former is also related to the pool of highly skilled labour that exists in urban centres and therefore attracts investment in R&D (Malecki 1979). Thus the probability of a high-technology plant to engage in innovation is influenced and dependent on the plant's location, its technological ability and its internal characteristics.

8.3.3 The Model

The logit binary choice model was employed in the empirical analysis, assuming two mutually exclusive alternatives: to either engage or not to engage in innovation (Pindyck and Rubinfeld 1981; Ben-Akiva and Lerman 1985). Thus, the model requires a specific choice that receives the value of 1. The alternative choice receives the value of 0 (Haynes and Fortheringham 1991).

The specification of the model is given in the following equation:

$$P_i = F(Z_i) = 1/[1 + \lambda^{-Z_i}] = 1/[1 + \lambda^{-(\beta_0 + \beta_1 R_j + \beta_2 A_{ix} + \beta_3 T_{iy} + \varepsilon_i)}] \qquad (8.1)$$

where:

P_i is the probability that plant i will innovate.

R_j location of plant j (j = 1,2,3). Three locations were defined: central area, R_1, intermediate area, R_2, and peripheral area, R_3.

A_{ix} attribute x of plant i (size, age, ownership type, annual turnover).

T_{iy} a measure of the technological capability of plant i (the number or proportion of employees engaged in R&D, the extent of investments in R&D).

β parameters to be estimated.

Equation (8.1) can be rewritten as follows:

$$P_i = \beta_0 + \beta_1 R_j + \beta_2 A_{ix} + \beta_3 T_{iy} + \varepsilon_i \qquad (8.2)$$

For estimating the firm's probability to engage in innovation, the maximum likelihood method was used. Concomitantly the extent of the influences of each of the explanatory (independent) variables on the dependent variable was estimated.

8.3.4 The Data

The data was collected through surveys conducted in both countries. In order to conduct the survey, instruments were carefully constructed for collecting the data on the plant level. Data concerning innovation activity, as well as information concerning the plant's characteristics such as age, size, ownership type and R&D activities, was included in the questionnaires.

In Israel, personal interviews were held with senior managers in each of the 86 plants selected for this study. These plants belong to fast-growing industrial branches, such as electronics, precision instruments, optics and electro-optics (Shefer et al. 2001).

In Ireland, data for the high-technology sectors is taken from a postal survey covering 400 high-technology plants in the Republic of Ireland and Northern Ireland (Roper and Hewitt-Dundas 1998). The survey was based on a stratified random sample, structured by plant sizeband and industrial sector. The overall response rate was 30 percent. A sample of 119 plants from the Republic of Ireland and Northern Ireland was included in the study. One key feature of the Irish sample was a significantly higher proportion of externally-owned firms than that in the Israeli sample. This reflects the underlying ownership pattern of high-technology industry in the two areas with Ireland host to a large number of US-owned computer and electronics plants (Roper and Frenkel 2000).

8.3.5 The Regions

One of the fundamental research questions is linked to the influence of location on the rate of innovation by high-technology plants in three different types of sub-regions: the metropolitan area, the intermediate zone and the peripheral zone.

In Israel the Northern region was chosen for the study as it represents a classic pattern of an area encompassing the three different types of sub-regions identified for the investigation. In 1997, some 1.5m people, comprising about 26 percent of the population of Israel resided in the Northern region which includes the Haifa metropolitan area, the main urban core in the North. The non-metropolitan area includes the intermediate zone, comprising the areas that surround the Haifa metropolitan area (on the fringe of the metropolitan area, within an acceptable commuting distance) and the peripheral areas, comprising the less developed areas of the Northern region. These areas are removed from the metropolitan influence and are not within an acceptable commuting distance (see Figure 8.1).

In Ireland the survey data covers both the Republic of Ireland and Northern Ireland. The central area consists of the two main urban areas, Belfast and Dublin. These two urban cores are characterised by a high population density and a high proportion of professional and technical expertise. The urban periphery surrounding the core areas of Belfast and Dublin conurbations is characterised by intermediate population densities and above average levels of professional and technical employment. Outside, and geographically distinct from the main urban centres of Belfast and Dublin, there are also important secondary centres characterised by relatively high population densities, where average proportions of people are employed in professional and technical occupations and where important university campuses are located (Derry, Coleraine, Limerick and Cork, Galway). Following Shefer and Frenkel (1998), and taking into account both the quantitative and qualitative characteristics of each of these areas, they were classified as intermediate zones Finally, the rural areas are characterised by below average population densities and lower than average proportions of people employed in professional and technical occupations. These areas include the secondary centres of population in the South and West of the Republic of Ireland and the North-West of Northern Ireland. This last group was classified as a peripheral area (see Figure 8.1).

8.4 RESULTS

8.4.1 A National Comparison

Variations in the characteristics of the high-technology plants in the two areas were examined using t-tests for a series of plant attributes. The results are presented in Table 8.1.

Significant statistical differences were found between high-technology plants in Israel and Ireland for all the attributes examined, except for the '% of export sales from turnover' (variable 7 in Table 8.1). These results reflect significant differences between Israeli and Irish high-technology plants. High-technology plants in Ireland are larger compared to those in Israel, as expressed by the number of workers and their annual turnover. On average, an Irish high-technology plant employs twice as many employees as does a parallel Israeli plant. This difference is even more noticeable when comparing size, as measured by the plant's annual turnover. The average turnover of an Irish high-technology plant is more than three times that of a comparable Israeli plant.

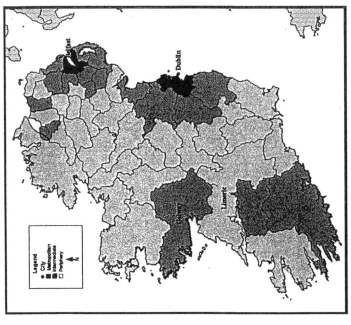

a. The Northern Region in Israel

b. The Republic of Ireland and Northern Ireland

Figure 8.1   The two research regions sub-divided into sub-areas

Table 8.1 t-tests for selected attributes of Israeli and Irish high-technology plants[†]

	Plant attributes	Ireland	Israel	t value
1.	Age of plant - number of years since establishment	18.3 (119)	15.3 (86)	1.754**
2.	Plant size - number of workers	223 (112)	113 (86)	2.788*
3.	Plant size - annual turnover (in million $)	43.8 (106)	13.7 (82)	3.001*
4.	Annual turnover per employee (in thousand $)	184.9 (102)	85.9 (82)	4.590*
5.	% growth in turnover in the last 3 years	52.6 (106)	23.5 (78)	2.721*
6.	Export sales (in million $)	28.74 (108)	9.98 (83)	2.570*
7.	% of export sales from turnover	49.5 (108)	51.4 (79)	−0.330
8.	R&D expenditure (in million $)	0.22 (107)	2.22 (86)	−2.602*
9.	R&D expenditure per worker (in thousands $)	1,265 (107)	15,362 (82)	−6.763*
10.	% of R&D expenditure from total turnover	1.0 (105)	29.6 (78)	−3.692*
11.	Number of R&D workers in the plant	2.4 (109)	22.5 (86)	−3.238*
12.	% of R&D workers from total employees	1.7 (109)	24.3 (86)	−8.813*

Notes:
[†] Figures in parentheses are the number of observations.
* Significant at the 5 percent level.
** Significant at the 10 percent level.

Source: Company Survey Data.

As might be assumed, the importance of exporting is especially significant for small countries such as Israel and Ireland, as may be noticed by the fact that about 50 percent of the annual turnover is export-linked. Because of differences in plant size, the volume of exports of an average Irish high-technology plant is three times that of an Israeli one.

However, Irish plants invest relatively little in R&D compared to Israeli plants where, on average, the latter invests ten times as much as its Irish counterpart. The investment in R&D shows that, in general, it accounts for about 30 percent of the turnover of a typical Israeli plant, compared to only 1 percent in Ireland. A notable difference also exists in investment in R&D as measured by the number of employees. The Israeli plant employs ten times as many R&D workers as does a comparable plant in Ireland. About a quarter of the employees in an Israeli high-technology plant are engaged in R&D, compared to less than 2 percent in an Irish high-technology plant.

In both areas, high-technology would appear to be a growing industry, evidenced by high rates of growth in turnover for the last three years. At the same time, the rates of growth of Irish high-technology plants are, on average, up to twice those of Israeli plants. The explanation for this apparently lies in the different types of high-technology industry in the two areas. Growth measured by an increase in turnover is greater in plants involved in production compared to those based mainly on R&D.

8.4.2 Inter-Regional Comparison

Variations for a series of plants attributes among the three sub-areas, within each of the two areas, are presented in Table 8.2. When we compare the results, we can see that in Israel for a large number of variables the variations among sub-areas are statistically significant compared to those found in Ireland. This is particularly true for the results obtained for the R&D variables 8-12. In Israel R&D expenditures of plants located in the metropolitan area are by far greater than those of plants located in the other two sub-areas. R&D expenditure of plants located in the intermediate areas is greater than that found in plants located in the peripheral areas. In Ireland no such variations were observed and thus no statistical differences were found in the expenditure on R&D of plants located in the three sub-areas. These results point to the significantly sharp differences which characterise the high-technology plants located in Israel, compared to those located in Ireland.[3]

In Israel plants located in the intermediate areas are significantly younger and faster growing than their counterparts located in the metropolitan and peripheral areas, while in Ireland, plants located in peripheral areas are relatively younger and they export significantly larger proportion of their output compared to those located in the metropolitan and intermediate areas.

Table 8.2 t-tests for selected attributes of Israeli and Irish high-technology plants by sub-areas[t]

	Region	Israel		Ireland	
Plant attributes		Mean	t value	Mean	t value
1. Age of plant	Metropolitan	17.5 (36)	2.822*	21.9 (29)	1.264
- number of	Intermediate	10.5 (34)		17.7 (52)	
years since	Metropolitan	17.5 (36)	−0.831	21.9 (29)	2.047*
establish-	Periphery	20.5 16)		16.2 (37)	
ment	Intermediate	10.5 (34)	−3.858*	17.7 (57)	0.590
	Periphery	20.5 (16)		16.2 (37)	
2. Plant size -	Metropolitan	123.2 (36)	0.176	140.5 (27)	−2.008*
number of	Intermediate	115.3 (34)		272.9 (49)	
workers	Metropolitan	123.2 (36)	0.676	140.5 (27)	−1.199
	Periphery	82.9 (16)		216.8 (36)	
	Intermediate	115.3 (34)	0.812	272.9 (49)	0.718
	Periphery	82.9 (16)		216.8 (36)	
3. Plant size -	Metropolitan	17.9 (34)	0.441	57.3 (27)	0.673
annual	Intermediate	13.7 (32)		40.8 (44)	
turnover (in	Metropolitan	17.9 (34)	1.025	57.3 (27)	0.882
million $)	Periphery	4.8 (16)		37.3 (35)	
	Intermediate	13.7 (32)	2.245*	40.8 (44)	0.204
	Periphery	4.8 (16)		37.3 (35)	
4. Annual	Metropolitan	87.6 (34)	−0.498	274.9 (25)	2.420*
turnover per	Intermediate	96.9 (32)		147.8 (42)	
employee	Metropolitan	87.6 (34)	1.778**	274.9 (25)	2.127*
(in thousand	Periphery	59.9 (16)		165.1 (35)	
$)	Intermediate	96.9 (32)	2.351*	147.8 (42)	−0.575
	Periphery	59.9 (16)		165.1 (35)	
5. % growth in	Metropolitan	21.3 (33)	−1.067	42.7 (24)	−0.359
turnover in	Intermediate	31.6 (29)		49.3 (45)	
the last 3	Metropolitan	21.3 (33)	1.085	42.7 (24)	0.915
years	Periphery	13.6 (16)		29.0 (34)	
	Intermediate	31.6 (29)	2.129*	49.3 (45)	1.865**
	Periphery	13.6 (16)		29.0 (34)	
6. Export sales	Metropolitan	14.0 (34)	0.577	33.3 (27)	0.550
(in million	Intermediate	9.4 (33)		25.1 (46)	
$)	Metropolitan	14.0 (34)	1.047	33.3 (27)	0.200
	Periphery	2.7 (16)		30.0 (35)	
	Intermediate	9.4 (33)	2.141*	25.1 (46)	−0.358
	Periphery	2.7 (16)		30.0 (35)	

Plant attributes	Region	Israel		Ireland	
		Mean	t value	Mean	t value
7. % of export	Metropolitan	51.1 (32)	−0.586	42.6 (27)	−0.252
sales from	Intermediate	57.2 (31)		44.8 (46)	
turnover	Metropolitan	51.1 (32)	0.845	42.6 (27)	−1.977**
	Periphery	40.7 (16)		61.1 (35)	
	Intermediate	57.2 (31)	1.382	44.8 (46)	−2.035*
	Periphery	40.7 (16)		61.1 (35)	
8. R&D	Metropolitan	4.43 (35)	1.826**	0.12 (24)	−0.797
expenditure	Intermediate	0.76 (31)		0.33 (48)	
(in million	Metropolitan	4.43 (35)	2.125*	0.12 (24)	−0.451
$)	Periphery	0.18 (16)		0.15 (36)	
	Intermediate	0.76 (31)	3.337*	0.33 (48)	0.828
	Periphery	0.18 (16)		0.15 (36)	
9. R&D	Metropolitan	22.9 (35)	1.823**	0.76 (24)	−1.080
expenditure	Intermediate	13.1 (31)		1.45 (47)	
per worker	Metropolitan	22.9 (35)	4.244*	0.76 (24)	−1.117
(in thousand	Periphery	3.2 (16)		1.35 (35)	
$)	Intermediate	13.1 (31)	3.344*	1.45 (47)	0.166
	Periphery	3.2 (16)		1.35 (35)	
10. % of R&D	Metropolitan	41.3 (33)	0.588	0.6 (24)	−1.293
expenditure	Intermediate	27.9 (29)		1.3 (46)	
from total	Metropolitan	41.3 (33)	2.120*	0.6 (24)	−0.894
turnover	Periphery	8.5 (16)		1.0 (35)	
	Intermediate	27.9 (29)	1.110	1.3 (46)	0.684
	Periphery	8.5 (16)		1.0 (35)	
11. Number of	Metropolitan	41.6 (36)	1.889**	1.7 (27)	−0.807
R&D	Intermediate	11.0 (34)		3.4 (48)	
workers in	Metropolitan	41.6 (36)	2.335*	1.7 (27)	0.525
the plant	Periphery	4.1 (16)		1.4 (34)	
	Intermediate	11.0 (34)	2.851*	3.4 (48)	1.109
	Periphery	4.1 (16)		1.4 (34)	
12. % of R&D	Metropolitan	35.4 (36)	2.421*	1.5 (26)	−0.687
workers	Intermediate	20.0 (34)		2.0 (48)	
from total	Metropolitan	35.4 (36)	4.675*	1.5 (26)	−0.260
employees	Periphery	8.5 (16)		1.5 (34)	
	Intermediate	20.0 (34)	2.321*	2.0 (48)	0.721
	Periphery	8.5 (16)		1.5 (34)	

Notes:
†   Figures in parentheses are the number of observations.
*   Significant at the 5 percent level.
**   Significant at the 10 percent level.

Source: Company Survey Data.

In Ireland the annual turnover per employee of plants located in metropolitan areas is significantly greater while in Israel it is significantly greater in plants located in the intermediate areas only in comparison to the periphery.

In short, significant variations among these three areas can be observed in Israel and Ireland for a large number of plants attributes. However, these variations are more pronounced in Israel compared to Ireland. This is particularly noticeable for the R&D variables, those that are often associated with the rate of innovation.

8.4.3 Innovation

Variation of the innovation patterns in Ireland and Israel is reflected in the relation between the frequency of innovation among the plants and their attributes located in each of the three sub-regions in the two areas. In this study we focus on plants that have generated product innovations during the past three years. Included in this definition are activities leading to the development of new products, the adoption of products which are new to the market, and the substantial improvement of existing products (development of the next generation of products). These activities emanate from in-house investments in R&D, or the purchase of outsourced R&D services. (Plants that dealt exclusively with developing or adopting innovative processes, or with adopting new products not requiring R&D investment, were not classified as innovative plants.)

At this stage a multi-variable analysis of variance and estimation of the logit model was performed. Three groups of explanatory variables were included in the model:

- *Location* - three dummy variables for identifying the plant's location were defined: (1) within a metropolitan area; (2) in an intermediate zone; (3) in a peripheral area.
- *Plant attributes* - this group encompassed a number of variables that characterise the plants included in the sample. We hypothesised that these variables influence the probability of the plant innovating. Among the variables included in this group are: age, size, ownership type, annual turnover and growth in turnover over the last three years.
- *Technological capability* - this group includes variables related to the level of investment by the plant in R&D, as measured by the number of employees in R&D or, alternately, by the annual expenditure on R&D (in-house R&D as well as outsourcing R&D services).

Table 8.3 presents the results of the analysis using the logit model. Four models are presented in the table. The division into four models stems from the desire to run alternative, highly correlated, variables. Thus, in order to avoid multi-collinearity, in model A and B expenditures in R&D were used and in models C and D the number of workers in R&D. Likewise in models A and C annual turnover was used as a proxy of the plant's size, and in models B and D, the total number of workers was used. Dummy variables were used for location in all the four models.

The results obtained for the two areas clearly indicate the positive influence of investment in R&D on the probability to innovate. All the four models indicate a high level of statistical significance, attesting to the considerable importance of the number of workers engaged in R&D or high expenditure in R&D. This result is consistent for both Israel and Ireland, despite the noticeable differences in the average investment per plant in R&D in Israel compared to Ireland (see Table 8.1).

In Israel, innovative plants prefer to locate in the metropolitan area. A statistically significant result was obtained for models A, C and D. This preference may stem from the innovative milieu which exists in the metropolitan area compared to that of the intermediate and peripheral areas. This is evidenced by the large pool of skilled labour that exists in the core area, the proximity to research and technological institutions, the availability of databases and the agglomeration of services.

In Ireland, on the other hand, no association was found between the plant's location and its tendency to innovate. This finding stems from the fact that in Ireland, in general, investment in R&D by high-technology plants is considerably less compared to that in Israel. A significant statistical association was found between the size of the plant and its rate of innovation. However the effect of the size variable is diametrically opposed in the two areas, stemming, apparently, from the different character of high-technology plants that emerge in the two areas.

In Israel small plants are more innovative than other plants. This can be vividly seen by the highly significant negative sign obtained for the estimated variables' coefficients of the annual turnover (models A and B) and the alternative model (models B and D). Furthermore, in Ireland the size of the plant, as measured by number of workers, is positively associated with the plant's innovation capability. This can be seen by the positive and significant signs of the estimated coefficient obtained for that variable in models B and D.

Table 8.3   Results of the dual-nation logit model analysis†

Independent variable	Israel				Ireland			
	Model A	Model B	Model C	Model D	Model A	Model B	Model C	Model D
Constant	-2.539 (1.444)**	0.1068 (0.909)	-7.386 (3.071)*	-1.444 (1.104)	-1.929 (0.919)*	-2.346 (0.979)*	-1.542 (0.849)**	-2.004 (0.911)*
R&D expenditure***	19.164 (6.106)*	2.524 (0.944)*	—	—	29.481 (10.903)*	32.443 (11.976)*	—	—
Number of workers in R&D	—	—	1.500 (0.179)*	0.441 (0.127)*	—	—	1.804 (0.622)*	0.006 (0.003)*
Location in metropolitan area (Dummy variable)	2.141 (1.114)*	1.203 (0.799)	4.183 (1.906)*	1.582 (0.912)**	-1.118 (0.772)	-0.324 (0.769)	-0.748 (0.716)	0.053 (0.725)
Location in intermediate zone (Dummy variable)	2.006 (1.378)	-0.351 (0.830)	4.738 (2.121)*	0.419 (0.943)	0.171 (0.811)	0.204 (0.771)	0.287 (0.814)	0.386 (0.781)
Annual turnover (in million $)	-0.609 (0.187)*	—	-0.446 (0.179)*	—	0.010 (0.007)	—	0.012 (0.007)	—
Size of firms (number of workers)	—	-0.011 (0.004)*	—	-0.159 (0.005)*	—	0.005 (0.003)**	—	0.006 (0.003)*
Age of firms (number of years)	0.060 (0.051)	-0.009 (0.032)	0.138 (0.083)	0.018 (0.034)	0.015 (0.024)	0.012 (0.025)	0.001 (0.023)	-0.004 (0.023)
Foreign ownership (dummy variable)	-2.572 (9.693)	0.334 (1.451)	-1.595 (7.758)	0.363 (1.670)	2.150 (0.715)*	2.019 (0.719)*	1.788 (0.686)*	1.636 (0.701)*

Independent variable	Israel				Ireland			
	Model A	Model B	Model C	Model D	Model A	Model B	Model C	Model D
Growth (% change in turnover in the last 3 years)	0.029 (0.027)	0.389 (0.021)**	0.040 (0.033)	0.044 (0.024)**	0.003 (0.034)	0.001 (0.003)	0.002 (0.003)	0.0002 (0.003)
N	74	76	76	78	92	95	90	94
-2 Log Likelihood	29.922	60.054	20.436	49.414	70.040	69.704	73.362	74.822
Goodness of fit	35.374	51.487	29.575	48.338	60.508	60.074	65.149	63.635
Cox and Snell - R^2	0.566	0.353	0.616	0.440	0.384	0.402	0.346	0.369
Nagelkerke - R^2	0.797	0.500	0.872	0.626	0.539	0.564	0.487	0.521

Notes:
† Figures in parentheses are the standard error.
** Significant at the 5 percent level.
* Significant at the 10 percent level.

The reason for the greater likelihood of innovation in the small plants in Israel may be connected to the existence of a large number of new plants at the infant stage, most of whose work is in R&D activities that lead to the development of new products. At a later, more mature stage, these plants transform from primarily R&D to production activities, taking in many production workers. In comparison, an opposite tendency prevails in Ireland, where the trend to innovate increases with the size of the plant. This finding is probably connected to the character of high-technology plants in Ireland, which, for the main part, are large compared to Israeli plants and deal mainly with production and less with R&D. The large plants are apparently also more prepared to take chances in developing new products compared to smaller ones, a fact connected also to the higher proportion of foreign ownership in large plants compared to the small ones. In large organisations there are more opportunities to transfer technology between plants. Foreign investors tend to build large production plants in Ireland, and they are prepared to invest more in innovative activities than local investors. This is manifested in the frequency of innovative plants amongst those 72 percent owned by foreign investors compared to 47 percent locally-owned plants.

No statistical association was found in either area between the age of the plant and its probability to innovate. This finding may be connected to the fact that the high-technology industry in both areas is relatively young, and its tendency to engage in, or not to engage in, innovation has not yet developed clear patterns. Statistically significant influence by foreign investors in Ireland on the innovative ability of high-technology plants was found in all the models that were tested. In comparison, no positive influence of foreign investors on the probability to innovate was detected in Israel. The explanation for this is partially connected to the low frequency of foreign investors in Israeli high-technology plants with only 36 percent of plants compared to 75 percent in Ireland.

In Israel, in contrast to Ireland, it was found that output growth, which characterised high-technology plants in recent years measured by the volume of sales, has a positive and statistically significant influence on the rate of innovation. This result occurred in two of the models, B and D, and at a level of significance of ($p < 0.10$). This finding concurs with the hypothesis that innovative plants tend to grow at a faster rate than those which are not innovative. In Ireland, on the other hand, since high-technology plants are mainly production plants, and for those concerned with innovation this activity is relatively marginal to the plant's production, the growth in sales does not influence the rate of innovation.

8.5 CONCLUSIONS

A comparative analysis of the characteristics of high-technology plants in Israel and Ireland indicates notable differences for most of the attributes tested in this study. High-technology plants in both areas are relatively young, mostly established since the second half of the 1980s, and relying to a very considerable extent on external markets for exporting their products. This is where the similarity between the high-technology industries in the two areas ends. All other characteristics examined indicate notable differences, indicative of the totally different character of the Irish high-technology industry compared to that in Israel.

High-technology plants in Ireland are large, established mostly by foreign investors. They concentrate primarily on production and very little on R&D. In comparison, the Israeli high-technology plants are small, engaged primarily in R&D, and were mostly established by local investors.

The results obtained from the multivariate empirical analysis for both areas indicate a connection between the likelihood of innovating and the level of investment in R&D. R&D incentive programmes could positively affect the willingness of high-technology plants to engage in innovation.

In Ireland, where there is no spatial policy regarding R&D incentives, locations were not found to have any influence on the tendency to innovate. The proportion of innovative high-technology plants in Ireland does not change according to location. However, in Israel, it was found that location does influence the frequencies of innovation, although it contradicts the progressive regional policy designed to gain support for R&D in peripheral regions. The results of the statistical analysis indicate the ineffectiveness of a support policy for R&D, which, in its regional preference, does not succeed in attracting innovative high-technology plants to peripheral areas.

The innovative milieu of the metropolitan region, expressed in a large pool of skilled labour and concentration of knowledge that contributes to an innovative environment, provides central areas with a comparative advantage over other areas (see our paper: Frenkel et al. 2001b). Furthermore, the spatial concentration of academic institutions, technological research institutes and other centres of knowledge in metropolitan areas increases the proximity and accessibility of high-technology plants to knowledge in these areas. Apparently the cumulative effect of these factors is greater than the power of the programmes designed to attract R&D activities to peripheral areas. In the intermediate areas, around the metropolitan area, we can discover the indigenous firms, including spin-offs from other firms (see for example selected paper in Breheny and McQuaid 1987).

Ireland's attractiveness for foreign investors may stem from the fact that Ireland is a member of the EU, holding a preferable position compared to Israel in attracting (American) foreign investors who prefer a location with a European market orientation. Ireland's conversion to a large production platform for high-technology products was also connected to the relatively large pool of cheap labour. Israel, on the other hand, is not so attractive to foreign investors, although it has developed new technologies and trained a large pool of skilled labour, as is manifested by the percentage of locally-owned firms. This difference between the two areas contributed to Israel's development as an R&D laboratory on a world-wide scale.

REFERENCES

Alderman, N. and M.M. Fischer (1992), 'Innovation and technological change: an Austrian-British comparison', *Environment and Planning A*, **24**, pp. 273-88.

Ben-Akiva, M. and R.L. Lerman (1985), *Discrete Choice Analysis: Theory and Application to Travel Demands*, Cambridge, Mass.: MIT Press.

Birnie, E. and D.M.N.W. Hitchens (1999), *Northern Ireland Economy: Performance, Prospects and Policy*, Aldershot, UK: Ashgate.

Breheny, M. and R.W. McQuaid (eds) (1987), *The Development of High-Tech Industries: an International Survey*, London: Croom-Helm.

Ciccone, A. and R.E. Hall (1996), 'Productivity and the density of economic activity', *American Economic Review*, **86**, pp. 54-70.

Davelaar, E.J. and P. Nijkamp (1988), 'The urban incubator hypothesis: re-vitalization of metropolitan areas?', *The Annals of Regional Science*, **22** (3), pp. 48-65 (special issue).

Dosi, G. (1988), 'Sources, procedures, and microeconomic effects of innovation', *Journal of Economic Literature*, **XXVI**, pp. 1120-71.

Felsenstein, D. (1994), 'University related science parks - seedbeds or enclaves of innovation?', *Technovation*, **14** (2), pp. 93-110.

Frenkel, A. (1997), 'Can regional policy affect firms' innovation potential in lagging regions?', Paper presented to the 37th European Congress of the Regional Science Association, Rome, Italy, 26-29 August.

Frenkel, A., D. Shefer, K. Koschatzky and G.H. Walter (2001a), 'Firm characteristics, location and regional innovation: a comparison between Israeli and German plants', *Regional Studies* (forthcoming).

Frenkel, A., D. Shefer and S. Roper (2001b), *Public Policies, Innovation and Locational Determinants of Hi-tech Firms: A Comparison Between Israel and Ireland*, Submitted for publication.

Haynes, K.E. and A.S. Fortheringham (1991), 'The impact of space on the application of discrete choice models', *Review of Regional Studies*, **20** (2), pp. 191-8.

Kleinknecht, A. (1996), *Determinants of Innovation*, London: Macmillan Press.

McAleese, D. and D. McDonald (1978), 'Employment growth and the development of linkages in foreign-owned and domestic manufacturing enterprises', *Oxford Bulletin of Economics and Statistics*, **40** (4), pp. 321-39.

Malecki, E.J. (1979), 'Agglomeration and intra-firm linkage in R&D location in the United States', *TESG*, **70**, pp. 322-31.

Nelson, R.R. (1986), 'The generation and utilization of technology: a cross industry analysis', Paper presented at the conference on '*Innovation Diffusion*', Venice, 17-21 March.

Nelson, R.R. (1993), *National Innovation Systems*, New York: Oxford University Press.

NESC (1982), *A Review of Industrial Policy*, A Report Prepared by the Telesis Consultancy Group, Dublin.

O'Farrell, P.N. and B. O'Loughlin (1980), *An Analysis of New Industry Linkages in Ireland*, Dublin: Industrial Development Authority.

O'Farrell, P N. and B. O'Loughlin (1981), 'New industry input linkages in Ireland: an econometric analysis', *Environment and Planning A*, **13** (3), pp. 285-308.

Pindyck, R.S. and D.L. Rubinfeld (1981), *Econometric Models and Economic Forecasts*, London: McGraw-Hill.

Roper, S. (1996), 'How much can regional policy increase firms' innovation capability?', Paper presented at the 36th European Congress of the 'European Regional Science Association', Zurich, 26-30 August.

Roper, S. (2001), 'Innovation, networks and plant location: some evidence for Ireland', *Regional Studies* (forthcoming).

Roper, S. and A. Frenkel (2000), 'Different paths to success? The growth of the electronics sector in Ireland and Israel', *Environment and Planning C*, **18**, pp. 651-65.

Roper, S. and N. Hewitt-Dundas (1998), *Innovation, Networks and the Diffusion of Manufacturing Best Practice: A Comparison of Northern Ireland and the Republic of Ireland*, Belfast, UK: NIERC.

Roper, S., B. Ashcroft, J.H. Love, S. Dunlop and K.V. Hofmann (1996), *Product Innovation and Development in UK, German and Irish Manufacturing*, Belfast, Northern Ireland: Economic Research Centres.

Rosenberg, N. (1985), 'The commercial exploitation of science by American industry', in K.B. Clarck, R.H. Hayes and C. Lorenz (eds), *The Uneasy Alliance: Managing the Productivity-Technology Dilemma*, Cambridge, Mass.: Harvard Business School Press.

Shefer, D. and E. Bar-El (1993), 'High technology industries as a vehicle for growth in Israel's peripheral regions', *Environment and Planning C*, **11**, pp. 245-61.

Shefer, D. and A. Frenkel (1998), 'Local milieu and innovativeness: some empirical results', *The Annals of Regional Science*, **1**, pp. 185-200.

Shefer, D., A. Frenkel, K. Koschatzky and H.G. Walter (2001), 'Targeting industries for regional development in Israel and in Germany - a comparison study', in M.L. Lahr and R.E. Miller, *Regional Science Perspectives in Economic Analysis*, Holland: Elsevier Publisher, pp. 207-30.

Suarez-Villa, L. and M.M. Fischer (1995), 'Technology, organization and export-driven R&D in Austria's electronics industry', *Regional Studies*, **29**, pp. 19-42.

Suarez-Villa, L. and P.-H. Han (1990), 'The rise of Korea's electronic industry: technological change, growth and territorial distribution', *Economic Geography*, **66**, pp. 273-92.

Suarez-Villa, L. and P.-H. Han (1991), 'Organization, space and capital in the development of Korea's electronic industry', *Regional Studies*, **25**, pp. 327-43.

Suarez-Villa, L. and C. Karlsson (1996), 'The development of Sweden's R&D-intensive electronic industries. Exports, outsourcing and territorial dispersion', *Environment and Planning A*, **28**, pp. 783-817.

Suarez-Villa, L. and R. Rama (1996), 'Outsourcing, R&D and the pattern of intra-metropolitan location: the electronic industry of Madrid', *Urban Studies*, (UK) **33** (7), pp. 1155-97.

Teubal, M. (1993), 'The innovation system of Israel: description performance and outstanding issues', in R.R. Nelson (ed.), *National Innovation Systems: A Comparative Analysis*, Oxford: Oxford University Press.

NOTES

1. The population of Israel numbered 6.0m in 1998, and that of the Republic of Ireland reached 3.7m, with an additional 1.6m people in Northern Ireland. The data is from the Statistical Abstract of Israel No. 55, 1999, and the Central Bureau of Statistics and Trade (1999) CSO of Ireland, respectively.
2. Here we focus solely on the Republic of Ireland. For industrial policy in Northern Ireland, see Birnie and Hitchens (1999). Throughout the rest of the chapter the term Ireland refers to both Northern Ireland and the Republic of Ireland. See Roper and Hewitt-Dundas (1998) for a discussion of differences in innovation behaviour between Northern Ireland and the Republic of Ireland.
3. See also Roper (2000) for a more detailed discussion of differences between the innovation behaviour of plants in the various Irish regions.

PART THREE

Human Capital

Introduction to Part Three

The role played by human capital in fostering regional growth is presently a major topic of research. Current theories of growth stress the role played by educational investments in increasing the pace of economic development. However, of particular interest to urban and regional economists is the relationship between such investments and the geography of growth. In order to understand these relationships it is necessary to consider the links between human capital gains and employment changes, both within regions and between regions. The three chapters in this part each consider the nature of these links from different perspectives.

In Chapter 9 Philip McCann and Stephen Sheppard examine the interaction between the individual's acquisition of human capital, the public provision of tertiary education, and the regional returns to such private and public investments. The link between these three issues is regarded as being the education-migration and employment-migration behaviour of students both prior to, and subsequent to, their higher education. The analysis is based on a large sample of UK university graduates, and the comprehensive data allow the sequential migration choices of the students to be modelled. The human capital characteristics of the student and also the quality of the education received are both shown to affect the employment-migration behaviour of the students, as do the local economic conditions in which the students originate, study and work. The results generated here provide for a reconsideration of the true regional economic impacts of higher education. Static income-employment multiplier approaches can significantly understate or overstate the regional benefits of public education investment, depending on whether the actual location of the benefits of the human capital acquisitions are incorporated.

In Chapter 10 Boris Portnov discusses the determinants of interregional labour flows. Migration models, and in particular disequilibrium models of migration, generally assume that interregional migration over substantial distances is related to the availability and returns to employment. As well as this, we know that the likelihood of migration is also related to human capital and amenity characteristics. Portnov combines these broad issues from the perspective of an employment-housing paradigm, in which the effects of in-migration on housing demand, and their consequent effects on land supply constraints are considered. Local land constraints under conditions of in-migration, can lead to the out-migration of many current residents, as well as hampering the further in-migration of new migrants. The result is that real estate cost appreciation can lead to simultaneous two way migration flows into and out of a region. Portnov analyses the net effects of these labour flows across a range of regions, and in particular discusses the situations where regional net migration flows are zero, even though gross migration flows are positive. The analysis focuses on three countries, namely Israel, Japan and Norway, which are relatively small geographically, and which also exhibit very high variations in regional population densities. For each of these countries, models of 'migration neutrality' are estimated across regions as a function of employment, climate-amenity, demographic and housing variables.

In Chapter 11 Joseph Persky and Daniel Felsenstein discuss the hierarchical interrelationships which exist between employment changes and human capital acquisitions. The approach they adopt is that of a 'job chain', in which individuals are regarded as moving into a newly vacated employment positions deemed to be superior to their previous positions. As one person moves up the employment ladder in order to take up a new job, this creates a new vacancy for someone else lower in the employment chain, which in turn provides a new opening for another person even further down in the chain. As each person moves up the employment chain, there are welfare gains which accrue to each mover within the chain. The process of moving up the employment chain provides the individual with a gain in human capital which. once acquired, is itself independent of the existence of the employment chain. As such, the net welfare effects of a movement up the job chain cannot simply be counted in terms of the income earned by the person at the top of the chain. Instead we must consider the aggregate effect of the incremental human capital gains to each job mover. This approach provides new insights into the impacts of public employment generation schemes, and allows us to consider 'trickle down' in a more comprehensive manner than would be possible from a standard multiplier model.

The three chapters highlight the complex nature of the relationship between human capital investments, regional labour markets and interregional labour market behaviour. The various approaches adopted and the techniques employed here point to ways of furthering our understanding of the interrelatedness of these issues. A sound understanding of this relationship is necessary to ensure that public policy can be effective as a means of promoting regional development.

9. Public Investment and Regional Labour Markets: The Role of UK Higher Education

Philip McCann and Stephen Sheppard

9.1 INTRODUCTION

In what ways does public investment in higher education affect the economy? Investigation of this question tends to focus on the way augmented human capital provides private returns for the person in whom it is embodied (Card 1995) or the returns to the aggregate economy from the collective educational investments (Blundell et al. 1999). From the perspective of the national economy it is implicitly assumed that all areas and sectors of the economy benefit from a general growth in national stock of human capital. For regional economists, the role higher education plays in encouraging specifically local economic development is rather more complex. Discussions from this regional perspective largely focus on the local direct expenditure-employment multiplier effects of higher education (Armstrong 1993). These rather static approaches tend to ignore the fact that the local provision of education and training may itself contribute to a growth in the local stock of human capital (Bennett et al. 1995), and may do so in a way that varies across regions.

The ability of higher education infrastructure to increase the stock of human capital within the local labour market will depend on the ability of the region to attract the appropriate labour and also to retain it. From the point of view of attracting appropriate labour, certain institutions may be better able to attract the most able students and scholars from a variety of areas. If the graduates of these institutions go on to relatively more successful employment than those of institutions less able to attract such candidates, this may imply that the rates of return to these institutions will be higher, when measured at the national level. However, in terms of the local rates of return to the public education investment, the relative performance will depend on the ability of the region to retain such graduates. For some areas, the retention rate of graduates in the local economy may be very high. In these cases, if local agglomerative forces are at work, the growth in human capital fostered by the local higher education institutions may engender further local growth in both public and private investments. The regional rates of return to the public investment in education will consequently be high. On the other hand, if no such local agglomerative forces are evident, then many of the potential gains to productive capacity may be lost to other areas as graduates look for employment elsewhere. There is some confirmation of this observation in the analysis of Quigley and Rubinfeld (1993), whose work suggests that in the US context there is less spending on public higher education in states where the population is more mobile. In such locations the reduced ability to retain students after graduation reduces the returns to public investment in higher education, and the state governments respond accordingly.

It is therefore clear that the existence of higher education institutions in the local economy is not of itself sufficient to ensure a growth in the local stock of human capital; what is also required is for the institutions to attract students of sufficient learning ability, and for the local labour market to retain them once they have graduated. The regional rates of return to public educational investment, therefore, depend crucially both on the migration behaviour of new students into the local economy, and also on the subsequent migration behaviour of these graduates.

With these arguments in mind, the object of this chapter is to discuss how the quality and location of public infrastructure in higher education is related to the migration behaviour of students. In order to do this we analyse data from two cohorts of UK graduates using the geographical information system MAPINFO. These data contain information about the characteristics of the individual graduate, and we combine this with information about the characteristics of the higher education institution attended, and the local economic environments of the domicile, education and employment locations. We then model the sequential migration moves from domicile to education and employment location as a function of these variables. In the next section we discuss UK labour market and migration behaviour. In Section 9.3 we will discuss the nature of the UK higher education sector, and indicate how various indicators of this sector can be interpreted within a human capital framework. In Sections 9.4 and 9.5, the data and methodology will be presented, and Section 9.6 will provide the results and discussion.

9.2 LABOUR MARKETS AND MIGRATION

The outcomes of the relationship between human capital, search costs, information and migration will depend in part on the personal characteristics of migrants and the spatial patterns of employment opportunities. The likelihood of migration is generally positively related to the education of the individual job-seeker (Schwartz 1976), as the returns to migration will tend to be higher for more skilled labour. At the same time, the likelihood of migration is generally positively related to the previous migration history of the individual (DaVanzo 1976). The hypothesised reason for this is that individuals with a more migratory history tend to be less psychologically tied to any particular local area, and as such are more footloose. At the same time, personal unemployment increases the likelihood of migration (DaVanzo 1978), and therefore the out-migration propensity of an area is correlated with the local unemployment rate. In the UK the strength of this relationship between local unemployment and spatial job-search appears to increase with the level of geographical peripherality and the severity of local cyclical downturns, and to decrease with search duration (Herzog et al. 1993) and housing tenure (Hughes and McCormick 1981). On the other hand, the effect of regional wage differences on migration behaviour is generally rather complicated to identify. This is because converting nominal wage indices to real wage indices involves the problem of identifying whether wage differences genuinely reflect real utility differences from employment, or alternatively reflect a partial compensation for regional amenity variations (Graves 1980; Evans 1990). In the case of UK labour markets, the situation is even more complicated by the fact that migration also appears to be something of an 'escalator' life-cycle phenomenon centred on the London labour market, in which young adults move to London to further their career prospects, only moving to more peripheral areas much later on in life (Fielding 1992).

9.3 THE UK HIGHER EDUCATION SYSTEM

The UK higher education sector is comprised of over one hundred institutions. This sector includes the traditional universities, which always had independent university charters, plus the 'new' universities, which prior to 1991 were polytechnics and technical institutes under the control of local and regional governments. There are only a handful of small private higher education institutions in the UK, such that the vast majority of the sector is funded by government expenditure. University fees are set nationally, and all undergraduate tuition fees are paid for by central government, except for a small fixed premium that is borne by students.

Students pay for the premium plus subsistence expenses from personal funds and/or a system of education loans, available at a subsidised rate set by the government. The annual tuition cost of higher education for UK students is thus independent of the institution or course, and differences in undergraduate educational investments depend solely on spatial variations in the cost of living between university locations. From the point of view of human capital theory, the initial cost of undergraduate educational investments is therefore only a function of location, plus variations in the length of the undergraduate course. Given that the vast majority of UK undergraduate courses are three years in length,[1] regional differences in the cost of living are the major factor that distinguishes the cost of human capital acquisition between institutions.

Although there have been some attempts to measure the private returns to education according to the subject studied and the level of attainment (Brewer et al. 1996; Blundell et al. 2000), there have been no attempts to measure differences in the returns to education in the UK context that considers the effect of the higher education institution attended. It is possible to provide an implicit index of the subject-independent attractiveness of an institution, because the UK higher education system exhibits an explicit quality ranking. This comes from the Research Assessment Exercise (RAE) carried out in 1992 and 1996 that ranks institutions according to academic research quality. The level of investment funding per student received by each institution from central government is largely dependent on the ranking of the institution. These rankings, which are published widely in the popular press, in part act as an indicator to potential students of the quality of the institution. Given that enrolment at UK higher education institutions is the result of a competitive process dependent on national exam results, the quality of the student applications is highly correlated with the RAE scores of the institutions. For all of these reasons, these scores act as an indicator to potential employers of the quality of the education received by the student, independent of the subject studied or the grade achieved. Therefore, from the perspective of the individual student, the RAE score can be regarded as an institution-specific indicator of returns to education.

Combining these arguments with the observations made in Section 9.2 suggests that the quality of the institution attended will have implications for graduate migration behaviour. In general, we would expect students attending higher ranked institutions to be more mobile, both in terms of the enrolment catchment area, and also their subsequent employment search area. This is because their returns to both education and spatial job search are expected to be higher, the higher is the ranking of the institution attended. In principle, the hypothesised effect of institution quality on migration behaviour would be expected to act independently of other factors, such as the attainment level of the individual student, and the local economic conditions of the student's domicile and educational environments. At the same time, human capital arguments imply that students will take advantage of spatial price variations, and will attend institutions where the cost of living is lower, for any given quality of educational institution. High quality institutions in low-cost areas would therefore appear to offer very high rates of return to the individual's investment in education.

As we saw in the introductory section it may be, however, that there is a relationship between the types and quality of educational establishments within a local area, the nature of the local labour market, and the efficiency of the job-search process. If the quality of the local higher education institutions contribute to the quality of the local labour market, it may be that areas with concentrations of high quality education institutions will also tend to be areas of high employment demand. For example, US data (Card 1995) suggests that growing up near a college or university increases both the individual earnings and the number of years of schooling eventually achieved. One possible explanation is that localised information spillovers and labour market hysteresis may contribute to the development of local agglomeration economies. In terms of our previous migration arguments, these arguments would imply that students graduating from institutions in areas with many high quality institutions, may tend to exhibit a lower on-migration propensity than students emanating from less prestigious institutions. The clustering argument would thus run counter to the spatial job-search argument discussed earlier, and would provide an institutional logic to the development of certain local labour markets. The net migration flows of students to any area, and thus the net human capital flows into the area, would thus be the result of a sequential pattern of migration, which itself is influenced by the location, density and quality of the educational institutions attended.

9.4 THE DATA

The data we employ are provided by the Higher Education Statistics Agency (HESA) and comes from the annual UK student leavers' questionnaire. The information given comes from a sample of two cohorts of students for the years 1994/95 and 1995/96,[2] broken down by gender (GENNUM), and provides information on the institution attended, whether the course was undergraduate or postgraduate (POSTGRAD), and the grade awarded (FIRST, TWOONE, TWOTWO, THIRD). The survey reports on their employment activities between six and twelve months after their graduation.

The HESA data give us a four digit standard occupational classification (SOC) and standard industrial classification (SIC 1992) description of the work activities in which the individuals are engaged, and classify whether the activities are full-time, part-time, permanent or temporary. At the same time, the HESA survey provides us with the postcode district details of the domicile, higher education institution, and first workplace locations of each student. Incorporating this postcode information into our GIS system, which allows us to identify the geographical centre point of each of the 2700 postcode districts,[3] we are able to map the sequential pattern of individual and aggregate student-graduate migration flows. Not all data points for every observation are consistent. Combining the data we end up with 89,710 observations from the two surveys for which all the individual, local area, and institution data outlined below are complete. Our combined sample represents just over 26 percent of the total sample of students surveyed over the two years, and 15 percent of the total national student populations graduating during these two particular years.

The data then permit us to identify student flows from domicile to location of higher education, and then from higher education to final employment. Our models below focus on the decision by students to acquire higher education locally versus away from their domicile, and after education the decision to accept employment near the education institution, to return to the original domicile location (if they left) or to move on to a third location. To begin with, it is helpful to get an overview of the nature of human capital flows within the UK generated by the higher education process. These can be seen in Figures 9.1 and 9.2 below. Both figures restrict attention to those flows between UK counties that averaged at least 100 individuals per year over the two years of our sample. In each figure, the left panel shows flows from domicile to higher education, and the right panel shows flows from higher education to first employment. The magnitude of the flow is proportional to the width of the arrows. The counties are shaded according to the number of higher education institutions located within.

Figure 9.1 shows flows that originate in London as pre-education domicile, and terminate in London for post-graduation employment. Figure 9.2 shows flows that originate from domiciles outside London, and terminate in employment outside London. One can compare flows and begin to see patterns in the data that are suggestive of the forces we have discussed above. For example, the flows into London for employment clearly swamp the flows out of London for higher education. This is in contrast to such cases as the flow between Glasgow and Edinburgh, where the flows from West to East to acquire higher education are only very slightly larger than the flow from East to West for employment.

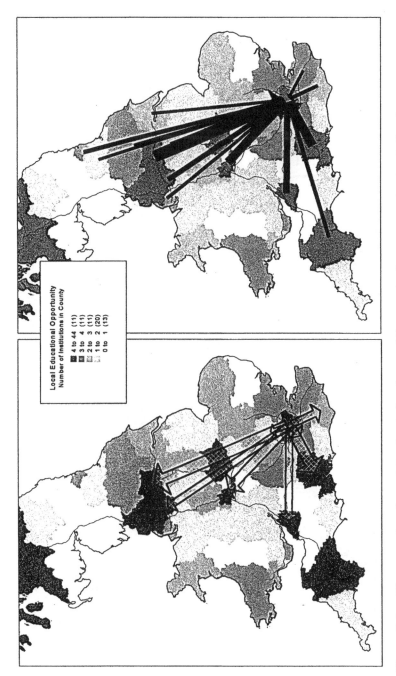

Figure 9.1   Flows to education originating in London, and flows to employment terminating in London

141

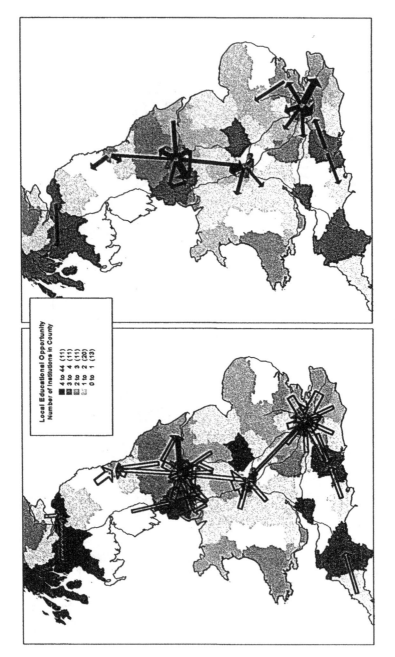

Local Educational Opportunity
Number of Institutions in County

- 4 to 44 (11)
- 3 to 4 (11)
- 2 to 3 (11)
- 1 to 2 (20)
- 0 to 1 (13)

Figure 9.2   Flows to education originating outside London, and flows to employment terminating outside London

In order to make use of the HESA data on migration and first employment within a human capital-search theory framework, it is necessary to impute long-run expected real wages to the occupations in which the students are currently employed (Naylor et al. 1998) in the locations in which the students are currently employed. The justification for this is that the existence of both technological lock-in effects and labour market hysteresis means that simply by taking a job at a particular location, an individual is more likely to stay in both that particular location and occupational grouping, than they are to move to any alternative occupation or location. Moreover, we assume that individuals are not systematically unaware of this.

In order to construct long-run real wage indices, we use national average occupational wages broken down by gender, and weighted by region and local county real estate costs, as a measure of the expected real lifetime occupational earnings. The 1995 and 1996 New Earnings Survey (NES), provide detailed nominal wage data broken down by gender and SOC. Average nominal levels are provided for up to three-digit SOC classifications, and nominal regional wages are given for 25 and 23 two-digit SOC groupings for men and women, respectively. Our basic spatial units of analysis are the fifty-four local authority district-based counties of England and Wales defined by the 1974 Local Government Act, plus the nine regional councils of Scotland as defined in 1975.[4] These are smallest areas for which all of the relevant information is available. Real wage indices (WAGE) are thus constructed by deflating nominal regionally-weighted wages by local county average real estate costs. The Land Registry of England and Wales provides residential real estate cost data for all of the English and Welsh counties, and Scottish Homes provides data for the Scottish councils. Both sources give us average current house prices by county for housing transactions during 1995.[5]

County unemployment (UE) and economic activity (EACT) data come from the Office for National Statistics. Current indices of the quality of the higher education institutions attended (RAE96) come from the 1996 Research Assessment Exercise. In order to allow for the effect of geographical centrality and peripherality on migration behaviour, we employ a measure of the distance of the domicile and education and final employment locations from London (DLOND), which are mapped within our GIS framework, and we also include population density measures (PDN) in order to allow for the urban hierarchy. Dummy variables allow for domicile and education locations in Scotland (SCOTDOM) and Wales (WALESDOM), in order to see if there are any cultural or linguistic effects on migration. Finally, we employ a variable that measures the number of higher education institutions within the domicile (DOMCOINS), education (EDUCOINS) and employment (FINCOINS) in order to pick up any possible educational clustering-agglomeration effects. The suffixes DOM, EDU and FIN represent variables with respect to the domicile, education and final employment locations, respectively.

9.5 METHODOLOGY

The modelling approach we employ reflects the fact that the migration process is a sequential decision-making process in two stages, one prior to higher education and the other after acquiring higher education. In order to model the first stage of this process, in which the student applicant decides whether to study in the home region or to migrate to another region, we assume that the potential migrant does not have complete information about the economic environment in all the various possible employment locations available. We can assume, however, that they do have relatively complete information about the economic environment in the locations of their original domicile, and also the location of the higher education institution. On the basis of the observable characteristics of the two locations, the institution attended and the characteristics of the individual, we use a mixed logit framework to model their education-migration decision on leaving secondary school and enrolling in higher education as a dichotomous choice in which the primary decision is whether to study in the domicile region or to migrate out of the region in order to study elsewhere.

In the second stage of the modelling process we split up the sample into those students who studied in their home region and those who studied in other regions. The justification for this is that the migration decision at this later stage will be somewhat different between these two sets of students. Students who had chosen to study in their home region will continue to perceive the employment-location decision as a dichotomous choice to remain in their domicile area or to move elsewhere as part of a national search. On the other hand, students who had moved away to study will have also acquired very good information about the local economic environment of the education institution, as well as that of their domicile region. As such, they will perceive the employment-location decision as a tripartite choice between remaining in their education location, returning to their domicile area, or moving to an alternative location as part of a national search process.

9.6 RESULTS AND DISCUSSION

The binomial logit model estimates of the initial decision by school-leavers or new graduates of where to continue their studies are given in Table 9.1.

From the perspective of the local economic environment, the logit estimates indicate that the probability of a student attending higher education outside of the domicile region is positively associated with the economic activity of the domicile region, the wage at the higher education location and the distance of the education location from London, and negatively associated with the wage at the domicile location and the distance from London of the domicile, the population density of the domicile, the unemployment rate and population density of the education location.[6] In other words, students from relatively high real wage, peripherally located, urban areas tend to study locally, whereas students from more central areas will tend to move to education only in other relatively buoyant areas characterised by a low levels of urban concentration, attracted by the prestige of the institution.

Table 9.1 Binomial logit model of the decision to go away (1) versus stay at home (0) for higher education

Variable	Comparison	Estimate	Std Error	t-value	$p{>}|t|$
CONST	1 vs 0	0.20227	0.4256	0.48	0.635
GENNUM	1 vs 0	0.03546	0.0205	1.73	0.084
UEEDU	1 vs 0	−0.06763	0.0091	−7.47	0
UEDOM	1 vs 0	−0.00527	0.0085	−0.62	0.536
DOMCOINS	1 vs 0	−0.00726	0.0018	−4.07	0
EACTDOM	1 vs 0	0.03454	0.0045	7.63	0
EACTEDU	1 vs 0	−0.00327	0.0044	−0.75	0.452
PDNEDU	1 vs 0	−0.00017	0	−18.2	0
PDNDOM	1 vs 0	−0.0004	0	−22.09	0
WAGEDOM	1 vs 0	−0.0412	0.0184	−2.24	0.025
WAGEEDU	1 vs 0	0.07665	0.0183	4.18	0
RAE96	1 vs 0	0.00253	0.0001	34.06	0
POSTGRAD	1 vs 0	−0.36708	0.0314	−11.68	0
FIRST	1 vs 0	0.06395	0.047	1.36	0.174
TWOONE	1 vs 0	0.44126	0.0295	14.94	0
TWOTWO	1 vs 0	0.5823	0.031	18.81	0
THIRD	1 vs 0	0.41001	0.0591	6.94	0
DLONDOM	1 vs 0	−0.00255	0.0001	−18.43	0
DLONEDU	1 vs 0	0.00037	0.0001	2.79	0.005
WALESDOM	1 vs 0	0.27899	0.0557	5.01	0
SCOTDOM	1 vs 0	−0.52991	0.0599	−8.84	0

From the perspective of human capital acquisition, the probability of a student attending higher education outside of the domicile region is also positively associated with the RAE ranking of the institution attended, and all exam grades below a class one undergraduate degree, and negatively associated with postgraduate study and the density of higher education institutions in the local area. The density of higher education institutions here represents in part the range of local choice alternatives. Scottish domiciled students are also more likely to attend higher educations institutions in their domicile region, whereas Welsh domiciled students are also more likely to attend higher education elsewhere. The Scottish and Welsh results reflect primarily institutional differences in education systems rather than cultural differences (McCann and Sheppard 2000b). The tendency of applicants to postgraduate courses to choose institutions in their domicile region may reflect attempts to reduce living costs by staying at home, given that very few grants are available for such educational investments.

The second stage in the sequential migration process is the employment-migration decision on graduation from higher education. For new graduates who attended higher education institutions in their domicile region, Table 9.2 presents the binomial logit model estimates of their decision of where to enter employment. In terms of local economic environments, the likelihood of moving away from the domicile and education region in order to enter employment elsewhere is positively associated with the economic activity and wage at the final employment location, and the distance of the domicile location from London, and negatively associated with the economic activity of the domicile economy, and the unemployment rate, the population density and the distance to London of the final employment location.

In terms of human capital acquisition, the likelihood of moving away for employment is also progressively associated with all academic grades and levels above a class three degree. Men are also more likely to move away for employment. Locally educated women are more likely to stay working in the domicile region, as are Scottish educated students. The effect of the density of higher education institutions on the employment-migration pattern of graduates educated locally is just marginally below the 5 percent significance level, but is sufficiently close to warrant reporting. Here, the likelihood of moving away from the domicile and education region in order to enter employment elsewhere, is positively associated with the density of education institutions in the domicile region, and negatively associated with the density of higher education institutions at the employment location.

In this case, the domicile wage, unemployment rate and population density, along with the RAE ranking of the institution attended, and third class degree qualifications, all appear to be unrelated to the employment-migration decision for students educated locally.

Table 9.2 Binomial logit model estimates of the decision to work locally (0)
or to move away for employment (1), for all students who had
attended higher education in their own domicile region

Variable	Comparison	Estimate	Std Error	t-value	$p > |t|$
CONST	1 vs 0	−1.0178	0.7688	−1.32	0.186
GENNUM	1 vs 0	0.18639	0.0415	4.5	0
UEDOM	1 vs 0	0.02873	0.0266	1.08	0.281
UEFIN	1 vs 0	−0.15598	0.026	−6	0
DOMCOINS	1 vs 0	0.00968	0.0052	1.87	0.062
FINCOINS	1 vs 0	−0.0099	0.0051	1.93	0.054
EACTDOM	1 vs 0	−0.05618	0.014	−4.03	0
EACTFIN	1 vs 0	0.06545	0.0129	5.05	0
PDNDOM	1 vs 0	0.00006	0.0001	1.12	0.263
PDNFIN	1 vs 0	−0.00033	0.0001	−6.19	0
WAGEDOM	1 vs 0	−0.07378	0.0591	−1.25	0.212
WAGEFIN	1 vs 0	0.29472	0.0589	5	0
RAE96	1 vs 0	−0.00001	0.0002	−0.09	0.931
POSTGRAD	1 vs 0	0.41756	0.0633	6.59	0
FIRST	1 vs 0	0.29343	0.0936	3.14	0.002
TWOONE	1 vs 0	0.2606	0.0612	4.26	0
TWOTWO	1 vs 0	0.13389	0.0652	2.05	0.04
THIRD	1 vs 0	0.09805	0.1275	0.77	0.442
DLONDOM	1 vs 0	0.00883	0.0005	17.76	0
DLONFIN	1 vs 0	−0.01029	0.0005	−22.25	0
WALESDOM	1 vs 0	0.1593	0.1171	1.36	0.174
SCOTDOM	1 vs 0	−0.39868	0.1238	−3.22	0.001

As we see in McCann and Sheppard (2000a), the highest positive out-migration elasticities are associated with the domicile distance from London and the activity rate at the employment location, while the highest negative out-migration elasticities are associated with the domicile activity rate and the distance from London and unemployment rate of the final employment location.

For the graduates who had moved away from their home region to study, the employment-migration estimates are given in Table 9.3. As we discussed above, these graduates will perceive the employment-location decision as a tripartite choice. For the decision not to return home for work,[7] in terms of local environmental factors the likelihood of entering employment at the education location is positively associated with the unemployment and activity rate of the education location, the wage at the domicile location, the unemployment rate and population density of the education and final employment locations, and negatively associated with the population density of the domicile location.

Table 9.3 Multinomial logit model estimates of the decision to return home to work (0), to work in the vicinity of the higher education institution attended (1), or to move away to a new employment location as part of a national job-search (2)

Parameter	Estimates				
Logit Variable	Comparison	Estimate	Std. Error	t-value	$p>|t|$
CONST	1/0	−5.34957	0.5666	−9.44	0
	2/0	−1.55747	0.4354	−3.58	0
GENNUM	1/0	−0.09299	0.0246	−3.77	0
	2/0	−0.14025	0.02	−7.01	0
UEEDU	1/0	0.03662	0.0112	3.26	0.001
	2/0	−0.04003	0.0086	−4.66	0
UEDOM	1/0	−0.00129	0.0107	−0.12	0.905
	2/0	0.00687	0.0089	0.77	0.44
UEFIN	1/0	0.04978	0.0117	4.24	0
	2/0	−0.01547	0.0097	−1.6	0.11
EDUCOINS	1/0	0.00831	0.0022	3.79	0
	2/0	−0.01504	0.0018	−8.41	0
DOMCOINS	1/0	0.01351	0.0027	5.01	0
	2/0	0.00767	0.0022	3.5	0
FINCOINS	1/0	−0.00265	0.0024	−1.11	0.266
	2/0	0.02391	0.0021	11.53	0
EACTDOM	1/0	−0.00145	0.0052	−0.28	0.781
	2/0	−0.0124	0.0043	−2.91	0.004
EACTEDU	1/0	0.04374	0.0058	7.48	0
	2/0	0.00436	0.0044	0.99	0.322
EACTFIN	1/0	−0.00488	0.0057	−0.86	0.388
	2/0	0.02147	0.0044	4.92	0
PDNEDU	1/0	0.00005	0	2.31	0.021
	2/0	0.00002	0	1.22	0.222
PDNDOM	1/0	−0.00047	0	−17.91	0
	2/0	−0.00043	0	−20.21	0
PDNFIN	1/0	0.00036	0	14.81	0
	2/0	−0.00005	0	−2.31	0.021

Parameter	Estimates				
Logit Variable	Comparison	Estimate	Std. Error	t-value	*p*>|*t*|
WAGEDOM	1/0	0.08463	0.0241	3.51	0
	2/0	0.20264	0.0203	9.97	0
WAGEEDU	1/0	0.03499	0.0245	1.43	0.154
	2/0	0.19454	0.0189	10.27	0
WAGEFIN	1/0	0.04375	0.0281	1.56	0.12
	2/0	−0.06745	0.0227	−2.98	0.003
RAE96	1/0	0.00216	0.0001	24.48	0
	2/0	0.00111	0.0001	15.63	0
POSTGRAD	1/0	−0.35521	0.0433	−8.21	0
	2/0	0.32691	0.0364	8.97	0
FIRST	1/0	0.06914	0.0626	1.1	0.269
	2/0	0.60928	0.052	11.73	0
TWOONE	1/0	−0.16048	0.0373	−4.3	0
	2/0	0.23964	0.0324	7.4	0
TWOTWO	1/0	−0.17333	0.0382	−4.54	0
	2/0	0.09251	0.0331	2.79	0.005
THIRD	1/0	−0.1587	0.067	−2.37	0.018
	2/0	−0.02565	0.057	−0.45	0.653
DLONDOM	1/0	0.00007	0.0002	0.42	0.672
	2/0	0.00095	0.0001	6.53	0
DLONEDU	1/0	−0.00158	0.0002	−8.14	0
	2/0	0.00048	0.0001	3.22	0.001
DLONFIN	1/0	0.003	0.0002	17.02	0
	2/0	−0.00223	0.0001	−14.95	0
WALESDOM	1/0	0.08853	0.0606	1.46	0.144
	2/0	−0.04612	0.0494	−0.93	0.351
SCOTDOM	1/0	−0.29454	0.1001	−2.94	0.003
	2/0	−0.24794	0.0869	−2.85	0.004
WALESEDU	1/0	0.01164	0.065	0.18	0.858
	2/0	−0.20493	0.0496	−4.13	0
SCOTEDU	1/0	0.39288	0.1048	3.75	0
	2/0	−0.06772	0.0879	−0.77	0.441

In terms of human capital acquisition, the likelihood of remaining in the education region is positively associated with the RAE ranking of the institution and the density of education institutions at both the education and domicile locations, and negatively associated with postgraduate study and all undergraduate degree classes below a first. Women are more likely to remain close to the education locations, and the likelihood of remaining in the education location is also associated with the distance of the employment and education location from London. Scottish educated students are also more likely to remain at the education location, although Scottish domiciled students are likely to return home.

In McCann and Sheppard (2000a) we see that the highest elasticities regarding the likelihood of remaining at the education location are positively associated with the activity rate at the education location and the distance from London of the employment location, and negatively associated with the activity rate at the final location.

In terms of the decision not to return home for employment, the likelihood of moving away from both the domicile and education locations in order to seek work as part of a national labour market search is positively associated with the activity rate of the employment location and the wage at the domicile and education locations, and negatively associated with education area unemployment rate, the domicile activity rate and population density, and the wage at the employment location.

In terms of human capital acquisition, the likelihood of moving away as part of a national labour market search is positively associated with the RAE ranking of the institution attended, the achievement of all academic grades above a class three undergraduate degree and the density of education institutions at the domicile and employment locations, and negatively associated with the density of education institutions at the education location. The likelihood of moving away is positively associated with the distance from London of the domicile and education locations, and negatively associated with the distance from London of the final employment location. Men are also less likely to move away to a new location for employment than women, as are Welsh educated and Scottish domiciled students.

As we see from McCann and Sheppard (2000a), the highest on-migration elasticities are positively associated with the activity level of the final location and the wages at the education and domicile locations, and negatively associated with the activity rates of the domestic and education locations and the distance of the employment location from London.

9.7 CONCLUSIONS

In terms of the interaction between higher education and labour markets, there are five major migration findings that come out of our results. The first general observation is that the higher is the ranking of the education institution, and the higher quality are the individual undergraduate students, the more migratory are the students admitted and the more migratory are the graduates produced. This is consistent with the human capital argument. Secondly, a high local concentration of higher education establishments in the domicile region tends to reduce the attractiveness of moving away to study. For those students who moved away for education, there does appear to be strong evidence of a relationship between the spatial clustering of education institutions and the attractiveness of the local labour market. Thirdly, UK graduate migration is primarily a function of job availability, which itself is a function of accessibility to London. All of this is consistent with the escalator observations (Fielding 1992). Fourthly, Scottish domiciled and educated students exhibit the lowest education and employment migration propensities, compared to both English and Welsh students. As we see elsewhere, this is due to differences in the education systems rather than cultural factors (McCann and Sheppard 2001b). The fifth major observation to come out of this research is that there are significant gender differences in terms of migration behaviour. For undergraduate student admissions, men are generally more mobile. However, for those students who do move away from home in order to enter higher education in other regions, women are consistently more migratory than men. Moreover, this result holds irrespective of whether we define on-migration as staying in the area of education or moving to an alternative location. The reason for this is that men appear consistently more likely to move back to their domicile region.

REFERENCES

Armstrong, H.W. (1993), 'The local income and employment impact of Lancaster University', *Urban Studies*, **30**, pp. 1653-68.

Bennett, R., H. Glennerster and D. Nevison (1995), 'Regional rates of return to education and training in Britain', *Regional Studies*, **29** (3), pp. 279-95.

Blundell, R., L. Dearden, C. Meghir and B. Sianesi (1999), 'Human capital investment: the returns from education and training to the individual, the firm, and the economy', *Fiscal Studies*, **20** (1), pp. 1-23.

Blundell, R., L. Dearden, A. Goodman and H. Reed (2000), The returns to higher education in Britain: evidence from a British cohort', *Economic Journal*, **110**, pp. 82-99.

Brewer, D.J., E. Eide and R.G. Ehrenberg (1996), 'Does it pay to attend an elite private college? Cross cohort evidence on the effects of college quality on earnings', NBER Working Paper W5613.

Card D. (1995), 'Using geographic variation in college proximity to estimate the return to schooling', in L.N. Christofides, E.K. Grant and R. Swidinsky (eds), *Aspects of Labour Market Behaviour: Essays in Honour of John Vanderkamp*, Toronto: University of Toronto Press.

DaVanzo, J. (1976), 'Differences between return and nonreturn migration: an econometric analysis', *International Migration Review*, **10**, pp. 13-27.

DaVanzo, J. (1978), 'Does employment affect migration? Evidence from micro data', *Review of Economics and Statistics*, **60**, pp. 504-14.

Evans, A.W. (1990), 'The assumption of equilibrium in the analysis of migration and interregional differences: a review of recent research', *Journal of Regional Science*, **30** (4), pp. 515-31.

Fielding, A.J. (1992), 'Migration and social mobility: south east England as an escalator region', *Regional Studies*, **26** (1), pp. 1-15.

Graves, P.E. (1980), 'Migration and climate', *Journal of Regional Science*, **20** (2), pp. 227-37.

Herzog, H.W., A.M. Schlottmann and T.P. Boehm (1993), 'Migration as spatial job search: a survey of empirical findings', *Regional Studies*, **27** (4), pp. 327-40.

HESA (1997), *Higher Education Statistics for the United Kingdom 1995/96*, Cheltenham: Higher Education Statistics Agency.

Hughes, G. and B. McCormick (1981), 'Do council house policies reduce migration between regions?', *Economic Journal*, **91**, pp. 919-37.

McCann, P., and S. Sheppard (2000a), 'Public investment and regional labour markets: the role of UK higher education', Department of Economics, University of Reading Discussion Paper Series C No 143.

McCann, P. and S. Sheppard (2000b), 'Human capital, higher education and graduate migration: an analysis of Scottish and Welsh students', Paper Presented at the 47th North American Regional Science Association Congress, Chicago.

Naylor, R., J. Smith and A. McKnight (1998), 'Determinants of occupational earnings: evidence for the 1993 UK university graduate population from the USR', Discussion Paper, University of Warwick: Department of Economics.

Quigley, J.M. and D.L. Rubinfeld (1993), 'Public choices in public higher education', in C. Clotfelter and M. Rothschild (eds), *Studies of Supply and Demand in Higher Education*, Chicago: The University of Chicago Press.

Schwartz, A. (1976), 'Migration, age and education', *Journal of Political Economy*, **84**, pp. 701-20.

NOTES

1. The exceptions to this are courses at Scottish institutions that generally last for four years, and courses in medicine, veterinary medicine, dentistry and

architecture that last for five years. All these courses combined account for only 13 percent of UK undergraduates (HESA 1997).

2. The definition of the survey cohorts are the 162,378 students who left higher education in the summer of 1994 and 180,417 students who left higher education in the summer of 1995 respectively. The surveys therefore account for 56.1 percent of the national total of 289,000 students who graduated between 01.10.94 and 31.7.95, and 58.1 percent of the national total of 310,790 students who graduated between 1.8.95 and 31.7.96.

3. The postcode districts have an average area of 84.9 sq. km and an average population of 21,162.

4. In England, seven of these counties are the metropolitan county councils covering the largest urban agglomerations of over one million people. In Scotland, the three separate island councils are combined into a single council for the purposes of our analysis. The average employment size of the areas is 330,825.

5. There is no aggregate UK spatial data for a particular volume or type of housing stock which can be used as a numeraire good for constructing real wage deflators which will allow for substitution between housing and other goods. However, the average price of local transactions, which is weighted by the number of individual transactions of each housing type and size, will partly reflect any such substitution behaviour. Furthermore, by 1995, housing prices in London and the South East were recovering from the 1991 slump and the income-house price ratios were moving closer to their long-run average levels. As such, the real wage estimates provided here for London and the South East, if anything actually underestimate the effect of local house prices on reducing local real wages in these areas.

6. In our sample 81 percent of students moved away to study and 19 percent remained in their home region.

7. In our sample, 32 percent of students who moved away to study returned to the domicile region, 20 percent stayed at their education location, and 48 percent underwent a national search.

10. Models of Migration Neutrality as a Tool of Regional Policy

Boris A. Portnov

10.1 INTRODUCTION[1]

'Migration neutrality' is defined as the state of equilibrium in which a region or community neither gains nor loses its population in migration exchanges with other areas (Figure 10.1).

Using preconditions for 'migration neutrality' as a reference line, planners and decision-makers can determine regional policies aimed at a more balanced distribution of a country's population through generating a 'migration push' in overpopulated regions and encouraging inward migration to development areas in which this growth is desirable.

In this chapter, this concept is examined by studying the patterns of interregional migration in three relatively small and unevenly populated countries - Israel, Japan, and Norway. The study attempts to answer the following questions:

- Is there a general mechanism through which disparities in regional development affect the patterns of interregional migration?
- Which aspects of regional inequalities (climate, employment, housing availability and so on) have the most profound effect on the rates and direction of interregional migration?
- Lastly, which planning policies and strategies are conducive to increasing the attractiveness to migrants of peripheral development areas, in which enduring population growth is desirable?

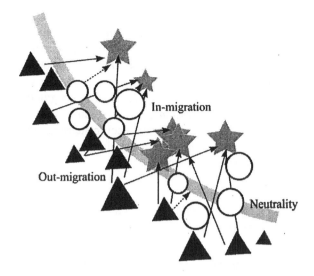

Figure 10.1 Migration neutrality as a general concept

10.2 MODELLING MIGRATION BEHAVIOUR

The neo-classical *human capital model* (Borjas 1989; Poot 1996) represents a common approach to modelling long-distance migration. This model suggests that individuals and families compare the present value of earnings at the present location with that at alternative locations and the costs of move. Richardson (1977) argues, however, that this cost-benefit approach appears to be oversimplified. In supporting this conclusion, he points out that this model rests upon several critical assumptions (homogenous labour, constant returns to scale, perfectly competitive labour markets, and absence of other, non-economic migration motives), which appear to be, in many cases, unsupported by empirical evidence.

De Jong and Fawcett's (1981) *value-expectancy model* represents an attempt to explain inter-area migration as a function of a broad array of both economic and non-economic (environmental, cultural and social) factors. This model, however, requires a precise specification of the *personally valued goals* that 'might be met by moving ... and an assessment of the perceived linkage, in terms of expectancy, between migration behaviour and the attainment of goals in alternative locations' (p. 47). Although this model may provide a perfect explanation of the behaviour of individual migrants, its ability to explain more general migration patterns appears to be considerably restricted.

Numerous empirical models of inter-urban and cross-district migration are also found in the recent literature on migration decision-making (see *inter alia* Michel et al. 1996; Portnov 1998; Portnov and Pearlmutter 1997; Moore and Rosenberg 1995; Greenwood and Stock 1990). These empirical models cover a wide range of migration variables (namely employment, housing, the level of urbanisation and climatic differences between geographic areas), and commonly employ multiple regression analysis as an analytical tool. While this technique often provides a good fit for specific statistical data at hand, it remains unclear, however, whether these models can be applied elsewhere, beyond their original 'time-area' framework.

10.3 HOUSING-EMPLOYMENT PARADIGM OF INTER-AREA MIGRATION

A simplified model of the way in which inter-regional inequalities may affect the patterns of interregional migration is represented in Figure 10.2. The model considers the phenomenon in terms of a simplified *employment-housing* paradigm and is based on a number of assumptions.

Suppose that labour is required in the area. This may be obtained by:

- employing commuters from other localities;
- employing current residents of the area (either currently unemployed, or workers from other industries in the locality), or
- attracting migrants from elsewhere (either residents of other districts or foreign immigrants).

The arrival of newcomers from other areas boosts the demand for housing. The response of the local market to this demand may, however, be time-lagged or inadequate. This, for instance, is the case if land for development is not readily available, as is often the case in overpopulated core areas. The shortage of land for new development may, in turn, increase housing prices, and this process may cause the outflow of current residents who cannot afford decent housing in the area to areas where housing is more available and affordable (Portnov and Pearlmutter 1997).

High housing prices may also hamper the influx of migrants to the area despite the availability of employment. The effect of this housing-employment imbalance on migration may, however, be weakened by various 'interfering' factors. These may include local amenities (mild climate, attractive landscape and so on), macroeconomic performance of the country as a whole, mass immigration, and the educational makeup of the local population (Milne 1993; Walker et al. 1992; Frey 1995; Portnov and Erell 1998).

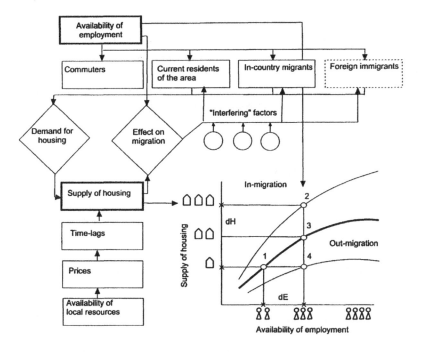

Figure 10.2 Employment-housing paradigm of inter-area migration

The chart incorporated in the model (Figure 10.2) provides a simplified illustration of this 'employment-housing' interlink and its effect on migration.

Suppose that a region has an established balance of employment and housing availability and a relatively low annual rate of net migration (Point 1). Now, assume that additional *employment opportunities* became available in the area (dE), and this employment growth is accompanied by an increase in the *availability* of *housing* (dH). Under these conditions, an influx of migrants to the region can be expected (see Point 2).

Although a response of the local housing market may be lagging or not sufficient (Point 3), such an insufficient supply of housing *may not* have an immediate effect on the existing level of a district's attractiveness to migrants: potential migrants and current residents of the area may still 'tolerate' high housing prices in the region as a necessary 'charge' for better employment opportunities, compared to other areas.

Assume, however, that due to, for instance, land shortage, supply lags or a high rate of foreign immigration, the availability of housing in the area dropped beyond this 'tolerability' level (Point 4). In this case, 'housing-driven' out-migration from the region may become increasingly likely.

As suggested, this hypothetical threshold of 'tolerability,' on which Points 1 and 3 are located, can be termed the *threshold of migration neutrality* (see the bold line in the chart). This threshold is a borderline *sui generis*: the area beneath this curve corresponds to negative net migration (*out-migration*), while the zone, which lies above this curve, is likely to match the state of predominant *in-migration* to the area.

10.4 CASE STUDIES

To test the employment-housing paradigm, introduced in the previous section, countries with uneven distributions of population and development are required. The reason is that the expected effect of the employment-housing interlink on the migration attractiveness of a geographic area is expected to be most prominent in densely populated areas, in which land resources for development are considerably restricted.

Although Israel, Japan and Norway differ in respect to a number of general development indicators - land area, population size, the overall rate of population growth and so on (Table 10.1), they appear to share a number of similarities essential for the present analysis. In particular, population densities in the core regions of these three countries are considerably high.

Thus, in the Tokyo prefecture of Japan, population density reaches nearly 5,400 people per km^2, while in the Tel Aviv district of Israel, this density exceeds 6,700 residents per km^2.

Although Norway is less densely populated, the concentration of population in the capital region of this country (the Oslo county) exceeds some 1,100 people per km^2.

The considerable disparities in population distribution are worth noting. While in Japan, population density in the country's core surpasses the national average by the factor of 16, corresponding ratios for Israel and Norway are even higher: 27 and 81, respectively.

*Table 10.1   Selected socio-economic indicators of the countries included in
the research set*

Indicator	Israel	Japan	Norway
Population size [1,000]	5,500	125,500	4,400
Land area [km^2]	21,946	374,744	324,220
Overall population density [per km^2]	246	335	14
Population density in the core[a] [per km^2]	6,717	5,384	1,144
Overall population growth rate [%]	2.11	0.21	0.47
GDP [$US per capita]	15,500	21,300	26.200
Maximum and minimum rates of migration during the past decade [%]	−0.91/5.87	−0.38/0.46	−2.59/2.80
Interregional inequalities:[b]			
• population density	1.55	1.00	3.06
• employment	0.36	0.91	0.47

Notes:

[a]   The Tokyo prefecture in Japan, Tel Aviv district in Israel, and Oslo prefecture in
Norway.

[b]   Williamson's unweighted inequality index.

Sources: CIA (1997); ICBS (1997); JSB (1997); NSD (1999).

10.5   GENERAL PATTERNS OF INTER-AREA MIGRATION

10.5.1 Israel

Two migration streams appear to exist simultaneously in Israel: while new
immigrants move predominantly to major metropolitan centres of the country
in which most jobs are available, the existing population of these areas tends
to move outward, to the less populated areas in which housing is more
available and affordable (Portnov 1998).

During the recent wave of mass immigration (1990-91), the overwhelming
majority of the new immigrants settled in the country's central areas - the
Haifa, Tel-Aviv and Central districts. Concurrently, two out of three of the
above central districts (Tel-Aviv and Haifa) experienced in these years a
substantial loss of their established population due to negative rates of in-
country migration (ibid.).

The influx of new immigrants (NI) to a particular district of Israel and the outflow of in-country migrants (IM) from this district appear to be interrelated, correlating, most likely, via housing prices. The mass influx of new immigrants to a particular locality boosts housing demand and increases housing prices. This, through a spiral process, may eventually cause the outflow of current residents who cannot afford decent housing in the metropolitan centres to areas of the country where housing is more widely available and more affordable (Portnov and Pearlmutter 1997).

In the area of employment, a similar 'push' effect of immigration on internal migrants is noted by a number of North American studies (see *inter alia* White and Liang 1993; Walker et al. 1992). The above noted 'housing competition' between immigrants and in-country migrants seems, however, to be a typical Israeli phenomenon caused by extremely high immigration rates, government housing subsidies to newcomers, and a lack of land for new development (Lipshitz 1997; Portnov 1998).

10.5.2 Japan

General patterns of in-country migration in Japan during the past decade (1985-95) exhibited two broad trends. First, similar to that in Israel, the relative migration attractiveness of the core districts of Japan (Kanto, Tokai, and Kinki) tended to decline, while that of the peripheral areas (Hokkaido, Tohoku and Kyushu district) tended to grow. Second, the absolute overall rate of net migration in both core and peripheral districts of the country tended to decrease (Abe 1996; Portnov 1999).

A number of possible explanations of these trends can be suggested. First of all, as Abe (1996) argues, the relative level of housing rent in the core districts of Japan grew in recent years at a considerably high rate due to continuously growing land prices. At the same time, the relative level of housing rent in virtually all the peripheral areas of Japan appeared to drop (JSB 1997). Other influencing factors can also be mentioned. One of them is the overall slowdown of the Japanese economy, which became apparent more or less since 1991. As Milne (1993) argues, the business cycle has a significant influence on interregional migration flows and people's propensity to migrate. In particular, the overall rate of in-country migration tends to decline in unfavourable economic years, when people prefer to refrain from costly long-distance moves (Portnov and Erell 1998). This explains why the overall rates of net migration by districts of Japan tended to drop. A decline in migration attractiveness of Japan's metropolitan regions may also be attributed, at least in part, to the aggressive policy of the Japanese government aimed at preventing the excessive accumulation of population and economic activities in the country's core areas (Abe 1996; Markusen 1996).

10.5.3 Norway

Although the countryside of Norway experienced negative net migration for years, the net migration losses were traditionally compensated by the high fertility of rural regions (Hansen 1981). The urban growth of the 1950s-1960s not only accelerated migration from the countryside to urban areas but also caused centripetal migration from peripheral regions to more urbanised core areas. The high rates of migration outflow (0.6-0.9 percent of the overall population per year) and the decreasing fertility rates created a situation in which the population of the northern and interior regions of the country started actually to decline (ibid.).

The discovery of oil in the North Sea and the first oil crisis of 1973 caused the creation of thousands of new jobs in the petroleum industry, primarily in the Rogaland and Hordaland counties on the western coast. The growth of industrial employment in these areas, as well as the decentralisation of the industries from the congested capital region to urban communities located some 100-200 km from Oslo, helped to reverse, at least partially, the progressive trend of the concentration of population in the Oslo-Akershus capital region.

The worsening economic conditions of Norway in the late 1980s, mainly caused by a rapid drop in oil prices, resulted in structural changes in the national economy towards reducing the numbers of economically active in mining, farming and fishing (Eika and Magnussen 1998). These changes affected adversely the traditional manufacturing base of the local regions and caused a further outflow of migrants from these regions to more economically prosperous central areas. As a result, Oslo and the surrounding municipalities in the Akershus county increased their migration surplus from 900 in 1989 to 5,200 in 1996, while net out-migration from the remote municipalities of North Norway reached 4,000-5,000 persons annually, or about 1.0 percent of their overall population (SN 1997).

10.6 RESEARCH METHOD

In order to test the proposed employment-housing paradigm of inter-area migration and to verify the existence of 'neutrality curves,' hypothesised in the previous discussion (see Figure 10.2), it was essential to confirm that employment and housing factors are indeed statistically significant in influencing the patterns of in-country migration in the countries under consideration. To accomplish this task, the analysis was carried out in two main phases.

The first phase included the collection and descriptive analysis of statistical data on inter-area migration and its possible determinants (employment, housing construction, housing prices, and climate).

The data for the analysis were obtained from the following sources:

- *Statistical Abstract of Israel (1985-1996)*; *Construction in Israel (1985-1996)* and *Climatic Atlas of Israel* (Bitan and Rubin 1991).
- Japanese Statistics Bureau: Japan, *Statistical Yearbook (1985-1997)*.
- Norwegian Social Science Data Services (NSD): *Municipality Database (1980-89)*.

In Israel and Japan, the data for the analysis were obtained for administrative districts (ten districts in Japan and six administrative districts of Israel).[2] In Norway, multi-year migration averages were available for individual municipalities (430 municipalities), which made it possible to perform the analysis using a finer spatial grain.

In the second phase of the research, multiple regression analysis (MRA) was used to identify and measure the significance of various factors on net migration rates (percent). Since the study was primarily focused on investigating the effect on migration of *inter-area* disparities in selected development data (employment, housing and so on), rather than on factors affecting migration in a particular district or community, a cross-section analysis was clearly preferred over a time-series analysis.

In *Israel* and *Japan*, the following factors were in the analysis as explanatory variables:

- Climate: The harsh climate of some geographic areas (that is extreme temperatures, high humidity, excessive precipitation and so on) places considerable limitations on regional amenities and human comfort (Portnov and Erell 1998). Climatically harsh areas may, therefore, be less desirable and attractive, at least theoretically, to migrants. As a proxy for the climatic harshness of the area, two different indicators were used. Since in Israel overheated conditions are commonly perceived as the main source of thermal discomfort, the mean annual number of days with heat stress (Bitan and Rubin 1991) was used as the index of a district's climatic harshness. At the same time, in Japan, the mean annual number of snowy and rainy days (JSB 1997) was used as a proxy for climatic harshness of the area.
- Economy: The annual change of per capita GDP was included in the analysis as an explanatory variable. As suggested, the rate of cross-district

migration may be affected by the overall economic performance of a country as a whole.

- Employment change: The average annual change of the number of employees in a district, percent.[3]

Table 10.2 Factors influencing inter-area migration in Israel, Japan and Norway (MRA: linear-log form)

Variable[a]	B	Tolerance[b]	T	Sig. T
Israel:				
Employment change	−0.0342	0.6807	−0.122	0.903
Climate	−0.6281	0.8722	−2.191	0.032
Housing construction	0.4782	0.7229	2.150	0.036
Economy	−0.5650	0.6316	−1.756	0.084
Immigration	2.3269	0.5271	6.703	0.000
Housing growth	0.3165	0.7584	1.891	0.064
Housing prices	−1.2376	0.9133	−2.808	0.007
(Constant)	2.7842		0.988	0.324
No. of obs	60			
R^2	0.7059			
F	19.8906			
Japan:				
Employment change	0.0702	0.8881	4.544	0.000
Climate	−0.1447	0.9180	−1.712	0.091
Housing construction	0.2541	0.9601	5.466	0.000
Economy	−0.0580	0.9789	−1.053	0.295
(Constant)	−0.1010		−0.167	0.868
No. of obs	30			
R^2	0.4379			
F	15.5789			
Norway:				
Housing change	0.609	0.335	6.607	0.000
Employment change	1.020	0.333	8.801	0.000
Constant	−1.822		−19.657	0.000
No. of obs	430			
R^2	0.608			
F	322.818			

Notes:

[a] Factors' initial values were logarithmically transformed.

[b] Collinearity diagnostics.

- Housing construction: The area of gross building of housing in a given year, 1,000 m^2.
- Housing change: A change of the annual rate of housing construction in a district, compared to the previous year.
- Housing prices: Since fully comparable data for Israel and Japan was unavailable, two proxies for housing prices were used. In Israel, housing prices in a district were approximated by the average market price of a standard housing unit. Concurrently, in Japan, average housing rent in the private sector was used. To narrow the differences caused by these two different estimation approaches, the absolute values for a district were normalised using the national average in a respective year as the conditional baseline.
- Immigration: Since in Israel foreign immigration is subject to substantial annual changes, the overall rate of immigration in a given year was included in the analysis as an additional explanatory variable. (Owing to relatively low rates of foreign immigration to Japan, this variable is included only in the Israeli model).
- In Norway, due to restrictions on data availability and comparability, the overall rates of annual net migration (percent) were compared directly with two policy variables - employment and housing change in municipalities.
- Employment change was calculated as the percentage of annual change between the number of employment opportunities available in the municipality at the end and beginning of the period under consideration.
- Housing change was measured as the annual change of per capita housing stock in the municipality (percent).

Three functional forms of regression models - double-linear, linear-log and double-log form - were tested. In the following discussion, the results of the best performing model (linear-log form) are reported (Table 10.2). The collinearity of explanatory variables was analysed and found to be within tolerable limits (Tol. > 0.25).

10.7 INFLUENCING FACTORS

As Table 10.2 shows, regression models for Israel and Norway appear to provide a relatively good fit ($R^2 = 0.706$ and $R^2 = 0.608$, respectively). For Japan, the fit is lower but also reasonably high ($R^2 = 0.438$). This implies that the explanatory variables included in the analysis appear to explain the interregional disparities in net migration rates relatively well.

Table 10.2 also shows that net migration balance in a district of Israel increases in line with the overall number of immigrants to the country *(immigration)* and the overall rate of *housing construction* in the area. At the same time, net migration is adversely affected by high *housing prices* and *harsh climate* of the area.

None of these relationships is totally surprising. For instance, the positive effect of *immigration* on migration balance of a region seems to be clear since foreign immigration is an essential component of a country's overall population growth: when foreign immigration increases, a district has, *ceteris paribus,* better chances to improve its migration balance.

The effect of *housing* (the rate of construction and housing prices) on migration rates is also in line with the initial research assumptions (Figure 10.2). However, it is somewhat surprising that, contrary to our initial assumption, the effect of *employment change* on migration balance of a region in Israel does not appear to be statistically significant (Table 10.2). This phenomenon may have two possible explanations. First, it can be attributed to the heterogeneity of the migrant population, and specifically to the presence of foreign immigrants that are less familiar with the local employment situation than in-country migrants. Second, relatively short aerial distances between various parts of the country should also be taken into consideration. These distances make it possible to commute on a daily basis across regional borders. This, in turn, may reduce the effect of employment change in a specific district on the general patterns of inter-area migration.

Indirectly, the latter assumption appears to be justified in the case of Japan and Norway (Table 10.2). Since commuting distances in these countries are far greater than those in Israel, it is not surprising that the effects of both *housing* and *employment change* on migration 'performance' of geographic areas appear to be highly statistically significant ($T > 4.5$, $P < 0.01$ in Japan and $T > 6.6$, $P < 0.001$ in Norway).

10.8 NEUTRALITY MODELS

Since the preliminary analysis confirmed that employment and housing change are indeed of statistical significance in influencing the rates of inter-area migration in two out of three countries included in the research scope, we shall try to construct the curves of 'migration neutrality' which were hypothesised in the previous discussion (see Figure 10.2). To this end, in each country a subset of cases with a relatively low level of net migration was formed. Considering the actual rates of inter-area migration in the countries in question (see Table 10.1), the conditional range of 'migration neutrality' was assumed to be ±0.25 percent for Israel and Norway and ±0.10 percent for Japan.

There were found *nine* such *neutrality* cases among 60 valid observations available for Israel, 15 cases among 30 valid observations available for Japan, and 130 cases among 430 valid observations available in Norway.

The selected subsets of cases were then diagrammed using their respective rates of employment-housing change (Figures 10.3-10.5).

10.8.1 District level: Israel and Japan

Although the level of administrative districts for which data are available in Israel and Japan makes it possible to perform only a general comparison, the models of migration neutrality obtained for these two countries appear to be a reasonably good fit and are relatively easy to interpret. In the case of Japan, for instance, a *2 percent* increase in employment (10/5 = 2) should be accompanied by a *6 percent* increase in new housing construction (30/5 = 6) in order to maintain the 'neutral migration' balance of the area (see Figure 10.3; dotted line). Concurrently, lower rates of housing construction in the region are likely to cause out-migration.

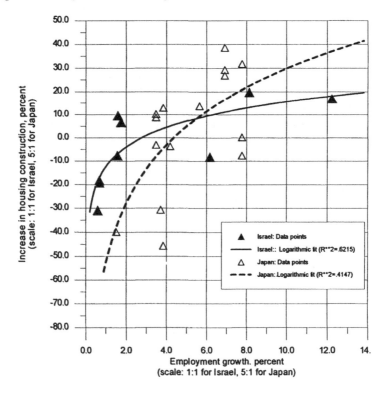

Figure 10.3   'Neutrality' curves for Israel and Japan

At the same time, in Israel the preconditions for 'migration neutrality' are as follows: if the number of jobs in a district increases by some 6 percent, this employment growth should be accompanied by a 10 percent increase in new housing construction in order to maintain the region's 'migration neutrality' (Figure 10.3; solid line). The rates of construction above this level may boost in-migration to the area, while lower rates are likely to cause out-migration.

10.8.2 Municipality Level: Norway

Although even the limited number of cases of 'migration neutrality' found in Israel and Japan allow us to conclude that, in principle, the band of migration neutrality can be identified and separated from other migration outcomes - predominant in-migration and out-migration - a larger number of cases is

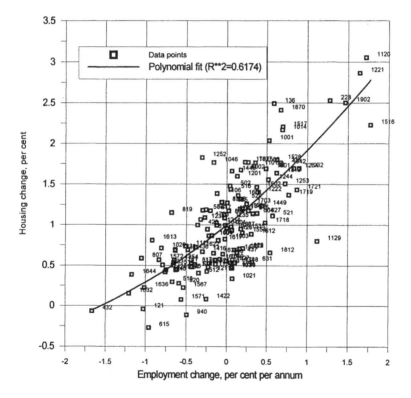

Note: Each symbol is a 10-year average for a municipality. The labels represent the identification numbers of municipalities in the Municipality Database of Norway.

Figure 10.4   Norway: neutrality band for 1980-89

needed for a generalisation. Since in Norway migration statistics are available for some 430 municipalities, this makes it possible to obtain enough observations for more rigorous testing.

As Figure 10.4 shows, similar to that in Israel and Japan, neutrality cases in Norway form a relatively dense cluster of observations allowing for a reasonably good fit (R^2 = 0.617). The relative position of this cluster corresponds to the following rates of employment and housing change: −1.5 + 2.0 percent (employment) and 0.0 + 3.0 percent (housing). Higher rates of these factors' change may cause in-migration to the area, while lower rates are likely to cause an outflow of migrants from a community.[4]

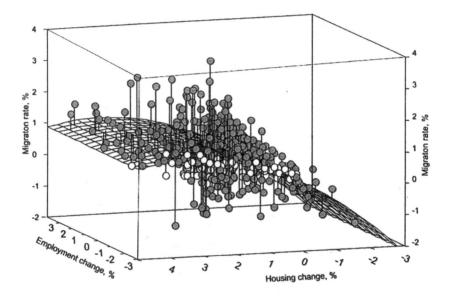

Note: Each dot represents a ten-year average of net migration for a municipality. Neutrality cases are marked by hollow dots.

Figure 10.5   Employment-housing paradigm of inter-area migration in
*   Norway - response surface*

Figure 10.5 helps to illustrate the relative position of 'neutrality cases' in relation to other migration outcomes - in-migration and out-migration. As this figure shows, the 'neutrality cases' (marked by hollow dots) form a cluster positioned between in-migration and out-migration cases, which are located above and below the response surface, respectively.

10.9 CONCLUSION AND POLICY IMPLICATIONS

According to a general migration theory, the predominant motive of interregional migration is job-related: long-distance migrants move to areas where more jobs are available, and wages are higher (Richardson 1977; Perroux 1983; LaLonde and Topel 1997). The present comparative analysis of interregional migration in Israel, Japan and Norway makes it possible to reconsider partially this notion. While the core regions of these countries account for the bulk of available jobs, the attractiveness of these areas to in-country migrants appeared to decline substantially in past years.

To explain this phenomenon, a '*housing-employment*' paradigm of inter-area migration is suggested. According to this paradigm the availability of employment in the core areas attracts in-migrants and this, in turn, boosts housing demand. The response of the local market to this demand is not, however, always adequate, due to, for instance, land shortage or an influx of immigrants. This inadequacy of response of the local housing market increases housing prices and causes the outflow of current residents (who cannot afford decent housing in the area) to areas where housing is more available and affordable. Expensive housing may also hamper a further influx of migrants to the core regions despite the availability of employment.

Based on this housing-employment paradigm, the notion of 'migration neutrality' is suggested. This is the state of migration in which a *region or community neither gains nor loses its population in migration exchanges with other areas.*

The analysis of empirical data made it possible to obtain the curves of migration neutrality (CMN) for the three countries included in the sample. Although further studies in other countries are required to establish the typical form of these curves, and to determine a country's settings that influence their parameters, it is suggested that these curves may represent a useful tool for urban and regional development planning. The areas of their potential use can be identified as follows:

- *Allocation of public housing construction.* CMN developed for a specific country and continuously updated may help the local decision-makers to determine the amount of public construction to be allocated in priority development areas in order to encourage inward migration.
- *Restricting further population growth in overpopulated, specifically core areas.* CMN may assist in formulating regional development policies aimed at stimulating out-migration from over-populated core regions. Knowing, for instance, country-specific preconditions for out-migration may lead to developing a set of restrictive regional policies aimed at

preventing further concentration of industrial development and housing construction in 'overdeveloped' areas.

* *Targeting economic activity towards economically distressed areas.* CMN may help to identify 'better-off' regions and regions with a high risk of out-migration. These data may inform public policies on the more effective distribution of geographically specific development priorities favouring regions that are currently in distress and other potentially 'problematic' geographic areas.

REFERENCES

Abe, H. (1996), 'New directions for regional development planning in Japan', in J. Aden and P. Boland (eds), *Regional Development Strategies: A European Perspective,* London: Jessica Kingsley Publishers, pp. 273-95.

Bitan, A. and S. Rubin (1991), *Climatic Atlas of Israel for Physical and Environmental Planning and Design,* Tel-Aviv: Ramot Publishing Co.

Borjas, G.J. (1989), 'Economic theory and international migration', *International Migration Review,* **23** (3), pp. 457-85.

CIA (1997), *The 1996 World Fact Book,* Internet Edition.

De Jong, G.F. and J.T. Fawcett (1981), 'Motivation for migration: an assessment and a value-expectancy research model', in G.F. De-Jong and R.W. Gardner (eds), *Migration Decision-Making. Multidisciplinary Approaches to Microlevel Studies in Developed and Developing Countries,* New York: Pergamon Press, pp. 13-53.

Eika, T. and K.A. Magnussen (1998), 'Did Norway gain from the 1979-85 oil price shock?', Discussion paper No.210, Oslo: Central Bureau of Statistics.

Frey, W.H. (1995), 'Immigration and internal migration 'flight' from US metropolitan areas; towards a new demographic Balkanisation', *Urban Studies,* **32** (4-5), pp. 733-57.

Greenwood, M. and R. Stock (1990), 'Patterns of change in the international location of population, jobs and housing: 1950 to 1980', *Journal of Urban Economics,* **28** (2), pp. 243-76.

Hansen, J.C. (1981), 'Settlement pattern and population distribution as fundamental issues in Norway's regional policy', in J.W. Webb, A. Naukkarinen and L.A. Kosinski (eds), *Policies of Population Redistribution,* Oulu: The Geographic Society of Northern Finland, pp. 107-27.

ICBS (1997), *Statistical Abstract of Israel 1996,* Jerusalem: Israeli Central Bureau of Statistic.

JSB (1997) *Japan. Statistical Yearbook,* Tokyo: Japanese Statistics Bureau, Management and Co-ordination Agency.

LaLonde, R.J. and R.H. Topel (1997), 'Economic impact of international migration and the economic performance of migrants', in M.R. Rosenberg and O. Stark (eds), *Handbook of Population and Family Economics,* Amsterdam: Elsevier, pp. 800-850.

Lipshitz, G. (1997), 'Immigrants from the former Soviet Union in the Israeli housing market: spatial aspects of supply and demand', *Urban Studies,* **34** (3), pp. 471-88.

Markusen, A. (1996), 'Interaction between regional and industrial policies: evidence from four countries', *International Regional Science Review,* **19** (1), pp. 49-77.

Michel, F., A. Perrot and J.F. Thisse (1996), 'Interregional equilibrium with heterogeneous labour', *Journal of Population Economics,* **9** (1), pp. 95-113.

Milne, W. (1993), 'Macroeconomic influences on migration', *Regional Studies* **24** (7), pp. 365-73.

Moore, E.G. and M.W. Rosenberg (1995), 'Modelling migration flows of immigrant group in Canada', *Environment and Planning A,* **27,** pp. 699-714.

NSD (1999), *Municipality Database,* Norwegian Social Science Data Services (NSD), Bergen, Norway.

Perroux, F. (1983), *A New Concept of Development: Basic Tenets,* London and Canberra: Croom Helm.

Poot, J. (1996), 'Information, communication and networks in international migration systems', *The Annals of Regional Science,* **30,** pp. 55-73.

Portnov, B.A. (1998), 'The effect of housing on migration in Israel', *Journal of Population Economics,* **11,** pp. 370-94.

Portnov, B.A. (1999), 'The effect of regional inequalities on migration: a comparative analysis of Israel and Japan', *International Migration,* **37** (3), pp. 587-615.

Portnov, B.A. (2000), 'Neutral migration models for Israel and Japan', *Journal of Ethnic and Migration Studies,* **26** (3), pp. 511-33.

Portnov, B.A. and E. Erell (1998), 'Long-term development peculiarities of peripheral desert settlements: the case of Israel', *International Journal of Urban and Regional Research,* **22** (2), pp. 216-32.

Portnov, B.A. and D. Pearlmutter (1997), 'Sustainability of population growth: a case study of urban settlement in Israel', *Review of Urban and Regional Development Studies,* **9** (2), pp. 129-45.

Richardson, H.W. (1977), *Regional Growth Theory,* London: Macmillan.

SN (1997), 'Greater Oslo winner in migration', *Weekly Bulletin of Population Statistics,* **34,** Oslo: Statistics Norway.

Walker, R., M. Ellis, and R. Barff (1992), 'Linked migration systems: immigration and internal labour flows in the United States', *Economic Geography,* **68** (3), pp. 234-48.

White, M.J. and Z. Liang (1993), 'The labour market competition of immigrants and the native-born: insights from internal migration', *Papers of American Sociological Association* (ASA).

NOTES

1. The chapter is based, in part, on two previous papers by this author: Portnov (1999; 2000).
2. Three statistical districts of Israel - Judea, Samaria, and the Gaza area - were deliberately excluded from the analysis due to an assumption that migrations to and from these areas are affected by political and ideological considerations rather than by 'routine' factors of in-country migrations.
3. Employment statistics for Japan is available in the Population Census held quinquenially. The most recent employment data are available for 1985, 1990 and 1995. This restricted the analysis to these three time periods.
4. It may be argued that changes in employment and housing simply follow population growth rather than actually cause migration. This assumption may indeed be correct for those cases in which the availability of housing and employment in a community increase. However, it seems to be unlikely that the availability of employment in a community may decline in response to out-migration (see cases with negative rates of employment in Figure 10.4). The opposite effect is more likely: migrants move away from less prosperous geographic areas characterised by a decline in employment.

11. A 'Job Chains' Model for Assessing Employment Creation in Local Labour Markets

Joseph Persky and Daniel Felsenstein

11.1 INTRODUCTION

The notion that the impact of economic growth 'trickles down' beyond the confines of the population, area or sector in which it is stimulated, is hardly new. 'Ripple through' effects of local economic development have been built into many regional growth models. They can be detected at the base of growth poles and growth centre theory (Perroux 1955), in the 'soft' institutionalist and evolutionary models of regional growth (Amin 1999) and pervading the new economic geography's focus on agglomeration, increasing returns and spillover effects (Krugman 1991).

Demand-side linkages have, of course, been a mainstay of regional analysis. Their percolation through the local economy in the form of new expenditures has been the focus of much attention through the estimation of Keynesian-type multiplier effects and input-output linkages. The ripple-through effect of the standard employment multiplier, relates to the indirect and induced expansion of an initial (demand-side) employment stimulus. However, another way of conceptualising the transmission of growth impulses is to look at them as occurring in chain-like sequences. The chain metaphor has been adopted by a variety of disciplines to examine movement whereby individuals progress up a chain to higher levels of welfare, and in so doing leave behind units (jobs, houses, cars) that successively percolate down the chain. The vacancy (job, house, car) rather than the individual becomes the focus in this kind of analysis. In this way, 'vacancy chains' are created. The maintenance of these chains is contingent on replacement: by occupying a vacancy, an individual simultaneously creates another vacancy. In the absence of replacement, the chain is terminated. Thus, for example, a new entrant to the housing market, a first time car-buyer or an immigrant taking a

173

new job cause the vacancy chain to end as they offer no vacancy as a replacement.

The chain metaphor can be a very useful instrument for examining changes in local labour markets, particularly those induced by public policy aimed at job creation. If a chain of jobs is triggered off whenever a new job is created (A moves to a new job *i* and vacates job *j* for B who moves in, thereby vacating job *k* for C), then the welfare gain is more than just the extra income accruing to A in the new position. At each completed step up the chain, workers move closer to their fully employed status. Workers can make employment and/or wage gains either in jobs newly generated by a subsidised programme or as a result of vacancies opened by job chains. Welfare increments pertaining to the programme are not just those directly generated by the new jobs. Rather they are represented by all the increases in welfare in all the chains opened up by the new job.

These 'job chains' are simply a sub-set of vacancy chains. Their effects, however, should not be confused with the standard multiplier effect. They are much wider-reaching, referring to the cumulative effect of a new job on all other jobs affected by the chain and not just the expansion of the direct impacts to include indirect and induced effects. In the job chains approach, each new job, whether direct, indirect or induced jobs, sets off its own chain.

However, to look at the impact of employment creation simply in terms of the length of the chains it sets off in the local labour market is to adopt a rather mechanistic approach. The contribution of a job chains model is not simply the estimation of the number of moves in a chain or even the different lengths of chain set in motion by different kinds of jobs. A more important contribution relates to the ability of a job chains model to estimate the welfare effects arising from the job chains set in motion. In order for public policy to make a difference, jobs have to be created for local workers who would not have employment opportunities in the alternative situation. The benefits of an employment programme have to trickle down to those local residents most in need.

To avoid a purely mechanistic perspective of employment on local labour markets we therefore need a model of job chains and the welfare gains arising from them. The remainder of this chapter presents a simple, linear theory of local labour market dynamics under conditions of less than full employment. The welfare effects of job chains and their measurement is at the centre of this approach.

11.2 JOB CHAINS AND THE ANALYSIS OF LOCAL LABOUR MARKETS

The vacancy chain model is the building block for understanding many social and economic phenomena that involve mobility and inter-dependence. In such a system, a move by an individual will always simultaneously affect all other parts of the system. While Harrison White's seminal book is often credited with introducing the notion of chain-reactions in diverse social systems (White 1970), the roots of the idea can be traced to early descriptive studies in the housing market literature (Firestone 1951; Kristof 1965).

The vacancy model has been used in different social science settings as an instrument for analysing how supply and demand conditions are matched and how a constant process of re-alignment between the two takes effect. In this way, a pool of dwellings is matched with a pool of house-buyers (Marullo 1985; White 1971), a pool of college football coaches with a pool of teams (Smith and Abbot 1983), a pool of clergy with a pool of parishes (White 1970) and even a pool of hermit crabs with a pool of shells (Chase et al. 1988). It is obvious that this model offers considerable insights in diverse settings.

In this literature much effort is expended in measuring and predicting chain lengths. Housing studies, for example, go to great effort to estimate the policy implications of adding different types of dwellings to the existing housing stock in order to determine which 'filters down' best (Marullo 1985; White 1971). The linear mathematics of Markov processes and Leontief multipliers provide ready-made tools for these analyses. Most of these studies, however, are rather devoid of any behavioural model to supplement the mechanics of chain formation. In the absence of a model of individual preferences for housing, the statistical regularities of chain lengths and housing moves remain rather sterile.

The application of the vacancy chains model to the labour market has yielded two distinct approaches. Sociologists' accounts of occupational mobility have adopted vacancy chain models to study both intra-organizational labour markets (Stewman 1986) and national occupational structures (Harrison 1988). The focus of these studies is on occupational advancement and the type of organizations that promote or hinder this. Thus Stewman (1986) uses extensive development of Markov chains in order show that the probability of advancement within organizations is higher at intermediate levels than at lower levels. Harrison (1988) shows on the basis of US data how the vacancy chain model can predict movement between different occupations nationally. Both these studies illustrate how the linear mobility model developed by White (1970) can be extended to labour market applications. However, this genre of application is lacking both a spatial and a behavioural dimension.

A contrasting application to the labour market context is that adopted by economists. In these studies, the vacancy chain is often embedded in wider models of labour market processes explaining cycles of labour turnover (Akerlof et al. 1988) or labour market crowding (Gorter and Schettkat 1999). While these studies focus little particular attention on local labour market processes, other literature that has local labour market dynamics as its focus, pays little attention to vacancy chains operating locally (Holzer 1989). Vacancies in the local labour market are considered as 'frictionally' or 'structurally' induced, the result of exogenous forces. The possibility of hysteresis-type effects and the endogenisation of these flows, is not really considered. This can occur when an exogenous demand shock triggers-off a chain reaction in the local labour market allowing workers to move up the jobs ladder and accumulate new skills that then position them on a higher rung in anticipation of the next round of moves. If vacancies and flows are considered the result of exogenous forces alone, this important insight is overlooked.

11.3   JOB CHAINS AND THE MODELLING OF LOCAL WELFARE GAINS

To move from intuitions to serious empirical work, we need to construct a formal model of job chains. In this section we consider the simplest possible job chain model, one in which all jobs can be ranked along a single dimension. The next section expands our work to a more general Leontief approach.

Consider a local economy in which each job grouping can be represented by a rung along a single well defined job ladder. A job vacancy is resolved in one of three ways:

- An employee occupying a job on the rung immediately below the vacancy moves up.
- An individual not currently employed along the ladder obtains the job in question. Such individuals might be drawn from the locally unemployed, those not currently in the labour force, or in-migrants to the community.
- The job disappears. The probabilities of these three outcomes (p_1, p_2, p_3) sum to 1.0 and are fixed for the system.

In this setting, a newly created job opens a vacancy at the corresponding rung of the job ladder. Whatever its position in the ladder, it will be filled either by someone in the immediately lower rung (1, above) or by someone not currently employed in the local economy (2, above). The rigidity of the given probabilities necessitates a well defined hiring multiplier, *m*, the expected number of local job vacancies created *and filled* as the result of the appearance of a new job on any rung on the job ladder.

To see this, consider the probability that a new job will give rise to at least one more vacancy that is subsequently filled. This probability is just given by the probability that the new job was filled by someone on the ladder, $[p_1/(1 - p_3)]$, times the probability that the job vacancy opened in this move was not destroyed, $(1 - p_3)$. This product is simply p_1. Now clearly the probability that this filled vacancy will give rise to another must also be p_1, and so forth down the line. The expected number of filled vacancies generated by the new job will be:

$$m = 1 + p_1 + (p_1)^2 + (p_1)^3 + \ldots = 1/(1 - p_1) \qquad (11.1)$$

Interestingly, the length of the chain depends only on p_1. This is true even though we count those moving onto the ladder in the same manner as those already on it. To appreciate this point, consider two sets of probabilities. Both have the same value for p_1, but in the first vacancies can only be filled from the job ladder, otherwise they disappear. This means $p_2 = 0$ and $p_3 = 1 - p_1$. In the second, jobs never disappear ($p_3 = 0$), but they may be filled from off the ladder ($p_2 = 1 - p_1$). For either set of probabilities the new job is filled. Now under the first case this must mean a vacancy is created. That vacancy in turn has a probability p_1 of not disappearing and being filled; and so on down the chain. For the second case we again start with a filled vacancy, but now there is a probability, $p_2 = 1 - p_1$, that it is filled from off the chain and produces no second vacancy. This means that the likelihood of a filled second vacancy is just p_1 again; and so on down the chain.

To use this multiplier to estimate welfare effects, we must assign an expected welfare gain to each worker who fills a vacancy. A worker moving up the ladder forgoes his or her present wage w', in order to obtain a higher wage w at the next rung up. From the individual's perspective the lower wage is the opportunity cost of the higher wage. His or her welfare gain is just the difference between the two wages. For simplicity assume the ratio d ($= w'/w < 1$) remains independent of the rung in question and incorporates any non-monetary differences in working conditions. In this context, filling a single vacancy from the rung below increases welfare by $(1 - d) w$, where w is the wage of the vacancy being filled.

But what of the welfare gains achieved by those who move into a vacancy from outside the labour force, from unemployment, or through migration? These are complex transitions; their welfare values have been long debated.

For the present exercise, we keep matters simple and conservative by assuming that these transitions render the same welfare gain as a move up the ladder, that is $(1 - d)$ w. This assumption sets the opportunity cost of individuals moving onto the job ladder at an amount equal to the wage of the job just below the one they take. Such a proposition can be plausibly defended for both in-migrants and entrants to the labour force, but very likely underestimates the gains of those moving out of involuntary unemployment.

Now the calculation is straightforward:

$$V = (1 - d)w[1 + d\,p_1 + (dp_1)^2 + (dp_1)^3 + ...] = [(1 - d)/(1 - d\,p_1)]w \quad (11.2)$$

where V represents the total expected welfare gain set off by the creation of a job paying a wage of w. This result has two interesting and interrelated implications. Under the assumptions of the simplest job chain model, a new job in a community will yield an expected welfare gain less than its wage, since $(1 - d) < (1 - d\,p_1)$. But under those same assumptions, a new job will generate a gain larger than that enjoyed by the worker who actually fills it, since the probability of vacancies being filled from existing jobholders is taken greater than zero (that is $p_1 > 0$).

This simple observation relates directly to the 'all or nothing' dilemma in evaluating wage and employment gains from local economic development programmes (Felsenstein and Persky 1999). On the one hand, impact analyses meticulously count all new wages arising from job creation as a local gain. In contrast, welfare economists claim that converting job counts into incomes represents 'a great deal of effort that could have been better spent asking different questions' (Courant 1994, p. 863). Many workers in subsidised jobs could have invariably found alternative employment. Their welfare gain is not represented by their wage but by a much smaller amount, that is the difference between the new wage and the workers reservation wage. This is usually taken as reflecting the opportunity cost of the new job and empirical estimates of this cost fluctuate greatly (Jones 1989).

We can push our simple model a bit further to explore the sensitivity of expected welfare gains, V/w, to the key parameters, p_1 and d. Figure 11.1 holds the latter constant, but allows the former to vary. Here we have set d at 0.8. The intercept on the vertical axis varies directly with $1 - d$. If no hiring is done from existing local employees, $p_1 = 0$, the only expected welfare gain is 0.2 times w. The welfare fraction rises slowly as p_1 increases away from zero, but then more quickly as p_1 approaches 1.0.

Keep in mind that p_1 is just equal to $1 - (p_2 + p_3)$. Thus if we fix one of these probabilities, Figure 11.1 can tell us how the welfare ratio varies with the other. Of course as the other probability rises we read the figure from right to left and not from left to right.

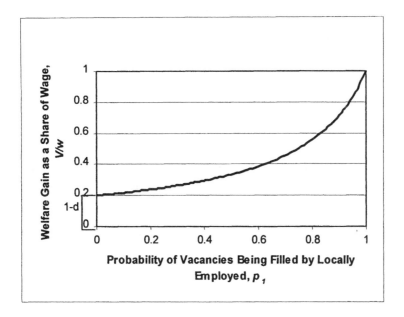

Figure 11.1   Welfare sensitivity

Can we go on to make an estimate of V/w? To carry out such an exercise with any confidence we need empirically established values for key parameters. We are currently working on an extensive project to measure these parameters. However, here we can make a few educated guesses to at least narrow the likely range. In this spirit, we set p_2 at about 0.3, perhaps divided more or less equally between in-migrants and local residents not employed in the recent past. In average times, p_3 is likely to be considerably smaller, say 0.05. This leaves us with an estimate of 0.65 for p_1. To allow a range for the crudeness of the estimate, we take p_1 to lie between 0.6 and 0.7.

These parameters imply that on average a job chain will have a length of about three filled vacancies so $m = 3$. On each link we assume that the worker (whether an in-migrant, unemployed, out of the labour force or previously employed) has a reservation wage (d) equal to 80-90 percent of his or her new wage. Putting these estimates of d and p_1 into our basic equation suggests that the welfare gain associated with an average new job will be between 20 percent and 40 percent of the new job's wage.

These figures reflect a considerable discount on wage gains calculated from simple impact models. Yet they also suggest that gains from economic development projects can be substantial. The simple model used here also provides a framework for handling differences across metropolitan areas in their unemployment rates and in-migration rates. However, the model cannot address the very real possibility that different new jobs generate different benefit ratios. Since our central question is the effectiveness of trickle down in the labour market, this deficiency must be corrected.

11.4 THE MECHANICS OF JOB CHAINS: A LEONTIEF MODEL

Our second, more general, model starts with the recognition that recruitment may look very different across the rungs of the job ladder. Some job vacancies will be filled only with workers already holding very narrowly defined skills/jobs, while others may draw on a wider range of candidates. If we can categorise all jobs into meaningful groupings on the basis of skill requirements, remuneration and conditions of work, then we can think of a new job vacancy as setting off a 'multiplier' effect as successive workers move from one job to another.

The inter-rung probabilities can be represented as a square (origin-destination) matrix $(\mathbf{Q})$ with elements, q_{ij}, which show the chance that a job vacancy of a j-type position is taken by a worker currently in an i-type position. Notice that the sum of these elements over i for a given j will be less than one. The difference will be made up largely by workers drawn from unemployment, out of the labour force and in-migration. Finally some vacancies will simply result in job destruction or disappearance. These terminating events play a role similar to primary inputs and imports in an input-output matrix. They act as leakages that dissipate the flow of demand in the local area.

We have strong theoretical reasons for modelling $\mathbf{Q}$ as a triangular matrix. In general, workers will not voluntarily move from a better job to a worse one. Of course many such moves do take place, but presumably they are involuntary. In the context of a chain begun by an economic development project, such involuntary moves effectively guarantee that job vacancies always move 'down' the job ranking. For example, consider the consequences of a project-created semi-skilled (type 2) job being taken by a worker who was fired from a high-skilled (type 1) job. The type 1 vacancy would occur whether or not the economic development project takes place. It is not part of the chain generated by the project. However, this high-skilled worker would presumably have been able to take a job at the semi-skilled level even in the absence of the development project. The counter-factual is not that the high-skilled vacancy would not have been created, but that a semi-skilled vacancy would have been taken by this worker. In this sense vacancies can only move 'down' and never 'up' the job ranking.

The **Q** matrix allows us to approximate the net consequences of job creation at each job level. A simple Leontief-type inversion of the locally based origin-destination matrix $(\mathbf{I} - \mathbf{Q})^{-1}$, will yield a multiplier-type matrix of m_{ij}'s which show the gross number of local i-type vacancies generated by a j-type vacancy. Summing down the columns of this matrix gives us the total number of links or vacancies per chain, triggered off by jobs of different types. Thus $M_j = \Sigma_i m_{ij}$ gives the total number of expected vacancies associated with a newly created j-type job including that initial vacancy. It seems natural to call M_j the length of a type j chain. A rough approach to estimating chain length has been presented above for the simple model (Section 11.3). Here, as there, the key to measuring the length of chains is estimating the probabilities of a chain being truncated by an in-migrant, unemployed worker or new entrant. But, since all of these can differ depending on the initial 'new jobs' level, expected chain length will also vary across levels.

Because **Q** is taken to be triangular, the chain lengths, M_j, are relatively easy to calculate in a recursive manner. In particular, if we rank skill levels from 1 as the highest to n as the lowest, then:

$$M_n = 1/(1 - q_{nn}),$$

$$M_{n-1} = [1/(1 - q_{(n-1)(n-1)})]\ [\ 1 + q_{n(n-1)}\, M_n\,],$$

$$M_{n-2} = [1/(1 - q_{(n-2)(n-2)})]\ [(1 + q_{(n-1)(n-2)}\, M_{n-1} + q_{n(n-2)}\, M_n)], \quad (11.3)$$

. . . .

As these formulae make clear, the actual values for the chain lengths will depend on the specifics of the **Q** matrix. We return to this point below.

Having sketched the theory of chain lengths, we turn to an analysis of differences in the expected increments in local welfare arising from the creation of different new jobs. Again we emphasise the importance of opportunity costs in evaluating welfare gains. In particular for each type of vacancy, i, the welfare gain is equal to $\Sigma_k\, q_{kj}(w_i - w_k)$, where $(w_i - w_k)$ represents the difference in wages between the new job i and the old job k. Notice we assume here that those changing jobs within the same occupational group, i, will experience no gain (or perhaps, only a negligible one), that is $w - w' = 0$. For in-migrants, unemployed or entrants who might take a vacancy at level i we assume that their reservation wage or opportunity cost is just equal to the wage of the group at the next lowest level, $i + 1$. This is essentially the same assumption as we used in Section 11.3. And again we take wages at each level to be a constant fraction, d, of the wages at the next highest level. Putting these elements together then suggests an overall expected gain of adding a j- type job (V_j) is given by:

$$V_j = \Sigma_i m_{ij} \left[(\Sigma_k q_{ki} (w_i - w_k) + (1 - \Sigma_k q_{ki})(w_i - w_{i+1}) \right].$$

$$= w_j \Sigma_i m_{ij} d^{-j} \left[(\Sigma_k q_{ki} (1 - d^{k-i}) + (1 - \Sigma_k q_{ki})(1 - d) \right]. \qquad (11.4)$$

Finally we can use the chains matrix to make calculations concerning the distribution of gains across various groups of workers. In particular we might ask for any given chain how much welfare gain goes to the lowest group of workers - those who would take the worst group-n jobs if they were available. Given the assumptions used in equation (11.4) this Rawlesian welfare measure, R_j, can be easily calculated for each j. The result is given in equation (11.5).

$$R_j = w_n m_{nj} (1 - q_{nn})(1 - d) \qquad (11.5)$$

The only term on the right-hand side of this equation to vary with j is m_{nj}. Hence, this measure of the distributional consequences generated by a new type j-job depends only on the number of vacancies of the lowest level that 'end' the job chain.

11.5 JOB CHAINS AND TRICKLE DOWN

A model built along the above lines can address a broad range of questions about economic development impacts. In particular, this generalised job chains approach can be used to explore the logic of trickle down to economic development. In general, a trickle down theory holds that the poor are best served by policies that directly improve the welfare of the more prosperous. Much economic development activity undertaken by state and local governments explicitly or implicitly invokes a trickle down perspective. In this view, subsidising high-skilled, well-paying jobs generates substantial positive spillovers for the less well trained, even though the latter are unable to directly qualify for the subsidised jobs. Of course these spillovers might take a number of forms. We make no general claim here to explore all of those. However, in the context of job chain analysis, we interpret the advocates of trickle down as asserting three related propositions:

- A job multiplier effect: The expected length of a job chain goes up as the skill level of the added job increases.
- An efficiency effect: The expected welfare gain associated with a job chain goes up as a proportion of the initial wage as the skill level of the added job increases.
- A distributional effect: Absolute gains to even the least skilled workers increase as the skill level of the added job increases.

Although our goal is ultimately to test these hypotheses by empirical means, we can make use of our simple model to explore the mathematical constraints on the trickle down process. We now consider each of the above propositions in turn.

11.5.1 The Multiplier Effect

Equation (11.3) governs the chain lengths or total vacancies generated by new jobs of various types. If there is a trickle down multiplier effect, then $M_n < M_{n-1} < M_{-n-2} < ...$

Sufficient, although not necessary, conditions to generate this result from equation (11.3) above, are that the q's fall monotonically as i and j rise or more formally:

Condition 1: $q_{ij} >= q_{(i+1)(j+1)}$ for all $j > i$, with strict inequality for $j = i$.

The intuition here is that more skilled jobs are more likely to be filled by those who are already employed at the given level or close to it. With relatively low unemployment rates among skilled workers, skilled jobs are less likely to draw directly on the unemployed. For a simple proof see Appendix 1.

11.5.2 The Efficiency Effect

We suspect that in the context of the other assumptions of the model, condition 1 is sufficient to guarantee the efficiency claim of trickle down. An exception that tends to support the spirit of this conclusion is the case of a diagonal **Q** matrix, that is all q_{ij} with i not equal to j are set to zero. Chains generated in such a matrix must be limited to those currently employed at the same level or experienced workers (unemployed, out of the labour force, or in-migrants) of the same skill group. Under these circumstances the welfare measure V_j/w_j equals $(1 - d)$ regardless of j. This would seem to be the worst case, meeting all the conditions of the model and case 1.

For a result more in the spirit of the job chains approach, allow $q_{ij} > 0$ for $i = j$ and $i = j + 1$, but $= 0$ for all other i and j. These are lower triangular matrices with only the diagonal and the elements immediately below the diagonal greater than zero. More intuitively, such a system fills job vacancies at level j only by workers at the same level, the level immediately below, or from the ranks of the j-level experienced workers not currently employed. Still we assume that condition 1 holds. Under these conditions, it is not difficult to show that the relative index of efficiency gain, V_j/w_j will be highest for the most skilled jobs, $j = 1$, and fall as j increases. See Appendix 2 for a proof.

11.5.3 The Distributional Effect

Condition 1, which guarantees longer chain length for more skilled jobs and supports the efficiency claims of trickle down, undermines the distributional claims. Using the measure suggested in equation (11.5) above, we know that the Rawlesian ranking of new jobs will depend only on the corresponding m_{nj}'s. It is a relatively easy matter to show that if the condition 1 holds then $m_{nn} > m_{nj}$ for all j. The multiplier for the lowest level job, m_{nn}, is just equal to $1/(1 - q_{nn})$. Hence, the creation of one new n-type job ultimately draws one new worker from the pool of the lowest skilled unemployed whose opportunity cost is less than w_n. But this is the maximum possible since the chain set off by any single new job will draw exactly one worker from outside the system. If $m_{nj} > m_{nn}$, then a total of more than one worker would be drawn into the system.

The above results are subject to a long list of provisos growing out of the various assumptions made along the way. The most critical of these concern our condition 1. While this condition seems highly plausible for the diagonal itself, our intuition becomes less firm as we move off the diagonal. Indeed a good argument can be made that for the most skilled jobs, vacancies cannot draw on workers currently holding positions of lower skill. Such a proposition would suggest the following:

$$\text{Condition 2:} \quad q_{ii} > q_{(i+1)(i+1)} \tag{2a}$$

$$q_{ij} <= q_{(i+1)(j+1)} \text{ for all } j > i \tag{2b}$$

$$1 - \Sigma_i q_{ij} < 1 - \Sigma_i q_{i(j+1)} \tag{2c}$$

Condition (2c), here, requires that we keep the ordering of jobs with respect to their propensity to draw on the non-employed. This will keep the distributional results discussed above. However, efficiency can now work against trickle down. Clearly, a convincing resolution must wait for empirical measurement.

11.6 CONCLUSIONS

The study of simple vacancy chains runs the risk of a mechanistic perspective on labour market dynamics. In such a story, a pool of workers and a pool of jobs exist and the issue is simply one of matching. No attention is given to markets, prices do not change and the vacancy model simply gives an account of the rippling-through effect that occurs sub-surface with the creation of new jobs. On the other hand, market models of this process where a price structure emerges and the market clears, can give a sterile perspective on what is essentially the dynamic process in which all of us make our career paths.

The model presented above has tried to break middle-ground. By looking at welfare gains from chains at different skill levels and by incorporating insights from opportunity cost theory, we have attempted to show that prices alone do not control the supply and demand for jobs. We have credited workers with more autonomy. Their decisions to in-migrate, re-enter the labour market or retire, affect the labour supply. Similarly, by assuming under-employment and a fairly rigid wage structure, we note that demand impacts on chains and on the welfare that accrues from chains set-off by different skill levels. Echoing Bartik's 'hysteresis' theory of local job growth (Bartik 1991), we note that both supply and demand shocks affect chain length and welfare impacts. In this view of labour market processes, short-run dynamics such as movement through a job chain have long-term effects. Once a chain is triggered off and workers start to move up to a new platform, they accumulate new levels of human capital that serve them in any further progressions along the job chain. Even if the external agent of change (the job chain), was removed, they would not return to their initial state. Local employment creation, via the chain process, can therefore lead to long-run changes beyond the initial effect of the job creation itself.

A further implication of the above is the inter-relatedness inherent in employment creation. Chains limit our ability to use targeting as an economic development strategy. The job chains model shows us that targeting one group in the population will always affect other sub-groups, as they are all inter-connected via job chains. At the very least targeting economic development efforts must be undertaken in a more sophisticated context; one that accounts for the ramifications generated through labour chains.

APPENDIX 1

Given: Q a $n \times n$ lower triangular matrix. M is the corresponding matrix of Leontieff multipliers, that is $M = (I - Q)^{-1}$. Define chain lengths as M_j, where $M_j = \Sigma_i m_{ij}$.

Proposition A1: if $q_{ij} \geq q_{(i+1)(j+1)}$ for all $j > i$, with strict inequality for $j = i$ (condition 1) then $M_n < M_{n-1} < M_{n-2} < \ldots$

Proof:

$$M_n = m_{nn} = [1/(1 - q_{nn})],$$
$$M_{n-1} = m_{(n-1)(n-1)} + m_{n(n-1)} = [1/(1 - q_{(n-1)(n-1)})] \ [1 + q_{n(n-1)} M_n],$$
$$M_{n-2} = m_{(n-2)(n-2)} + m_{(n-1)(n-2)} + m_{n(n-2)} =$$
$$= [1/(1 - q_{(n-2)(n-2)})] \ [(1 + q_{(n-1)(n-2)} M_{n-1} + q_{n(n-2)} M_n)],$$

Or in general:

$$M_j = [1/(1 - q_{jj})] \ [\Sigma_{i=j} \ (q_{(i+1)j} M_{i+1})]$$

Clearly $M_n < M_{n-1}$ since $[1/(1 - q_{(n-1)(n-1)})] > [1/(1 - q_{nn})]$, by condition 1.
Assume all M_k up to j fall into the required pattern, that is $M_n < M_{n-1} < \ldots < M_{j+1} > M_j$.
But clearly:

$$M_j = [1/(1 - q_{jj})] \ [\Sigma_{i=j} \ (q_{(i+1)j} M_{i+1})]$$
$$> [1/(1 - q_{(j+1)(j+1)})] \ [\Sigma_{i=j} \ (q_{(i+1)j} M_{i+1})] \qquad \text{(by condition 1)}$$
$$> [1/(1 - q_{(j+1)(j+1)})] \ [\Sigma_{i=j} \ (q_{(i+2)(j+1)} M_{i+1})] \qquad \text{(by condition 1)}$$
$$> [1/(1 - q_{(j+1)(j+1)})] \ [\Sigma_{i=j} \ (q_{(i+2)(j+1)} M_{i+2})] \qquad \text{(by hypothesis)}$$
$$> [1/(1 - q_{(j+1)(j+1)})] \ [(\Sigma_{i=j} \ (q_{(i+2)(j+1)} M_{i+2})) - q_{n(j+1)} M_n]$$
$$\qquad\qquad\qquad\qquad\qquad\qquad \text{(subtracting a positive term)}$$
$$= [1/(1 - q_{(j+1)(j+1)})] \ [(\Sigma_{i=j+1} \ (q_{(i+1)(j+1)} M_{i+1}))] \qquad \text{(collecting terms)}$$
$$= M_{j+1}$$

a contradiction. q.e.d.

APPENDIX 2

Given: Q a $n \times n$ lower triangular matrix. **M** is the corresponding matrix of Leontief multipliers, that is **M** $=(\mathbf{I} - \mathbf{Q})^{-1}$.

Proposition A2: if $w_{i+1} = dw_i$; $q_{ii} > q_{(i+1)(i+1)} > 0$; $q_{i(i+1)} > q_{(i+1)(i+2)} > 0$; all other $q_{ij} = 0$, then $V_n/w_n < V_{n-1}/w_{n-1} < V_{n-2}/w_{n-2} < ... < V_1/w_1$

Proof: Start from equation (11.4):

$$V_j = w_j \, \Sigma_{i=j} m_{ij} \, d^{i \cdot j} \, [(\Sigma_k q_{ki} \, (1 - d^{k \cdot i}) + (1 - \Sigma_k q_{ki})(1 - d)]$$

Given the assumptions about zeroes in the **Q** matrix it follows that:

$$V_j/w_j = \Sigma_{i=j} m_{ij} \, d^{i \cdot j} \, [(q_{(i+1)i} \, (1 - d) + (1 - q_{ii} - q_{(i+1)i})(1 - d)]$$

$$= \Sigma_{i=j} m_{ij} \, d^{i \cdot j} \, [(1 - q_{ii})(1 - d)]$$

It is also relatively easy to show that the same assumptions imply: $m_{jj} \, (1 - q_{jj}) = 1$ for all j and that for $i > j$, $m_{ij} = m_{jj} \, \Pi \, q_{k(k-1)} \, m_{kk}$, where the product is taken from $k = j + 1$ to i. Hence:

$$V_j/w_j = (1 - d)$$
$$+ \, m_{jj} \, q_{(j+1)j} \, (1 - d)d$$
$$+ \, m_{jj} \, q_{(j+1)j} \, m_{(j+1)(j+1)} q_{(j+2)(j+1)} \, (1 - d)dd$$
$$+ ...$$

From this expression once can see that V_{j+1}/w_{j+1} has one less term in its summation and, given the hypotheses, each of the remaining terms is smaller.

REFERENCES

Akerlof, G.A., A.K. Rose and J.L. Yellen (1988), 'Job switching and job satisfaction in the US labor market', *Brookings Papers on Economic Activity*, **2**, pp. 495-594.

Amin, A. (1999), 'An institutionalist perspective on regional economic development', *International Journal of Urban and Regional Research*, **23** (2), pp. 365-78.

Bartik, T.J. (1991), *Who Benefits from State and Local Economic Development Policies?*, Michigan: W.E Upjohn Institute for Employment Research, Kalamazoo.

Chase, I.D., M. Weissburg and T.H. DeWitt (1988), 'The vacancy chain process: a new mechanism of resource allocation in animals with application to hermit crabs', *Animal Behavior*, **36**, pp. 1265-74.

Courant, P.N. (1994), 'How would you know a good economic development policy if you tripped over one? Hint: don't just count jobs', *National Tax Journal*, **47** (4), pp. 863-81.

Felsenstein, D. and J. Persky (1999), 'When is a cost really a benefit? Local welfare effects and employment creation in the evaluation of economic development programmes', *Economic Development Quarterly*, **13** (1), pp. 46-54.

Firestone, O.J. (1951), *Residential Real Estate in Canada*, Toronto: University of Toronto Press.

Gorter, C. and R. Schettkat (1999), *On Musical Chairs and Matching Models: Do Employed Job Seekers Crowd-Out the Unemployed?*, Amsterdam: Department of Regional Economics, Free University (unpublished).

Harrison, R.I. (1988), 'Opportunity models: adopting vacancy models to national occupational structures', *Research in Social Stratification and Mobility*, **7**, pp. 3-33.

Holzer, H.J. (1989), *Unemployment, Vacancies and Local Labor Markets*, Michigan: W.E. Upjohn Institute for Employment Research, Kalamazoo.

Jones, S. (1989), 'Reservation wages and the cost of unemployment', *Economica*, **56**, pp. 225-46.

Kristof, F.S. (1965), 'Housing policy goals and the turnover of housing', *Journal of the American Institute of Planners*, **31**, pp. 232-45.

Krugman, P. (1991), 'Increasing returns and economic geography', *Journal of Political Economy*, **99** (3), pp. 483-99.

Marullo, S. (1985), 'Housing opportunities and vacancy chains', *Urban Affairs Quarterly*, **20**, pp. 364-88.

Perroux, F. (1950), 'Economic space: theory and applications', *Quarterly Journal of Economics*, **64**, pp. 89-104.

Smith, D.R. and A. Abbott (1983), 'A labor market perspective on the mobility of college football coaches', *Social Forces*, **61**, pp. 1147-67.

Stewman, S. (1986), 'Demographic models of internal labor markets', *Administrative Science* Quarterly, **31**, pp. 212-347.

White, H.C. (1970), *Chains of Opportunity: System Models of Mobility in Organizations*, Cambridge, MA: Harvard University Press.

White, H.C. (1971), 'Multipliers, vacancy chains and filtering in housing', *Journal of the American Institute of Planners*, **37** (2), pp. 88-94.

PART FOUR

Physical Infrastructure

Introduction to Part Four

The policy of providing physical infrastructure has long been seen as a cause and a consequence of economic development in a region. In this part, four chapters consider the importance of road, housing and building infrastructure for regional development. A range of models and techniques are used to explore the complexity of the two-way interaction between investment and behaviour.

One of the main infrastructure investments to promote regional development has been in roads. This is considered by Raphael Bar-El in Chapter 12. Road investment in the Tel Aviv metropolitan region, and other urban regions of Israel over the last two decades, has responded, with a lag of two or three years, to an increasing population and labour force. However, there is no such response in the peripheral, low population density Southern region. Here road area constructed per resident or per worker has constantly declined since 1978, potentially impeding the ability of this region to compete in attracting economic activities. This is despite the region gaining population, employment and economic activity in relative and absolute terms. The research shows that a policy of infrastructure investment which responds to revealed needs (such as congestion) may lead to a distorted regional allocation of public expenditures. This may lead to discrimination against the peripheral region and an unconscious policy of public-led regional economic concentration.

In Chapter 13 Ronald McQuaid, Scott Leitham and John Nelson show that it is important to disaggregate different types of firms when analysing the importance of infrastructure and other factors upon location decisions. They consider the location choice of industrial and commercial firms in Scotland in terms of the *ex ante* decision making process. The importance of motorway connections varied considerably between UK- and non-UK-based firms. UK branch plants were found to rate motorway links the highest, underlining the dominance of road links for the distribution of goods and services and intra-firm travel in the UK. In contrast, overseas branch firms found road links to be less important, being outweighed primarily by factors such as workforce and premises.

The conclusion is that, for many types of firm, road infrastructure is probably most significant at a fine geographical level, with the general location being determined by workforce and other agglomeration economies, inputs and market sectors. The study suggests that stated preference techniques add useful insights, which are likely to complement other techniques such as revealed preference, in modelling and understanding the impact of physical infrastructure and other factors upon location choice.

The relationship between infrastructure and behaviour is complex and interactive. In Chapter 14 Yoram Shiftan integrates a residential choice model, estimated using a recent stated preference survey conducted in the Metropolitan Area of Portland, Oregon, USA, with a set of activity-based travel demand models for the area in order to evaluate the effects of potential land use policies on regional travel. The estimated stated preference model shows that land use policies can affect people's residential choice in a way that favours urban area growth over suburban growth. In total the model application forecasts that 4.2 percent of the Portland metropolitan area households will move from a suburban location to within the Urban Growth Area boundary under the proposed policies.

Paradoxically, when the results of the residential choice model are incorporated into the Portland activity-based travel demand model system, only a marginal if not actually counterproductive effect on regional travel is shown. Such an activity-based model system represents an important improvement over trip- and tour-based models commonly used and provides behavioural insights that are not possible with conventional four-step transportation modelling approaches.

Housing investment is a significant part of a region's infrastructure, especially in terms of labour market responsiveness and employment. However, in Israel the housing market is changing and the share of public housing is unlikely to contribute to the expanding need for rentals for single parent households, divorcees and other non-standard households. Hence, Elia Werczberger in Chapter 15 argues that it is important to improve policies to revive the commercial private housing rental sector. Three facets of the rental market are examined: the changing government policy, the main characteristics of rental housing and the demand for renting.

A tenure choice logistic regression model and a simple demand model for private sector housing are developed which include demographic and socio-economic characteristics between households, geographical conditions. The former model suggests that seven variables are significant in tenure choice: age of household head, his/her education, marital status, ethnic background, religion, labour force participation, student and district. The strong differences between regions are clear with, for instance, public housing less likely to be chosen than ownership in the Tel-Aviv area compared to every other district. The demand for private sector housing uses OLS to estimate a log-linear equation utilising household expenditure survey data. Policy suggestions are to reduce uncertainty for commercial landlords to make the new rental market attractive to investors and to make long-term investment in older rental housing profitable.

Together the chapters increase our understanding of the relationships between regional development, physical infrastructure and the behaviour of individuals, firms and government. They provide some answers but, of course, raise many new questions and suggestions for future research in this area.

12. Infrastructure Investment and Regional Underdevelopment

Raphael Bar-El

12.1 INTRODUCTION

The combined trends of globalisation and technological change have exposed peripheral regions to a new and challenging situation. On the one hand increased accessibility to markets, easier diffusion of technologies, and higher mobility of production factors offer greater opportunities to marginal regions. On the other hand, they expose them to fierce competition with stronger regions. While the dispute amongst scholars about the existence of convergence or divergence processes between regions is still open (see for example: Barro and Sala-i-Martin 1991; Fagerberg and Verspagen 1996; Quah 1996), it is quite widely accepted that the provision of infrastructure in a region is one factor contributing to its competitiveness (Aschauer 1989). In fact, in many cases this factor has been found to explain the level of convergence or divergence.

One role of public policy is to assure the appropriate allocation of public infrastructure between regions in a country, in order to provide the necessary tools for the development of a competitive ability. A government may decide to provide a region with more or less of its 'fair' share of public infrastructure, in line with long-term economic or non-economic objectives. We assume here that there is no hidden government agenda and that the regional allocation of public infrastructure is based on economic rationale.

Given this assumption, the problem is how to evaluate the most appropriate regional distribution of public expenditure for infrastructure. Theoretically, public infrastructure should be allocated first to a region in which the expected return is the highest, in terms of economic or social national objectives. In practice, there is little possibility of achieving acceptable estimates of expected marginal returns to investment in infrastructure in each region. Standard public policy responses are often geared towards the needs of infrastructure users: alleviating traffic congestion, responding to demands from economic activities and so on. However, using these demand-oriented parameters for allocating infrastructure may be misleading and inefficient. The reason is that there are no real free market conditions for infrastructure investment, since demand is not conditioned by a direct price to be paid by the user (Bar-El 2000). Furthermore, revealed need for infrastructure, such as the existence of unemployment or slow levels of economic development in a region, does not generally lead to the appropriate reaction. The common reaction in this situation is short-term direct intervention through the attraction of firms to the region, the provision of incentives or other measures of this kind. The provision of infrastructure is considered as a policy measure that is beneficial over the long term, and therefore is not given top priority in the treatment of acute employment problems.

All this is based on the notion that infrastructure is an endogenous variable within the overall regional economic system. It is determined within the system as a consequence of changes in population, in economic activity and so on. However, an alternative perception is that, in part at least, infrastructure is exogenously determined. It is externally set by decision makers, and used by them as a normative planning measure in order to influence economic activity. In this case, policy makers may initiate infrastructure investment in a region that does not demonstrate any demand.

Using the case of a peripheral region in Israel, this chapter illustrates the consequences of a policy responsive to the need for infrastructure, and deduces the need for a more normative policy. It shows that regional infrastructure expenditure as a response to demand pressures may lead to a process of polarisation and therefore impose a serious publicly-generated constraint on the ability of the peripheral regions to compete and develop.

12.2 SOME METHODOLOGICAL CONSIDERATIONS

The general approach of this chapter is the comparative analysis of infrastructure time series data against changes in population in different regions. Many methodological issues need to be addressed. The first involves the operational definition of infrastructure. While infrastructure has many components such as roads, airports, power supply, water supply, communication networks, and so on, components are assembled into one operational measure of infrastructure. Here we restrict ourselves to one single component (road area) and ignore others such as regional road distances, road quality, construction costs and so on.

We do not allow for any depreciation effect, since our data do not include expenses for road maintenance, and we therefore assume that the newly constructed roads exist across all the years covered in this study. Since the depreciation rate is quite low anyway, it is not expected to differ considerably between regions and since we refer only to newly constructed roads, ignoring the depreciation effect is not really significant.

Another question regarding the road area relates to its measurement as a flow or as a stock variable. The flow is represented by the road area built each year, and the stock is represented by the total surface of roads existing at each given time. Since economic activity is linked to total available infrastructure, we prefer the stock measurement. However, data are collected only from a certain year (1978), in which there already existed an initial stock of roads. The distribution of road surface between regions is not available at any reasonable starting year, and consequently there is no way to use real stock data by region. Any assumption of a given distribution would distort the quantitative analysis since the growth of road stocks, as measured by the percentage increase, would heavily depend on the assumed initial stock.

We prefer therefore to only use 'new stocks' of road infrastructure, accumulated since 1978. The relationship between new stocks and other variables will be analysed on the same basis: population increase since 1978, or new labour force or new employment supply. This is not an optimal solution, since the influence of 'old stocks' continues for many years, and cannot be disregarded. In addition, stock variables may not be reliable in the first years of collected data, because of annual fluctuations in infrastructure building. The influence of such flow fluctuations diminishes at later years, when the flow data adds to a relatively high stock data. We shall therefore use the stock data in a time series beginning in 1983, that is after a five year accumulation of infrastructure.

Another methodological issue deals with the definition of infrastructure intensity and its operational mathematical definition. Some accepted definitions are the quantity of infrastructure at time t in relation to the area of the region, or to its population, or to its labour force:

$$RIA_i = R_i / A_i$$
$$RIP_i = R_i / P_i$$
$$RIL_i = R_i / L_i \tag{12.1}$$

where R_i, A_i, P_i, L_i are respectively the stock of road area accumulated in region i since the base year (1978), the area of region i, the population and the labour force accumulated in the region since the base year. RIA_i, RIP_i, and RIL_i are road intensity, as measured in terms of total stock of road area, in relation to area, population or labour force in region i.

As simple as such definitions may look, they imply the strong and problematic assumption that the road infrastructure of a region is intended to serve that region only. The fact is that roads in one region serve other regions as well, and may contribute to their economic development. Consequently, a higher *RIP* measure in a region does not necessarily mean better infrastructure for that region - this may be the case in a peripheral area with an urban population and a large hinterland area used by the population of other regions. Theoretically, the relevant road infrastructure intensity for a region should be calculated as some weighted combination of roads in the region itself and roads in other regions, with smaller weights for more distant regions. For the intensity measure in relation to population, the appropriate measure would be:

$$WRIP_i = \sum_r \alpha_{ri} R_r / P_i$$
$$\sum_r \alpha_{ri} = 1 \qquad\qquad (12.2)$$

where $WRIP_i$ is the weighted roads intensity in region i, α_{ri} is the weight for relevant roads in each region r of the country to region i. The total of all weights is equal to 1. It is of course expected that the highest weight would be for α_{ii} ($r = i$). This measure of road intensity is theoretically the most valid, since it reflects the relevance of all road infrastructure in all regions to the users in region i. The problem with this measure is the estimation of the α_{ri} parameters. This requires a separate econometric study, which is beyond the scope of this chapter. Here, we restrict ourselves to the non-weighted version of the road intensity measure, while keeping in mind that no absolute comparison of this measure can be done across regions.

12.3 THE REGIONAL DISTRIBUTION OF POPULATION IN ISRAEL

The population of Israel is divided into six districts (see Table 12.1). The main metropolitan area is Tel-Aviv, located in Tel-Aviv district, which also includes other smaller cities, which are part of the continuous urban area of 'Greater Tel-Aviv'. The Tel-Aviv district has a population of 1.1m, concentrated in an area of 170 km^2. Thus, 20 percent of the population is concentrated in less than 1 percent of the country's area, representing a high density of 6,700 persons/km^2. The Central district includes a wide area surrounding the Tel-Aviv district. Its population is comparable to (but somewhat greater than) that of the Tel-Aviv district, although it is distributed over an area almost eight times larger. Most of the population is urban, distributed among centres located within commuting distance of Tel-Aviv, the largest being Rishon Lezion, which has a population of around 175,000.

Table 12.1   Distribution of area, population and population density in 1998 (by district)

District	Area Km^2	Area Percent	Population 1998 Thousands	Population 1998 Percent	Population density Persons/km^2
Jerusalem	627	3.1	709	12.2	1,131
North	3,325	16.4	1,014	17.5	305
Haifa	854	4.2	782	13.5	915
Centre	1,242	6.1	1,333	23.0	1,073
Tel-Aviv	170	0.8	1,139	19.6	6,702
South	14,107	69.4	827	14.2	59
Nation	20,325	100.0	5,805	100.0	286

In fact, the Tel-Aviv and Central districts can be considered together as one metropolitan area. This is because of the small distances between and within the two districts, and because of the very strong employment relationships between them. Many people who work in Tel-Aviv chose to live in the Central district, within commuting distance and at a lower congestion level. Together they could be considered a 'metropolitan area based region' (MBR), and we will refer to them as the 'metropolitan region' (Parr 1999). This region covers about 7 percent of the total area of the country, but contains 43 percent of the population.

Other major urban concentrations in Israel are Haifa and Jerusalem. Haifa is surrounded by the Northern district, and together these two districts may also be regarded as a MBR. The Jerusalem district includes the capital and its hinterland (a third MBR). Finally, the Southern district, which covers most of the land area of the country, has an extremely low population density. Most of its population lives in small towns, and the largest urban centre, Beer-Sheva. This city could probably be viewed as an auxiliary metropolitan area, which can be expected to become the focus for a wider MBR.

Until 1990 the peripheral Southern district grew more or less at the national average rate and maintained a constant share of 12 percent of the national population. Over the last decade, this region has grown more rapidly registering a population index of 190 (the population of year 1977 being defined as 100), as compared with an index of 159 nationally, and a growth in the share of the national population to 14 percent. Over this period, the district of Tel-Aviv grew at the slowest rate, and its population has remained more or less constant over the last seven years. Conversely, the central district has shown rapid growth, attracting inhabitants from Tel-Aviv, but is still second, in terms of growth rate, to the Southern district. The share of the latter district is expected to continue to grow in the future, from 14 percent today to about 17 percent in year 2020 (Bar-El 2001).

We classify the six districts into three main regions. One is the metropolitan area based region (MBR) and includes the district of Tel-Aviv and the Centre district. A second region includes the districts of Jerusalem, Haifa and the North, and will be denominated as 'other'. This broad region includes the two other main urban centres of Israel, Jerusalem and Haifa, and their rural hinterland. The Northern district does include peripheral areas, but most of its population is located at commuting distance from the city of Haifa. The third region is defined as the Southern district, and is regarded as peripheral, although some parts of it are within commuting distance to Tel-Aviv.

12.4 ROAD INFRASTRUCTURE: INVESTMENT TRENDS

The development of road infrastructure is presented in terms of accumulated stock values, in relation to the three parameters mentioned above: area of the region, accumulated population and accumulated labour force. First, the basic data on road construction during the period of 1978 to 1998 are presented in Table 12.2.

About 30 square km of roads were built in the 21 year period between 1978 and 1998, more or less equally distributed across the three main regions. The calculation of the annual rate of growth is somewhat problematic, as we begin with a value of zero at the first year. Growth rates are therefore calculated from 1983 onwards, after a substantive accumulation of roads in the preceding five years.

The results show that the average growth of the constructed area nationally is 9.6 percent. It should, however, be remembered that this raw number does not mean much by itself, since it is heavily dependent on an arbitrary decision regarding the initial year for calculation. The importance of the results lies in the comparison across regions. The growth rate in the metropolitan area in and around Tel-Aviv and in the 'other' regions (Jerusalem, Haifa and their hinterlands), is much higher than that of the peripheral Southern region.

Table 12.2   *Accumulated road area constructed between 1983 and 1998 by region, absolute total (in km^2) and annual rate of growth by periods (using 1978 base)*

	83-98 %	83-89 %	90-92 %	93-98 %	Total area (sq. km)
National	9.6	8.1	8.8	11.9	30.3
Metropolitan	11.5	9.3	11.2	14.4	10.1
Other	11.4	8.5	8.4	16.4	8.0
South	7.7	7.4	7.7	8.0	12.3

Source: Calculated from the *Statistical Abstracts of Israel* for various years.

This is also true for each separate time period. The first period covers more or less the launch of an economic stabilisation programme, the second period covers a period of mass migration to Israel and rapid demographic growth, and the third period covers mostly a time of rapid economic growth. This third period is also characterised by the most rapid growth in road infrastructure stock. With respect to the regional distribution of the road infrastructure growth, two main points can be made:

• The growth rate is consistently lower in the Southern peripheral region.
• The gap between the regions is especially high during the period or rapid growth of road infrastructure. After 1992, while other regions experienced accelerated growth, the Southern peripheral region maintained a consistent rate. Over this period of rapid economic growth nationally, the infrastructure growth in the periphery was about half that of the metropolitan region and of the other urban regions.

This growing gap between the periphery and other regions in road infrastructure is further demonstrated in Figure 12.1, showing the trend of road intensity as measured by the share of roads in the total regional area (*RIA$_i$*).

The figure shows a rapid increase of road density in the metropolitan region, as compared with a lowest increase in the Southern region. The trend lines estimated for each region on an exponential basis are the following:

$$RIA(N) = 0.0003e^{0.0876x} \qquad R^2 = 0.9762$$
$$RIA(M) = 4E\text{-}05e^{0.1227x} \qquad R^2 = 0.9562$$
$$RIA(O) = 7E\text{-}05e^{0.1013x} \qquad R^2 = 0.9551$$
$$RIA(S) = 0.0016e^{0.0638x} \qquad R^2 = 0.9659 \qquad (12.3)$$

where x represents the year (two last digits), *RIA(N)* stands for the road intensity in relation to area nationally, and the others stand for the road intensity in each region. The figure clearly shows the rapidly increasing road infrastructure in the Metropolitan region, as compared with a lowest rate in the Southern region. All equations show high R^2 levels with highest coefficients on x in the Metropolitan region (0.1227), and a lowest level in the Southern region (0.0638).

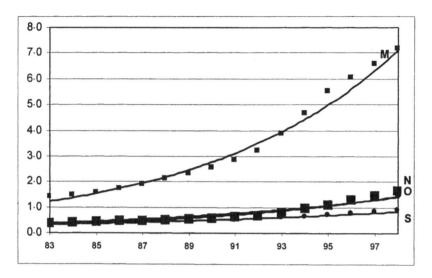

Figure 12.1   Road area density (RIA), *by regions and years*

A consequence of these trends is a decreasing share of the Southern region in the total road area infrastructure accumulated since 1983 (starting with 1978 as the base). This is shown in Table 12.3, for years at the beginning and end of each period.

Table 12.3   Distribution of accumulated road area since 1978 (base) by region and selected years (in percent)

Years	83	89	92	98
Nation	100	100	100	100
Metropolitan	25	27	29	33
Other	22	21	21	26
South	53	52	50	41

The share of the Southern region was 53 percent in 1983 (compared to 69 percent of the national land area), and diminished constantly until reaching 41 percent in 1998. The most significant decrease was after 1992. At that time, the share of the metropolitan region sharply increased, as well as the share of other urban regions, although at a slower rate.

It is important to emphasise that these findings do not represent any declared (or undeclared) public policy of reducing the relative allocation of public expenditure for roads in the Southern region. On the contrary: the public policy rhetoric has always been one of support for this region, and explicitly the reinforcement of infrastructure investment. Moreover, over the period in which the share of the South in road area decreased most dramatically (after 1992), public declarations became increasingly strident. Public sector investment in road construction in the metropolitan area increased rapidly over the years as a response to demand pressures and not as part of any structured plan.

12.5 POPULATION ELASTICITY OF INFRASTRUCTURE INVESTMENT

The decreasing share of the peripheral region in total accumulated road area may theoretically be the consequence of decreasing relative need for infrastructure in this region. Road infrastructure has both a consumption dimension (responding to needs of consumers for travel for leisure or other social activities) and a productive dimension (for the transportation of products and of production factors). We shall use population change as a rough indicator of the consumption dimension, and labour force as a rough indicator of the production dimension.

Between 1978 and 1998, population rose nationally by about 2.2 million with a final population of 5.6 million. The distribution of this population in four selected years across regions is presented in Table 12.4.

Table 12.4   Distribution of accumulated population since 1978 (base) by region, at various years (in percent)

Years	83	89	92	98
Nation	100	100	100	100
Metropolitan	37	38	39	36
Other	51	50	47	46
South	12	13	14	18

This table shows that the decreasing share of the peripheral region in the stock of road infrastructure is clearly not a result of a decreasing population share. The accumulated share of the Southern region in nationally population since 1978 grew constantly over this period, from 12 percent in 1983 to 18 percent in 1998. At the same time, a slight decline in the metropolitan region's share can be discerned and a sharp decline of the other urban regions in total population - all this in the context of a rapid increase in their share of road infrastructure.

The response of road construction to increasing population may be estimated through the parameter of population elasticity of infrastructure. This may be defined as:

$$per_{i,t} = (\Delta R_{i,t} / R_{i,t-n}) / (\Delta P_{i,t} / P_{i,t-n}) \qquad (12.4)$$

where:

$per_{i,t}$ is the population elasticity of road infrastructure in region i at time t,

$\Delta R_{i,t} / R_{i,t-n}$ is the percentage growth of road area in the region during a period of n years, from time $t - n$ to time t,

$\Delta P_{i,t} / P_{i,t-n}$ is the percentage growth of population in the same region at the same time.

The data for the rate of growth of accumulated population since 1978 are presented in Table 12.5, and the elasticities in Table 12.6.

Elasticities are calculated here for average time periods, rather than on an annual basis, because of frequent fluctuations. Even using groups of years we find heavy fluctuations, with a decreasing elasticity at the second period and an increasing elasticity at the last period. National elasticity, as an average for the whole period between 1983 and 1998, reached only 0.87. This coefficient (<1) implies a lower increasing rate of road accumulation than population accumulation, or a decreasing intensity of road coverage per population. Normally, a coefficient higher than 1 indicates that the population growth is accompanied by income and consumption growth per capita, leading to an increasing demand for road area. This demand growth is explained by increasing use of vehicles per person, and higher levels of personal mobility. An elasticity coefficient of less than 1 clearly indicates therefore an insufficient response of road construction to population growth, assuming there is no drastic change in alternative transportation systems.

Table 12.5   Accumulated population between 1983 and 1998 (1978 base) by region, absolute total (in thousands) and annual rate of growth by periods

	83-98 %	83-89 %	90-92 %	93-98 %	Population 1998 (thousands)
Nation	11.1	10.5	19.7	7.8	2162
Metropolitan	11.1	11.1	20.8	6.4	779
Other	10.8	11.1	17.3	7.4	992
South	12.1	7.3	24.8	11.9	392

Source: Calculated from the *Statistical Abstracts of Israel* for various years.

Table 12.6   Population elasticities of road infrastructure ($per_{i,t}$), by periods

	83-98	83-89	90-92	93-98
Nation	0.87	0.77	0.45	1.53
Metropolitan	1.04	0.83	0.54	2.24
Other	1.05	0.77	0.48	2.21
South	0.63	1.02	0.31	0.67

The average elasticity for the whole period, shows an extremely low level in the Southern region (0.63), while in the metropolitan area and in other urban regions estimated elasticity is higher than 1. It is not clear whether coefficients of 1.04 or 1.05 as found in those regions actually reflect an adequate response to the increase in consumption per capita, but there is little doubt that the coefficient of 0.63 for the South indicates a severe decrease in road intensity. This constantly decreasing road intensity in relation to population in the southern region is clearly identified by the ratio of accumulated road area per accumulated population between the years of 1983 and 1998, as shown in Figure 12.2.

The estimated regression lines for each region are:

$$
\begin{aligned}
RIP(N) &= 243e^{-0.0311x} & R^2 &= 0.6016 \\
RIP(M) &= 11e^{0.0003x} & R^2 &= 0.0000 \\
RIP(O) &= 15e^{-0.0088x} & R^2 &= 0.0655 \\
RIP(S) &= 103e^{-0.0857x} & R^2 &= 0.9514
\end{aligned}
\tag{12.5}
$$

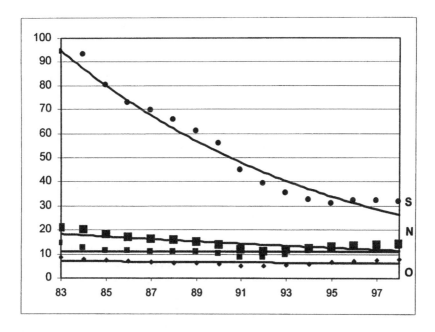

Figure 12.2   Road intensity in relation to population (RIP: m² per person), by regions and years

Of all the regions, only the results for the South show a clear negative tendency (with a very high correlation coefficient): a decreasing area per person across all the years. The total road area per person is still higher in the South than in other regions (due to the special geographical structure of this region), but the gap decreases continuously, from almost 100 m² per person in the South in relation to around 10 m² in the other regions (a ratio of 10:1) in 1983, to about 30 m² to 10 m² (a ratio of 3:1) in 1998.

As already stated, it is clear that the road infrastructure in one region impacts all other regions that use it, and this sharp decline in the road area per person in the South constitutes a deterioration of the conditions for the population in all regions. However, assuming that the existence of infrastructure in each region is mostly relevant to the region itself, we can conclude that the road infrastructure conditions in the South have suffered a real and substantive deterioration in relation to other regions. In any case, the decreasing road intensity in the Southern region, to the extent that those roads serve as a link to the other regions, constraints the potential of integration of the South into the national economy.

12.6 LAGGED POPULATION ELASTICITY OF ROAD INFRASTRUCTURE

Examining the elasticities by periods reveals generally high fluctuations, with low levels at the first periods, and a higher level later on. Such fluctuations may be the result of a lag between changes in population and late responses in road construction. Such a lag may also explain the low correlation coefficients received for two out of the three regions.

A measure of a lagged road infrastructure intensity in relation to population is defined as:

$$RIP_{i,t} = R_{i,t} / P_{i,t-l} \tag{12.6}$$

where $RIP_{i,t}$ is lagged road infrastructure intensity in relation to the population in region i, $R_{i,t}$ is accumulated road area in the region at time t, and $P_{i,t-l}$ is population of the region at time $t - l$, assuming that investments in road infrastructure respond to population increase after a lag of l years.

The correlation between road intensity and years is calculated at three alternatives of lags, using the same exponential function. The results for each region at each lag option are presented in Table 12.7 (each lag year decreases the number of observations by 1).

Table 12.7 R^2 of lagged road intensity in relation to population, by region, at three options of lags

	Lag of (years)			
Region	0	1	2	3
Nation	0.60	0.52	0.28	0.45
Metropolitan	0.00	0.31	0.87	0.98
Other	0.07	0.06	0.44	0.75
South	0.95	0.96	0.94	0.83

The results show an increasing correlation, reaching highest levels at a lag of three years for the metropolitan region and for the other urban regions, from the original level of about 0 with no lag. In the Southern region, the high level of correlation observed with no lag remains with a lag of one or two years, and even decreases with a lag of three years. A tentative conclusion is that while there is a road construction response to increasing population in the metropolitan area and in other urban areas, with a lag of about two or three years, this does not happen in the peripheral area of the South. Even the high correlation levels observed with no lag or with a lag of one or two years cannot indicate the existence of a structured policy of response to population change, because the observed relationship is negative. There is no logic in a conscious policy of decreasing road intensity as a response to increased population. The more probable explanation is the existence of a historic trend of slow increases in road construction in the periphery in relation to other regions.

The estimated regressions based on a three year lag clearly show a positive response of road infrastructure to changes in population in the metropolitan region and in other urban regions, and a lack of response (with a negative trend) in the peripheral region:

$$
\begin{aligned}
RIP(N) &= 3e^{0.0144x} & R^2 &= 0.4508 \\
RIP(M) &= 0.06e^{0.0555x} & R^2 &= 0.9831 \\
RIP(O) &= 0.1e^{0.0442x} & R^2 &= 0.7454 \\
RIP(S) &= 4773e^{-0.0517x} & R^2 &= 0.8273
\end{aligned}
\tag{12.7}
$$

The population elasticity of road infrastructure calculated on the basis of a three year lag also shows a lower level of fluctuations between the years. The lagged elasticity may be defined as:

$$
per_{i,t(l)} = (\Delta R_{i,t} / R_{i,t-n}) / (\Delta P_{i,t-l} / P_{i,t-l-n})
\tag{12.8}
$$

where:
$per_{i,t(l)}$ is the population elasticity of road infrastructure in region i at time t, with a lag of l years,
$\Delta R_{i,t} / R_{i,t-n}$ is the percentage growth of road area in the region from time $t - n$ to time t,
$\Delta P_{i,t-l} / P_{i,t-l-n}$ is the percentage growth of population in the same region l years earlier.

Table 12.8   Three years lagged population elasticities of road infrastructure ($per_{i,t(l)}$), by regions and periods

	86-98	86-89	90-92	93-98
Nation	1.17	0.93	1.53	1.17
Metropolitan	1.69	2.18	1.68	1.42
Other	1.40	0.88	1.48	1.72
South	0.75	0.80	1.54	0.56

For the whole period (between 1986 and 1998), the elasticity of road construction to population growth is higher than 1 in the metropolitan region and in the other urban regions, while it is clearly lower than 1 in the Southern region (Table 12.8). In this region, the elasticity was greater than 1 for a short period of 1990 to 1992, but has been less than 1 over the last few years. The high elasticity coefficient over the 1990-92 period (1.54) probably reflects a shorter lag in the adjustment of road infrastructure in the Southern region over this period. The same coefficient calculated on the basis of a two-year lag is only 0.85.

12.7 CONCLUSION

Regional investment of public expenditure for infrastructure is probably a crucial element in the economic development of the regions. However, the policy measures that are required in order to achieve an optimal allocation are not yet clear. The prevailing policy 'rule of the thumb' is to respond to revealed needs for infrastructure, such as reflected by demand pressure (for example, increasing traffic congestion). This analysis shows that such a policy approach may lead to discrimination against poorer peripheral regions.

Israeli data for the last two decades show the existence of a public response to increasing population (and labour force) in the metropolitan region and in other urban regions, with a lag of two or three years. However, such a response does not exist in the peripheral Southern region. Therefore, despite declared government policy support to the South, we find that the relative share of road infrastructure investment in that region decreased constantly over the years.

Most theoretical explanations for this situation do not supply a reasonable answer. One could be the existence of a 'natural' process of degeneration of the peripheral regions, loosing population and economic activity, and therefore being indifferent to infrastructure supply. This is not the situation in this case: data actually show that the peripheral Southern region is in a process of increasing its share in national population and labour force. A second explanation could be the process of a centralisation of economic growth, with an increasing dependence of the South upon employment in other regions. This also is not the case, and data on inter-regional commuting to work do not show any significant change over the years.

In fact, recent years have seen an increasing gap between the peripheral South and the metropolitan and other regions, mainly in terms of unemployment. Capital and other incentives in the periphery provide only short-term solutions, and many economic activities do not find the conditions for sustained growth in the region (Schwartz 1987; Bregman et al. 1999). While it is difficult to unequivocally prove the existence of a direct link between road infrastructure investment and the level of economic development of a peripheral region, other factors such as education and labour force skills are certainly important.

We have seen here that a policy infrastructure investment in response to revealed needs may lead to a distorted regional allocation of public expenditures and to the discrimination of the peripheral region. This may result in an unconscious policy of public-led regional economic concentration. A more 'normative' policy of allocation of infrastructure should be considered. This requires further research of the contribution of infrastructure to regional economic growth.

REFERENCES

Aschauer, D. (1989), 'Is public expenditure productive?', *Journal of Monetary Economics*, **23**, pp. 177-200.

Bar-El, R. (2000), 'Convergence, divergence and non efficiency of public infrastructure spatial allocation', *Region and Development*, **12**, forthcoming.

Bar-El, R. (2001), 'Promoting regional growth and convergence in the long-term master plan for Israel', in D. Felsenstein and M. Taylor (eds), *Promoting Local Growth: Process, Practice and Policy* (forthcoming).

Barro R.J. and X. Sala-i-Martin (1991), 'Convergence across states and regions', *Brookings Papers on Economic Activity*, **1**, pp. 107-82.

Bregman A., M. Fuss and H. Regev (1999), 'Effects of capital subsidization on productivity in Israeli industry', *Economic Review*, Bank of Israel, **72**, pp. 77-101.

Fagerberg, J. and B. Verspagen (1996), 'Heading for divergence? Regional growth in Europe reconsidered', *Journal of Common Market Studies*, **34**, pp. 431-48.

Parr, J.B. (1999), 'The metropolitan area in its wider setting', in A.A. Summers, P.C. Cheshire and L. Senn (eds), *Urban Change in the United States and Western Europe, Comparative Analysis and Policy* (Second edition), pp. 215-42, Washington: The Urban Institute Press.

Quah D.T. (1996), 'Regional convergence clusters across Europe', *European Economic Review*, **40**, pp. 951-8.

Schwartz, D. (1987), 'The government's role in private investment', in R. Bar-El, A. Ben David-Val and G.J. Karaska (eds), *Patterns of Change in Developing Rural Regions*, London: Westview Press.

13. Public Investment in Physical Infrastructure and Inward Investment Location Choice: a Stated Preference Experiment

Ronald McQuaid, Scott Leitham and John D. Nelson

13.1 INTRODUCTION

Attracting increased international and inter-regional inward investment and supporting industrial development has often been used to justify investment in road transport infrastructure (CEC 1993; DoT 1996). However, uncertainty surrounds the relationships between new or improved transport infrastructure, accessibility and the location decisions of industrial and commercial firms (see for example: Banister and Berechman 2000; Button 1994; McQuaid 1995; Shefer and Shefer 1999; Vickerman et al. 1999).

A large number of factors influence the location of businesses and inward investors in particular (Hood et al. 1994). It is important to distinguish between factors that influence the choice of a specific region, or country, from those that influence the choice of specific sites within that region (Breheny and McQuaid 1987). Generally, major factors affecting inter-regional location depend upon the characteristics of the business, the locality and the type of connections with other areas and organisations.

These key factors include: the type of production and organisation; access to markets, suppliers and capital; access to knowledge and technology, especially for more advanced industries; the labour supply in terms of both quantity, quality, costs and so on and the implications of these for production and other costs and value creation; agglomeration economies and economies of scale (Krugman 1998; Anas et al. 1998); government incentives, regulations and support; the local business climate, including taxation and the community's attitude towards business; physical infrastructure; inter- and intra-organisational and institutional links and networks; good communications and accessibility; and factor costs (although in countries such as the UK business taxes are centrally, not regionally, controlled).

For choices at the international level, relevant factors also include political stability, exchange rates and associated risks, financial support packages, language and international communications. At the intra-regional level of choice certain factors such as the specific site and property characteristics and costs, the image the business wishes to project, and local transportation access may also be particularly important for both firm and employees or potential employees (McQuaid et al. 2001).

Transport plays a particularly important role in location and is discussed more fully in the following section. When analysing the likely influence of transport infrastructure in the UK benefits have been calculated mainly in terms of user time savings (Mackie 1996). Two main ways of collecting data to estimate predictive models for travel demand or mode choice when assessing investment or planning strategies are revealed preference (RP) methods (Fridstrom and Elvik 1997) or stated preference (SP) methods (see for example: Horowitz and Louvière 1990; and Shiftan's Chapter 14 in this book on residential choice). While RP methods observe choices and decisions actually made by people, SP approaches analyse peoples' statements about how they would respond when faced with different choices, and so are used mainly for new or unique decisions, such as choosing a new industrial location. However, both methodologies have a number of advantages and disadvantages (Hensher 1994). Although SP has been widely applied in transport studies there have been few studies of the importance of transport on industrial location choice (see for example: Ouwersloot and Rietveld 1996; Rietveld 1994; Hagashi et al. 1986).

In SP experiments, hypothetical scenarios can be used as a forecasting tool applied to fixed or varying choice sets, as a way of estimating the utility functions specified in discrete choice modelling, where economic agents are generally assumed to maximise their utility when making choices. It is therefore useful for considering influences on the potential future decisions concerning industrial location. This chapter presents an SP experiment considering the *ex ante* choice of industrial and commercial firms concerning their future location using a case study in the Strathclyde region of Scotland. Using SP techniques, it investigates the importance of certain levels of service, in terms of small differences in the accessibility afforded by road links, compared to the importance of factors affecting premises and cost.

The next section considers the role of transport in industrial (inter-regional) location. Section 13.3 then considers the theory underlying the design of an SP experiment concerning multi-plant firms. Section 13.4 discusses the characteristics of the survey sample and the scenario and its attributes. Section 13.5 presents the results of the SP influence of transport and other factors upon the location choices of firms. The final section presents conclusions.

13.2 TRANSPORT AND INDUSTRIAL LOCATION

Transport infrastructure is important for the location of many industries in terms of: transport costs for goods; travel costs for staff, suppliers, customers, (including tourists); time (especially when an industry is organised in a manner such as 'Just-in-Time'); risk and uncertainty (if delivery is highly reliable then the time a delivery takes need not be a significant disadvantage); and need for liaison between supplier and customer; and need for suppliers to access market information directly. However the importance of these factors is likely to vary by industry, ownership and associated links to other parts of the organisation, and the characteristics of the region. Schmenner (1982) found that branch plants in the US emphasised transportation facilities and utilities, although as highway access is nearly ubiquitous in the US it does not rank highly as a location factor (see also Button et al. 1995). Vickerman (1998) also suggests that once a minimum threshold of accessibility is reached the relationship between accessibility and firm location and behaviour may change.

When considering the relationships between transport infrastructure and economic development, a wide range of approaches have been used. Two frequently used techniques in evaluating the economic impact of transport infrastructure are input-output analysis (for example Hewings and Jensen 1985; Batey et al. 1993) and econometric modelling (for example Glickman 1977; Rietveld 1989). In addition there have been a number of empirically based location studies, often ranking a set of location factors for their importance.

For instance, Hummon et al. (1986) investigating the importance of transport to US high technology industries found that 80 percent of firms thought that the transport of materials and products to and from markets and suppliers was 'very important' or 'important'. Some 68 percent rated access of personnel to others similarly, and 80 percent considered the importance of transport in creating a pleasant working environment as at least 'important'. Toft and Mahmassani (1984) report a survey of US high technology firms where transport was ranked sixth in inter-regional location choices (60 percent 'significant' or 'very significant') and fifth in intra-regional decisions (76 percent 'significant' or 'very significant'). More generally, CEC (1990) surveyed a large number of firms throughout the EU and found that transport and communications were amongst the most important factors influencing location decisions.

The influence of company structure and decision-making processes is also identified as a major factor in the location decision (for example branch versus single plant operator). Walker and Calzonetti (1990) analysed the plant location 'search processes' of US manufacturing using discriminant analysis on survey data. They concluded that transport becomes a factor only at the micro level of location search but firms with high transport costs were more likely to undertake a location search. In other words, the type of industry and function of the plant are crucial to the importance attributed to transport when making a location decision. However, it is difficult to make generalisations due to inter-industry differences, various types of move and assessing the impact of different factors on industrial location.

Researchers have also used observational and secondary data to investigate the statistical associations between the firm location and socio-economic data using discrete choice methodologies, concluding that transport infrastructure is one of several significant factors affecting the choice of a State location (Friedman et al. 1992). Henley et al. (1989) use a number of discrete choice models to contrast the actual economic attractiveness of a location with the attractiveness perceived by the establishments. The results indicate that perceptions about locations provided a good explanation for the distribution of location but the measurable reality of these perceptions was less explanatory, emphasising the importance of perceptions in location decisions. In order to estimate the level of significance that transport plays in the operation of firms it is also important to investigate company costs structures and their logistical strategy and behaviour.

Finally, the ECMT (1991) concluded that transportation costs are secondary to factors such as labour, although certain transportation infrastructure may be a necessary, though not a sufficient, condition for the location or development of firms in a specific area. In terms of company costs, previous studies suggest that a low proportion of overall costs are spent on transportation. Hence, a reduction in transportation costs will have minimal effects except in the few industries where transport makes up a much higher proportion of total costs. However, different factors affect different types of firm with those relocating intra-regionally behaving differently from inward investors, that is those moving inter-regionally (Leitham et al. 2000). While most studies place transport as a generally significant factor in location decisions greater knowledge is needed of how this varies between different types of firm. The next section considers the theory behind one approach to analysing location behaviour - stated preference.

13.3 THE THEORY UNDERLYING THE STATED PREFERENCE SCENARIO FOR MULTI-PLANT FIRMS

The analysis of SP results takes a variety of forms in terms of the estimation of the utility attached to each attribute level, and therefore each discrete alternative. Regression and ANOVA options exist, but the most common approach uses discrete choice models and more particularly the logit function (Multinomial Logit Models) (for example Bates 1988; McQuaid et al. 1996; Pearmain et al. 1991), although there may be difficulties in interpreting the changes in probabilities from unit changes in independent variables (Petersen 1985). This is therefore a probabilistic approach estimating the probability of each alternative being chosen, although consideration must be taken of the 'scaling problem' when producing forecasts of *actual* rather than *relative* utilities of alternatives (Beaton et al. 1998; Wardman 1991). A choice experiment is a first order ranking task (Hensher 1994).

This chapter seeks to explore how location factors influence the choice of firms from an *ex ante* perspective using hypothetical scenarios of possible future location factors. So in order to investigate further the relationship between transportation and industrial location and operation, an in-depth computer-based 'face-to-face' survey was carried out. This involved firms who had recent experience of location choice through moving from another region or country.

In this experiment, the choices are between different hypothetical locations, described by sets of attributes for each of the scenarios. Discrete binary choice methods (that is pairwise choices between two options) are used as this is the simplest way to present the alternatives in this application. In choosing attributes, it is important to use factors that will create a realistic choice for the respondent. These attributes are determined from theoretical models, previous knowledge and *a priori* reasoning, although considerations of parsimony limit the attributes selected. Clearly, a problem arises in terms of the number of pairs that each respondent would have to consider if the number of alternatives is large and there would be a danger of 'respondent fatigue'. This problem is resolved by assuming that respondents are transient in their choices and that certain interaction effects among the attributes are not statistically significant. Respondents are also only presented with pairs where neither option is obviously dominant.

In this study the computer-based experimental design packages SPEED and ALASTAIR were used to administer the experiment (Bradley and Daly 1994). ALASTAIR (Steer Davies Gleave 1991) employs a logic in the perceived attributes, for example, cheapest or most expensive, which are used to assess choices made by respondents and decide which pair of alternatives to present in turn. Once the program has ranked the alternatives according to the responses, the process terminates.

In the application of SP techniques to the current study, four (re)location scenarios were developed, but only the inward inter-regional location one is reported here (the others concerned intra-regional relocations, the expansion of firms to satellite premises and inter-regional relocation scenarios). The scenario described to the respondent and a series of paired choices were presented on the screen, which the computer evaluated adaptively from previous responses and an initial ranking of the various attributes. This process produces an estimated ranking of all the alternatives, whilst recording all the details of the individual pairs presented and choices made. In the analysis that follows, these responses are analysed using multinomial logit techniques to evaluate how each level of each attribute affects the probability of an alternative, and therefore a location, being selected. The output from the SP surveys comprises both a recording of the alternatives presented and the choices made, and a ranking of the alternatives generated by the program based on the choices made by the respondent. The choices from each respondent are then aggregated for analysis.

The stated preference analysis program ALOGIT Version 3.2 (Hague Consulting Group 1992) is used for the estimation of the utility functions associated with the choice games, utilising a maximum likelihood formulation. The estimation procedure uses a logit model which defines the probability of choosing an alternative as a function of its total utility in relation to that of the other alternatives, that is,

$$P_1 = exp\ (V_1)\ /\ \{exp\ (V_1) + exp\ (V_2) + \ldots\ldots\ldots + exp\ (V_k)\} \quad (13.1)$$

in which the V's represent the utilities of each of the alternatives 1, 2, ... k (in this case there are 16 alternatives which occur in the scenario - see below). Each alternative is assigned a share of the probability exactly proportional to the exponential of its utility. The partial utilities (or parameter estimates) estimated in ALOGIT are then assessed for their statistical significance. Since the models estimated use only discrete variables, a dummy variable method is used and the partial utilities are estimated with respect to a 'base' case for each discrete variable. The value (or utility) of the base (which can be defined as any level for any variable) is implicitly set at zero.

The analysis used for each game initially estimates the utility function of the location choices based on all the discrete choices aggregated. Models are then estimated based on sub-groups of firms with similar characteristics, or for those giving similar responses. In this latter case, a cluster analysis was used on the 'rankings' of the alternatives generated by the software, supplemented by the use of likelihood ratio tests. This produces groups of respondents exhibiting similar responses and gives an indication of the main differences of emphasis within the responses to the scenario.

Goodness of fit of the models is assessed using a range of output statistics from the ALOGIT program. The most appropriate are comparisons of the final likelihood values with the base likelihood with both zero coefficients and with constants, values known as ρ^2 (for example, McFadden 1979). These values show the fraction of the base likelihood that the model has 'explained', arguably comparable with the R^2 statistic from linear regression. In models with no clearly defined choice situation (for example, car versus bus mode choice would be a clearly defined choice situation) or when the alternatives are generic, the ρ^2 comparison with zero coefficients may be appropriate. It is therefore this value which is given below. The value of ρ^2 indicative of a good model is dependent on the complexity of the choices faced by the respondents, with higher values of up to 0.4 being expected for very clear choices (such as between modes) and lower values of < 0.1 deemed acceptable for more complex choices (Hague Consulting Group 1992). The values reported for the models below fall towards the top end of this range, and are therefore deemed a satisfactory fit.

In terms of interpretation, the partial utilities for one level of each factor can be added to establish a total utility for that location. A linear additive utility function was used throughout, as there was no *a priori* reason to expect an alternative form since all variables were discrete. The logit function can then be used to estimate the probability that this location would be chosen in comparison with a set of similarly defined locations. The magnitude and statistical significance of the partial utilities indicate the significance of individual levels of location factors in terms of influencing the probability of a location being chosen. The partial utilities (that is, the parameter estimates) are therefore of greater interest in interpreting these models.

13.4   THE STATED PREFERENCE SURVEY AND EXPERIMENT

Forty interviews were carried out with senior managers at the premises of firms in Western Scotland (see Leitham et al. 2000). Initially all firms were shown a list of factors and asked which they considered (*ex post*) to be important in deciding upon their current location. Table 13.1 shows the percentage of firms stating that the factor was considered important in their location decision.

Table 13.1   Percentage of firms considering location factors important

Rank	Location factor	Percentage of firms considering factor important
1	Road links	75
2	Lease/property costs	72
3	Site/building layout	72
4	Image of location	70
5	Access to markets or clients	68
6	Government/financial assistance	42
7	Access to suppliers	40
8	Proximity to previous location	35
9	Quality of staff	32
10	Air links	28
11	Access to related industries	25
12	Bus links	8
13	Access to public	8
14	Rail links	5

Note: n=40

The first five factors of road links, property costs, site/building layout, location image and access to markets are by far the most significant. The top four are in identical order to an earlier wider study of 939 firms (Button et al. 1995). Government assistance and accessibility to suppliers was cited as important by around 40 percent of respondents, while around a third cited quality of staff, and proximity to previous location. Air links are considered important by 28 percent of all firms, but this figure is much higher for foreign-owned branch plants and firms with international markets and suppliers. This information helps to lay the context for the SP analysis of the narrower group of branch plants below.

Some 24 of the firms were intra-regional and 12 inter-regional relocators and the others new firms or take-overs. The inter-regional relocators were part of multi-plant organisations, so the location of the corporate headquarters was identified, in addition to the location of other plants or offices in the organisation (in order to determine likely inter-plant transport needs). Each respondent was then asked to consider a hypothetical location decision scenario concerning a location scenario and then presented with varying pairs of hypothetical locations with different attributes. From each pair of locations they were asked to select a preferred one. The attributes, and their levels, used in the SP scenario were defined as: road links (with three attribute levels of 30, 15 or 5 minutes to a motorway); site/building layout (with attribute levels of poor, average and excellent); property costs (more expensive, similar to present and less expensive); image of location (poor or high); public transport provision (poor or good); quality of staff (moderate or excellent). Regional aid was excluded as all locations surveyed had equal eligibility for such support. This scenario produced 257 discrete choices. It should be noted that these relate primarily to intra-regional location choices (that is once the regional or Scottish location had been chosen), so the access to most markets and broad profitability of locations were similar for the firms. Hence, in this sample there was not a choice between high cost and high sales versus low cost low sales locations.

Accessibility factors were largely encompassed in the 'road links' factor, this being seen as a proxy for the accessibility of the location generally. This point was clarified with the respondent where necessary. The 'public transport' factor was also included in order to obtain a comparison of transport modes. Staff factors were included in some scenarios where the recruitment of labour was likely to be an important issue. Most of the location factors used as attributes can only be realistically described using qualitative judgements, due to the wide range of types of firms interviewed and the different types of locations and premises at which they were based. For example, property costs were impossible to quantify without knowledge of respondents' actual property costs and likely elasticities of demand, so a simple relative scale linked to the respondents' current costs was employed.

The respondent was given the following instructions: 'Imagine that your company has identified a potential market in a different part of the country in which you think it would be beneficial and profitable to operate. You have therefore decided to set up a branch operation located in this new area, whilst continuing your current operations at these premises.' They then had to choose between pairs of locations (defined by different levels of the same variables as specified in the experimental design, that is the parameters were all generic), while assuming that premises of a suitable size and nature existed at each of the hypothetical locations along with the necessary utilities.

An orthogonal fractional factorial design for the scenarios outlined above results in a set of sixteen discrete alternatives, that is sixteen differently defined locations which were specified for each scenario in the ALISTAIR software. The design assumes no important interactions and allows an estimation to be made of the effect of each level of each attribute in the analysis. No interactions were specified in the design due to the computational restrictions of the process (including that some interactions would lead to a loss of orthogonality) and as there were no particular interactions which were of specific interest in the experimental design. By creating a realistic and relevant choice situation for the respondent it was possible to reduce the problem of 'errors in responses' as in reality people may not always act later as they said they would in surveys. There was little or no incentive for the respondents to give deliberately misleading responses (particularly as the study was seen as being independent and not carried out for a government agency) and other responses made by the firms during the interview and a prior survey were checked for consistency.

13.5 RESULTS OF THE STATED PREFERENCE EXPERIMENT

A logit analysis of the choices aggregated together produced the model utilising the base parameter levels of: poor image of the location, moderate quality of local workforce, poor public transport, Motorway 30 mins, poor building quality, higher property costs. The results were a linear utility function based upon the average for all firms and incorporating the following parameters: IMAGOOD - good image; STAFEXEL - excellent local workforce; PTGOOD - good public transport; ROAD15 - Motorway 15 mins; ROAD5 - Motorway 5 mins; BUILADEQ - adequate building quality; BUILEXEL - excellent building quality; PROPSAME - similar property costs; PROPLOWE - lower property costs.

$$\text{Utility}_i = 0.2433 \text{ IMAGOOD} \quad + 1.233 \text{ STAFEXEL} \quad + 0.2858 \text{ PTGOOD}$$
$$(1.1) \qquad\qquad (5.4)^* \qquad\qquad (1.3)$$

$$+ 0.2766 \text{ ROAD15} \quad - 0.049 \text{ ROAD5} \quad + 1.648 \text{ BUILADEQ}$$
$$(0.7) \qquad\qquad (-0.1) \qquad\qquad (5.2)^*$$

$$+ 0.9754 \text{ BUILEXEL} \quad + 0.5558 \text{ PROPSAME} \quad + 0.9826 \text{ PROPLOWE}$$
$$(3.7)^* \qquad\qquad (2.0)^* \qquad\qquad (3.0)^*$$

$$\rho^2 = 0.2521 \qquad\qquad\qquad (13.2)$$

t-statistics are in brackets. * Significant at the 5% level.

All statistically significant parameters (at the 5 percent level) have signs in the expected direction. Unsurprisingly building quality (both the adequate and excellent variables, with the former having the largest coefficient) and similar or lower property costs were found to be significant. Lower property costs are preferred to similar (that is, similar to current) property costs.

Since branch plants are not relocating, they are not expecting to increase costs relative to their previous location for a given quality of accommodation, and they may seek the lowest cost properties for their new plant. The relatively large and significant coefficient for an excellent workforce indicates the importance attached to recruiting new staff for branch operations. Four factors were found to be non-significant, relating to image, to public transport and surprisingly to both 5 and 15 minutes from motorway access. The lack of significance of motorway access may be due to the availability of major non-motorway trunk roads or that access to the motorway system is a relatively small part of long journeys.

The results were further disaggregated into those branches of parent companies based in the UK and those based elsewhere (equations (13.3) and (13.4)). The disaggregation was defined from the analysis of the responses of branch firms to previous questions in the survey which showed UK or foreign ownership as being the most important factor in determining distinctly different attitudes towards location for branch plants, as suggested by previous studies noted above. This selection of 'groups' was supplemented using likelihood ratio tests, in order to determine if the addition of a firm to the model added significantly to its explanatory power (for example Ben Akiva and Lerman 1985).

The base parameter levels are as follows: moderate quality of local workforce, poor public transport, motorway 30 mins, poor building quality, higher property costs, poor image.

Non-UK-Based Parents Utility$_i$ =

$$
\begin{array}{lll}
0.8372 \text{ IMAGOOD} & + 1.722 \text{ STAFEXEL} & + 0.5458 \text{ PTGOOD} \\
(2.2)^* & (4.2)^* & (1.4) \\[2mm]
- 0.056 \text{ ROAD15} & - 0.6256 \text{ ROAD5} & + 1.760 \text{ BUILADEQ} \\
(-0.1) & (-1.1) & (3.4)^* \\[2mm]
+ 1.331 \text{ BUILEXEL} & + 0.5395 \text{ PROPSAME} & + 0.6287 \text{ PROPLOWE} \\
(3.1)^* & (1.1) & (1.3)
\end{array}
$$

$$\rho^2 = 0.3487 \tag{13.3}$$

UK-Based Parents Utility$_i$ =

$$
\begin{array}{lll}
-0.203 \text{ IMAGOOD} & + 1.722 \text{ STAFEXEL} & + 0.2101 \text{ PTGOOD} \\
(-0.6) & (2.8)^* & (0.7) \\[2mm]
+ 1.460 \text{ ROAD15} & + 2.068 \text{ ROAD5} & + 2.021 \text{ BUILADEQ} \\
(2.2)^* & (2.3)^* & (3.9)^* \\[2mm]
+ 1.142 \text{ BUILEXEL} & + 1.338 \text{ PROPSAME} & + 2.131 \text{ PROPLOWE} \\
(2.5)^* & (2.9)^* & (3.7)^*
\end{array}
$$

$$\rho^2 = 0.2455 \tag{13.4}$$

t-statistics are in brackets. * Significant at the 5% level.

Some distinct differences between the types of firms are revealed, although as the logit models' coefficients are scaled relative to the standard deviation of the errors the absolute coefficients are not directly compared across the models. Those firms with non-UK parents place the greatest emphasis on an adequate or excellent building quality, workforce and image being significant (the other factors are not statistically significant). Those with UK parent companies were similarly concerned with an adequate or excellent building quality, workforce. Also of importance were motorway access time, with almost immediate access (under 5 minutes having the highest coefficient) and property costs (with lower costs having a larger coefficient than the same costs).

The emphasis on low property costs, an adequate building and quick motorway access is consistent with the lack of significance for the good image variable. This suggests that UK-based plants focusing more on a functional cost-minimising role, with business development and image building more important at the head office (that is, where the decision is made to create and locate the branch plant). Conversely, foreign-based firms making large investments in another country are keen to be visible, and to be seen as an asset by local communities, thus image is important to these firms. Non-UK parents are arguably likely to be more involved in developing new business and markets. Thus, a high profile location and good image of their location may be of direct competitive advantage in terms of customer perception and attracting suitable mobile staff to the operation. This may also explain why property costs are less important, although property costs may be considered by such firms in terms of international comparisons and the total investment package.

The lack of importance attached to motorway access time by foreign-based branch plants may be seen as something of a surprise finding, given the emphasis on 'infrastructure' projects in regeneration packages and drives to attract inward investment. These findings would suggest that the level of accessibility to roads may generally not be an issue considered in the location decision of international inward investors for whom motorway access time is not seen as a significant factor, although the type of industry and function will be important. Perhaps access to motorway is seen as nearly ubiquitous or local access is relatively insignificant compared to journey times for inter-regional or international links. These findings suggest that funds would be best used to provide quality premises at attractive prices, and to ensure that the workforce can meet the expectations of inward investors. By the necessarily subjective definitions used in this study, they were found to perceive an important difference between a 'moderate' and an 'excellent' workforce. Thus, in terms of transport, it is clear that different links to the motorway could influence the decision of UK-based branch plants. However, there is not evidence to suggest that differences in motorway access time have any effect on the location decisions of overseas investors when deciding between competing locations.

This suggests that further research would be useful in order to distinguish how the logistical organisation of firms affects their location decisions (see for instance: McKinnon and Woodburn 1996). The statistical scope of the stated preference survey prevented the use of an air or sea links factor in the games, but this factor may be important for overseas branch plants. Varying levels of road links, however, were not recognised as a proxy for access to airports or seaports in the stated preference games.

These results appear to vary from those shown from the *ex post* results in Table 13.1, but as they are slightly different samples and variables, no direct comparison is suggested. For the combined sample (equation (13.2)) only variables related to property costs and quality appear significant, although for non-UK-based firms image is significant (equation (13.3)) and for UK-based branches roads are significant (equation (13.4)).

13.6 CONCLUSIONS

In this chapter, stated preference techniques were used in order to estimate the weightings attached to various commonly defined location factors, in terms of the *ex ante* decision-making process. The evidence suggests that it is important to disaggregate different types of firms when analysing the importance of transport upon their location decisions.

Motorway connections varied considerably in importance between UK- and non-UK-based firms, partly due to the different sectors predominant in each group. UK branch plants rated motorway links the highest of any of the groups of firms, underlining the dominance of road links for the distribution of goods and services and intra-firm travel in the UK. In contrast, branches of overseas firms found road links to be an unimportant factor, being outweighed primarily by considerations of workforce and premises.

Motorway access and property costs were only significant for UK-based branches and not for non-UK parent firms. The results suggest that good road communications are seen as crucial for UK branch firms with an inter-regional base. On the evidence of these findings, it is realistic to conclude that road access could be a crucial factor in determining actual location. However, once an inter-regional decision has been taken, more local decisions may be determined by workforce and other agglomeration economies, inputs, market sectors and so on. Hence, the implications are mixed in terms of the justification of new transport investment in road and transportation infrastructure on economic development grounds, and the use of road improvements to create an attractive environment for overseas manufacturing plants is not supported.

Further research is needed into the logistical organisation of firms' operations as evidence in this chapter suggests that this will affect how transport issues influence their decisions and to improve our understanding of modal choice. Comparing on a like-for-like basis is relatively difficult, since roads are ubiquitous in nature and other transport modes are 'nodal' in nature. In a straight comparison between modes, road links will normally be considered the most important (particularly as road links facilitate rail and air travel). Straight modal comparisons can therefore be problematic. Also the relationship between economic development and wider environmental, social and employment changes need to be more fully incorporated into models and analysis.

Finally, SP techniques can help take account of the rich diversity of current and future transport and other trade-offs by firms locating inter-regionally. They can add useful additional insights, which are likely to complement other techniques, such as revealed preference, in modelling and understanding the impact of transport infrastructure and other factors upon location choice. Additionally, as the chapter shows, SP can be useful in disaggregating various types of firms whose investment decisions are influenced by different factors, so helping to develop more appropriate and targeted policies.

REFERENCES

Anas, A., R. Arnott and K.A. Small (1998), 'Urban spatial structure', *Journal of Economic Literature*, **36**, pp. 1426-64.

Banister, D. and J. Berechman (2000), *Transport Investment and Economic Development*, London: UCL Press.

Bates, J.J. (1988), 'Econometric issues in SP analysis', *Journal of Transport Economics and Policy*, **22**, pp. 59-70.

Batey, P.W.J., M. Madden and G. Scholefield (1993), 'Socio-economic impact assessment of large-scale projects using input-output analysis: a case study of an airport', *Regional Studies*, **27** (3), pp. 179-91.

Beaton, P., C. Chen and H. Meghdir (1998), 'Stated choice: a study in predictive validity using an aggregate truth set', *Transportation*, **25**, pp. 55-75.

Ben Akiva, M. and S.R. Lerman (1985), *Discrete Choice Analysis*, Cambridge, MA.: MIT Press.

Bradley, M.A. and A.J. Daly (1994), 'Use of the logit scaling approach to test for rank-order and fatigue effects in stated preference data', *Transportation*, **21**, 167-84.

Breheny, M. and R.W. McQuaid (1987), 'The development of the UK's centre of high-technology', in M. Breheny and R.W. McQuaid (eds), *The Development of High-Tech Industries: an International Survey*, London: Routledge, pp. 297-354.

Button, K.J. (1994), 'What can meta-analysis tell us about the implications of transport?', *Regional Studies*, **29**, pp. 507-17.

Button, K.J., S. Leitham, R.W. McQuaid and J.D. Nelson (1995), 'Transport and industrial and commercial location', *The Annals of Regional Science*, **28**, pp. 189-206.

Commission of the European Communities (CEC) (1990), *Europe 2000 Outlook for the Development of the Community's Territory: A Preliminary Overview*, Brussels: Commission of the European Communities.

Commission of the European Communities (1993), *White Paper on Growth, Employment and Competitiveness*, Brussels: Commission of the European Communities.

Department of Transport (DoT) (1996), *Transport: The Way Forward - The Government's Response to the Transport Debate*, London: Department of Transport.

European Conference of Ministers of Transport (ECMT) (1991), *Transport and the Spatial Distribution of Activities*, ECMT, European Research Centre Round Table 85, Paris: OECD.

Fridstrom, L. and R. Elvik (1997), 'The barely revealed preference behind road investment priorities', *Public Choice*, **92**, pp. 145-68.

Friedman, J., D.A. Gerlowski and J. Silberman (1992), 'What attracts foreign multinational corporations? Evidence from branch plant location in the United States', *Journal of Regional Science*, **32** (4), pp. 403-18.

Glickman, N.J. (1977), *Econometric Analysis of Regional Systems*, New York: Academic Press.

Hague Consulting Group (1992), *ALOGIT User Guide, Version 3.2*, The Hague: Hague Consulting Group.

Hagashi, Y., T. Isobe and Y. Tomita (1986), 'Modelling the long-term effects of transport and land use policies on industrial location behaviour - a discrete choice model system', *Regional Science and Urban Economics*, **16**, pp. 123-43.

Henley, A., A. Carruth, A. Thomas and R.R. Vickerman (1989), 'Location choice and labour market perceptions: A discrete choice study', *Regional Studies*, **23** (4), pp. 431-45.

Hensher, D.A. (1994), 'Stated preference analysis of travel choices: the state of practice', *Transportation*, **21**, pp. 107-33.

Hewings, G.J.D. and R.C. Jensen (1985), 'Regional, inter-regional and multi-regional input-output analysis', in P. Nijkamp (ed.), *Handbook of Regional Economics*, Amsterdam: North Holland.

Hood, N., S. Young and E. Peters (1994), 'Multinational enterprises and regional economic development', *Regional Studies*, **28**, pp. 657-77.

Horowitz, J. and J.J. Louvière (1990), 'The external validity of choice models based on laboratory choice experiments', in M.M. Fischer, P. Nijkamp and Y. Papageorgiou (eds), *Spatial Choice and Processes*, Amsterdam: North Holland.

Hummon, N.P., L. Zemotel, A.G.R. Bullen and J.P. DeAngelis (1986), 'Importance of transportation to advanced technology industries', *Transportation Research Bulletin 1076*, Washington DC.

Krugman, P. (1998), 'What's new about the new economic geography?', *Oxford Review of Economic Policy*, **14**.

Leitham, S., R.W. McQuaid and J.D. Nelson (2000), 'The influence of transport on industrial location choice: a stated preference experiment', *Transportation Research*, **34A**, pp. 515-35.

Mackie, P.J. (1996), 'Induced traffic and economic appraisal', *Transportation*, **23**, pp. 103-19.

McFadden, D. (1979), 'Quantitative methods for analysing travel behaviour of individuals. Some recent developments', in D.A. Hensher and P.R. Stopher (eds), *Behavioural Travel Modelling*, London: Croom Helm.

McKinnon, A.C. and A.G. Woodburn (1996), 'Logistical restructuring and road freight traffic growth: an empirical assessment', *Transportation*, **23**, pp. 141-61.

McQuaid, R.W. (1995), 'The economic debate: theory and practice', in D. Banister (ed.), *Transport and Urban Development*, London: E & FN Spoon, pp. 59-64.

McQuaid, R.W., S. Leitham and J.D. Nelson (1996), 'Accessibility and location decisions in a peripheral region of Europe - a logit analysis', *Regional Studies*, **30**, pp. 589-98.

McQuaid, R.W., M. Greig and J. Adams (2001), 'Unemployed job seeker attitudes towards potential travel-to-work times', *Growth and Change*, **32**, 4 (forthcoming).

Ouwersloot, H. and P. Rietveld (1996), 'Stated choice experiments with repeated observations', *Journal of Transport Economics and Policy*, **30**, pp. 203-12.

Pearmain, D., J. Swanson, E. Kroes and M. Bradley (1991), *Stated Preference Techniques; A guide to practice, 2nd edition*, London: Steer Davies Gleave.

Petersen, T. (1985), 'A comment on presenting results from logit and probit models', *American Sociological Review*, **50**, 130-31.

Rietveld, P. (1989), 'Infrastructure and regional development: a survey of multiregional economic models', *Annals of Regional Science*, **23**, pp. 255-74.

Rietveld, P. (1994), 'Spatial economic impacts of transport infrastructure supply', *Transportation Research*, **28A**, pp. 329-41.

Schmenner, R.W. (1982), *Making Business Location Decisions*, Englewood Cliffs: Prentice-Hall.

Shefer, D. and D. Shefer (1999), 'Transport infrastructure investments and regional development: literature review', in P. Rietveld and D. Shefer (eds), *Regional Development in an Age of Structural Economic Change*, Aldershot: Ashgate.

Steer Davies Gleave (1991), *ALASTAIR User Documentation Version 1.5*, London: Steer Davies Gleave.

Toft, G.S. and S. Mahmassani (1984), 'Transportation and high technology development', *Transportation Research Bulletin*, **984**, Washington DC.

Vickerman, R.W. (1998), 'Transport provision and regional development in Europe: towards a framework for appraisal', in D. Banister (ed.), *Transport Policy and the Environment*, London: Spon, pp. 128-57.

Vickerman, R.W., K. Spiekerman and M. Wegener (1999), 'Accessibility and economic development in Europe', *Regional Studies*, **33**, pp. 1-16.

Walker, R. and F. Calzonetti (1990), 'Searching for new manufacturing plant locations: a study of location decisions in Central Appalachia', *Regional Studies*, **21**, pp. 15-30.

Wardman, M. (1991), 'Stated preference methods and travel demand forecasting: an examination of the scale factor problem', *Transportation Research*, **25A**, pp. 78-89.

14. Can Land Use Policies Reduce Regional Travel?

Yoram Shiftan

14.1 INTRODUCTION

Many researchers and planners believe that concentrated land use and mixed land use design have the potential to reduce the number of motorised trips and the length of these trips. The expectation is that such urban design will reduce transport externalities including air pollution, noise and congestion. Concentrated land use makes it easier to provide good public transit service, and therefore can achieve higher transit share. A mixed land use design can result in auto trips being replaced with walking trips either from home or work. The potential for shopping and personal errands near either the residential area or the work place can also contribute to shifts in mode from auto to transit with the home-work trip by eliminating the need to combine activities that may require automobile use.

In terms of land use policy aimed at reducing auto travel, the hypothesis is that integrated strategies that encourage people to live in higher-density residential areas can result in reduced motorised travel. The reduction in travel can be a result of fewer trips, shorter trips, or shifts from single-occupancy vehicles to public transit, walking and/or cycling. Potential policies include zoning changes, tax incentives, or other mechanisms designed to reduce housing prices in such areas, as well as improvements in school quality, safety and transit service.

There is a large body of research showing that living in higher density neighbourhoods contributes to reduced motorised travel, for example Cervero and Kockelman (1997), Newman and Kenworthy (1989, 1999), Holtzclaw (1990), Frank and Pivo (1994), Kitamura et al. (1997) and many others. However, there are also some doubts as to whether land use configuration itself affects travel patterns, or whether people with different travel behaviour preferences select different types of neighbourhoods to live in. Bagley and Mokhtarian (2000) suggest that the association commonly observed between land use configuration and travel patterns is not one of direct causality, but is due primarily to the correlation between each of these variables with others. Furthermore, when attitudinal, lifestyle and sociodemographic variables are accounted for, neighbourhood type has little influence on travel behaviour. Dunphy and Fisher (1996), analysing the 1990 U.S. National Personal Transportation Survey data, showed that there are significant differences in the household characteristics of persons living at different density levels - characteristics that are themselves important determinants of travel preference. Overall, there is no consensus regarding the effect of urban form on travel behaviour, a situation that has lead to an on-going debate as to whether land use policies should control urban sprawl.

The purpose of this chapter is to test the effect of land use policies encouraging people to move to higher-density neighbourhoods on regional travel through a case study of the city of Portland, Oregon. A package of land use policies, including improved land use, school quality, safety and transit service in the city centre is introduced, and its effect on household redistribution and regional travel is tested through a combination of a residential choice model and an activity-based travel model.

14.2 METHODOLOGY

The methodology of this chapter combines two research initiatives into a framework designed to evaluate the effect of land use policies on regional travel. A residential choice model, estimated using a recent stated preference survey conducted in the Portland, Oregon Metropolitan Area is combined with a newly developed set of activity-based travel demand models for Portland in order to perform this evaluation.

Activity-based modeling treats travel as being derived from the demand for personal activities. Travel decisions, therefore, become part of a broader activity scheduling process based on modeling demand for activities rather than merely trips. In activity-based modeling, the basic travel unit is a tour defined as the sequence of trip segments that start at home and end at home. For a more detailed discussion of activity-based models and their development, see, among others: Ettema and Timmermans (1997), Axhausen and Garling (1992) and Ben-Akiva and Bowman (1998). For a detailed discussion of the advantages of activity-based models for travel demand management analysis, see Shiftan and Suhrbier (1998).

The overall methodology is shown in Figure 14.1. A package of land use policies is introduced. The residential choice model is then run as an independent module, given the package of land use policies and the current distribution of households, in order to calculate a revised distribution of households by zone. The residential choice model is then run in conjunction with the activity-based travel demand models using a household sample enumeration forecasting procedure to determine the effect of changes in residential locations on various transportation variables.

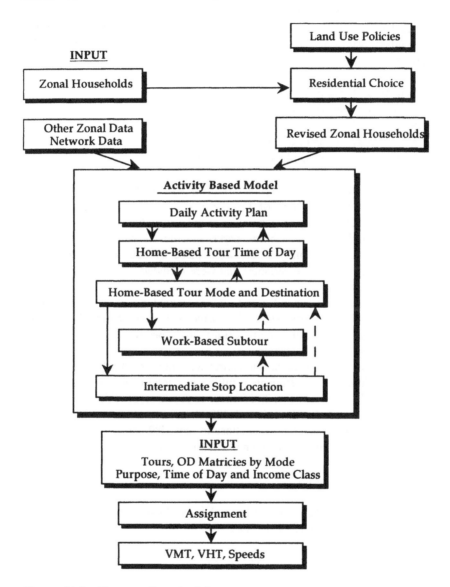

Figure 14.1　The overall methodology

14.3 THE RESIDENTIAL CHOICE MODEL

14.3.1 The Survey

The residential choice model was based on a stated preference survey conducted in Portland that included a series of eight experiments in which the respondent was asked to choose one of five possible future residential options:

- Single-family residence to purchase;
- Multi-family residence to purchase;
- Single-family residence to rent or lease;
- Multi-family residence to rent or lease; or
- Move out of the Portland metropolitan area.

The alternatives were presented to the respondents using 19 property characteristics including: type of dwelling and community, residence and lot size, parking availability, purchase or rental price, types of shops in the community and their accessibility, parks and bicycle paths, school quality and safety, and accessibility to the work place by auto and by transit. A detailed description of the variables that were included in the model appears in Table 14.1.

Personal data were appended and include variables such as age, income, number of vehicles, possession of a driver's licence, type of dwelling, number of employees, number of working hours per week, and children by different age group and education.

A total of 611 completed questionnaires were returned. Each questionnaire included eight choice experiments resulting in a total of 4,888 observations. Out of the 4,888 observations, 2,056 chose to purchase, of which 1,576 chose to purchase a single-family unit and 480 chose to purchase a multi-family unit. Of the 1,271 respondents that chose to rent, 789 chose to rent a single-family unit and 482 chose to rent a multi-family unit.

14.3.2 Model Estimation

The model is specified as a multinomial logit (MNL) where the utility of each residential location is specified as:

$$U_i = V_i + \varepsilon_i \qquad (14.1)$$

Where U_i is the utility of residential alternative i for a given household; V_i is the systematic component and ε_i is its random component. The systematic component of the utility can be written as:

$$V_i = \beta' X_i \tag{14.2}$$

Where X_i is a vector of attributes for alternative i, some of which interacted with household characteristics, and where β is a vector of coefficients.

In the MNL model, ε_i is Gumbel distributed independently and identically across alternatives, where the probability that alternative i will be chosen is:

$$p(i) = \frac{exp(\mu V_i)}{\sum_{i \in L} exp(\mu V_i)} \tag{14.3}$$

Where μ is the scale parameter, and L is the set of available alternatives.

Table 14.1 presents the model estimation results. The first column of the table lists the variables in the model. The second column defines the variables. The third column shows the estimated coefficients and the fourth column shows the t-statistics for a test of the equality of the coefficient to zero. Values larger than 1.645 in absolute values are significantly different from zero at the 5 percent level. A brief discussion of these results is follow, and the next section provides a more detailed discussion of the variables of interest (see Table 14.1 for a list of the abbreviations).

Table 14.1   Model estimation results

Variable	Description	Coefficient	t-statistic
ConsPS	Constant specific of the choice to purchase a single-family residence.	0.400	(2.2)
ConsPM	Constant specific of the choice to purchase a multi-family residence.	−0.585	(−3.1)
ConsRS	Constant specific of the choice to rent a single-family residence.	−0.577	(−3.1)
ConsRM	Constant specific of the choice to rent a multi-family residence.	−1.280	(−6.4)
SinglHouse	A dummy variable for single-family residence equal to 1 if the residence is a single house and equal to 0 if it is a duplex or row house.	0.144	(2.4)

Variable	Description	Coefficient	t-statistic
Condo	A dummy variable for multi-family residence equal to 1 if the residence is a condo, and equal to 0 if it is an apartment.	0.182	(2.6)
Res size	Residential size in square feet.	0.178e–2	(4.5)
Lot size	Lot size in square feet (for single-family residence only).	0.930e–4	(1.6)
Att Garage	A dummy variable equal to 1 if the residence has an attached garage, and equal to 0 otherwise (for single-family only).	0.349	(4.9)
Det Garage	A dummy variable equal to 1 if the residence has a detached garage, and equal to 0 otherwise (for single-family only).	0.330	(4.6)
Driveway	A dummy variable equal to 1 if the residence has a driveway but no garage, and equal to 0 otherwise (for single-family only).	0.202	(2.8)
Garage	A dummy variable equal to 1 if the residence has a garage, and equal to 0 otherwise (for multi-family residence only).	0.441	(3.3)
CarP/ Ressp[1]	A dummy variable equal to 1 if the residence has either a carport or a reserved uncovered space (for multi-family residence only).	0.330	(2.6)
Most Own	A dummy variable equal to 1 if the mix of residential ownership is mostly home ownership, and equal to 0 if it is mostly rental.	0.137	(3.3)
Comm-Square	A dummy variable equal to 1 if the area has a community square with shops, restaurants, movie theatre, etc., and equal to 0 otherwise.	0.145	(2.5)
SpecShop	A dummy variable equal to 1 if the area has some specialty shops in addition to some basic shops but no community square, and equal to 0 otherwise.	0.133	(2.3)
BasicShop	A dummy variable equal to 1 if the area has only basic shops, and equal to 0 otherwise (more special shops or no shops at all).	0.112	(1.9)
Exel VGD S[2]	A dummy variable equal to 1 if school quality is either very good or excellent, and equal 0 otherwise.	0.216	(4.2)
Good School	A dummy variable equal to 1 if school quality is good, and equal to 0 otherwise.	0.115	(2.0)

Variable	Description	Coefficient	t-statistic
AbvAvg-Safe	A dummy variable equal to 1 if neighbourhood safety is above average, and equal to 0 if it is average.	0.098	(2.4)
Bic Path	A dummy variable equal to 1 if the area has bicycle path, and equal to 0 if not.	0.064	(1.6)
LoclShp-Prc	Price of shopping locally relative to the area average (10% below, same, 10% more or 20% more).	−0.317e−2	(−1.7)
WlkTmLcShp	Walking time to local shops in minutes.	−0.604e−2	(−3.3)
TrvTmWrBu	Travel time to work by public transportation in minutes.	−0.441e−2	(−3.8)
MontRate-LM[3]	Monthly rental rate in dollars for low- and medium-income households (less than $60k) for rental choice only.	−0.011	(−11.2)
MontRate HI	Monthly rental rate in dollars for high-income (greater than $60k) for rental choice only.	−0.407e−2	(−3.0)
PurPrcLI	Purchase price in thousands of dollars for low-income (less than $30k) for purchase choice only.	−0.059	(−10.2)
PurPrcMI	Purchase price in thousands of dollars for medium-income (between $30k and $60k) for purchase choice only.	−0.047	(−9.4)
PurPrcHI	Purchase price in thousands of dollars for high-income (more than $60k) for purchase choice only.	−0.928e−2	(−9.4)
MontRate NI	Monthly rental rate for observations, missing income, and equal to 0 otherwise.	−0.013	(−6.9)
PurPrcNI	Purchase price for observations, missing income, and equal to 0 otherwise.	−0.040	(−5.6)
Rentrent	A dummy variable equal to 1 if the household is currently renting and chooses to continue to rent or lease, and equal to 0 otherwise.	1.906	(23.0)
Single-single	A dummy variable equal to 1 if the household is currently living in a single-family unit and chooses to live in a single-family unit, and equal to 0 otherwise.	0.394	(4.7)

Variable	Description	Coefficient	t-statistic
Childmove	Number of children under 18 years old for those choosing to move out of the metropolitan area, and equal to 0 otherwise.	0.158	(2.4)
Hhsize-move	Household size for those choosing to move out of the metropolitan area, and equal to 0 otherwise.	0.207	(7.1)

Notes:

n = 4888

Initial value of likelihood = −7866.93

Final value of likelihood = −6684.71

- The *SinglHouse* variable yields a positive and significant coefficient, indicating that single family residents prefer a single house over a duplex or row house. Similarly, the positive and significant coefficient of the *Condo* variable shows that multi-family residents prefer a condo to an apartment.

- The *Res size* and *Lot size* variables indicate that people prefer both larger residences and larger lots.

- The *Att Garage, Det Garage and Driveway* all yield significant and positive coefficients, indicating the importance of parking for single-family residences. The relative size of these variables shows that people prefer housing with an attached garage to a unit with a detached garage. Similarly, people prefer a unit with a detached garage to a unit having only driveway parking and prefer a unit with a driveway to a unit without parking. In a similar way, the significant positive coefficients of the *Garage* and *CarP/Ressp* variables show the importance of parking for multi-family residents. The coefficient of the *Garage* variable is higher than that of the *CarP/Ressp* variable showing that people prefer a garage to a carport or a reserved uncovered space.

- The *Most Own* variable yields a significant positive coefficient, indicating that people have a preference for neighbourhoods in which most people own their residence, since there is lower turnover in such neighbourhoods and residents tend to take better care of the neighbourhood.

- The *CommSquare, SpecShop* and *BasicShop* variables all yield significant positive coefficients, indicating the importance of local shops in the area. Community square has a higher coefficient than specialty shops, and specialty shops has a higher coefficient than basic shops showing the preference people have for a neighbourhood with a larger variety of shops and entertainment facilities.

- The *Exel VGD S, Good Schools,* and AbvAvgSafe yield significant and positive coefficients, indicating the importance people place on school quality and safety in residential choice.
- The *Bic Path* coefficient is not significant at the 5 percent level, but the sign suggests that the availability of bicycle paths increases the attractiveness of the area for residents.
- The *LoclShpPrc* and *WlkTmLcShp* variables yield negative and significant coefficients, showing that people pay attention not only to the type of shops in the community, but also to their prices relative to the area average, and to the distance they have to walk to these shops.
- The *TrvTmWrBu* has a negative and significant coefficient showing that people are more likely to choose residential location with shorter travel time to work by bus. Travel time to work by auto, however, was not significant.
- The cost variables *MonthRateLM, MontRateHI, MontRateNI, PurPrcLI, PurPrcMI, PurPrcHI* and *PurPrcNI* are all negative and significant. The exception is purchase price for high-income households, where the t-statistics value of 1.6 shows that cost is a more significant factor for low- and medium-income households. This is also shown in the absolute value of the coefficients. There was no significant difference between the coefficient of monthly rate for low-income people and for medium-income people, and were therefore combined into one variable.
- The *Rentrent* and *singlesingle* coefficients are positive and significant, indicating that current behaviour best explains future choices. People who are currently renting are more likely to continue to rent, and people who are currently living in a single-family unit are more likely to continue to live in a single-family unit.
- The number of children under 18 (*childmove*) and household size (*hhsizemove*) variables are positive and significant, showing that the larger the household and the more children under 18 in the household, the more likely it is that the family will move out of the metropolitan area.
- Other variables that were tested in the model and were found to be not significant included: bus fare and travel time to local shops; community type - urban versus rural or mixed use; housing mix - mostly single-family versus mostly multi-family; age of development; and the availability of local parks.

14.3.3 Policy Implications

A good way to interpret the model estimation results is through the notion of consumer willingness to pay. The willingness to pay for any attribute i (WTP_i) is the ratio between the marginal utility of the attribute and the marginal utility of price (in a negative sign), as shown in the following equation:

$$WTP_i = -\frac{\frac{\partial U}{\partial X_i}}{\frac{\partial U}{\partial P}}$$ (14.4)

Where P is the price of the residence and X_i is the ith attribute.

The willingness to pay shows the tradeoff, or the marginal rate of substitution, between cost and the attribute, and shows how people value different attributes in choosing a residential location. The willingness to pay for different housing characteristics is summarised in Table 14.2.

Many of the variables in the model indicate the value that people place on what is typically characterised as suburban sprawl. Table 14.2 shows that people are willing to pay for parking more than any other feature tested in this model. Even low-income people are willing to pay an additional $3,400 for a unit with a driveway over one without it, and an additional $2,200 for a unit with a detached garage over a unit with a driveway. These values increase proportionally for people with medium and high income. Depending on their income level, people are willing to pay between $30 to $192 for an additional square foot of residence, and between $1.60 to $10 per additional square foot of lot. Travel time to work by auto is not a significant variable in the model, showing willingness to commute for a suburban location. In choosing a residential location and type of housing, individuals make tradeoffs among competing priorities. For example, the willingness to pay for a large size residence, a larger-size lot and better availability of parking are representative of important suburban-style attributes. These tendencies must be overcome if people are to be attracted to pedestrian- and transit-friendly development patterns.

Looking at the willingness to pay for neighbourhood attributes that characterise higher-density neighbourhoods, medium-income households are willing to pay between $2,400 and $3,100 for different types of local shops. This is equal to what they are willing to pay for an additional 60 to 80 square feet of residential space. People also are willing to pay more for a residence with better transit service.

At higher densities, greater purchasing power makes it profitable for more types of business. Conversely, the more types of shopping and community services that are available increases the probability that people will choose these areas for their residence. The model also shows the importance of walking time to local shops. It is important to have both a variety of shops and to have these shops within a short walking distance; both characteristics can be achieved only in a high-density development.

Table 14.2 Willingness to pay for residential attributes ($)

Variable	Low-Income Purchasing	Medium-Income Purchasing	High-Income Purchasing	Low/Medium-Income Renting	High-Income Renting
SinglHouse	2,455.2	3,078.9	15,520.6	12.7	35.3
Condo	3,094.6	3,880.7	19,562.4	15.9	44.6
Res size*	30.3	38.0	191.6	0.2	0.4
Lot size*	1.6	2.0	10.0	0.01	0.02
Att Garage	5,952.3	7,464.2	37,626.6	30.7	85.7
Det Garage	5,633.4	7,064.4	35,611.1	29.0	81.1
Driveway	3,444.2	4,319.0	21,771.9	17.8	49.6
Garage	7,520.9	9,431.3	47,542.6	38.8	108.3
CarP/Ressp	5,621.5	7,049.4	35,535.7	29.0	80.9
Most Own	2,334.2	2,927.1	14,755.3	12.0	33.6
CommSquare	2,477.4	3,106.7	15,660.7	12.8	35.7
SpecShop	2,271.1	2,848.0	14,356.5	11.7	32.7
BasicShop	1,907.9	2,392.6	12,060.8	9.8	27.5
Excel VGD S	3,674.3	4,607.7	23,227.0	18.9	52.9
Good School	1,962.5	2,461.0	12,405.7	10.1	28.3
Bic Path	1,091.7	1,369.0	6,901.3	5.6	15.7
AbvAvgSafe	1,665.5	2,088.5	10,528.1	8.6	24.0
LoclShpPrc	−54.1	−67.8	−342.0	−0.3	−0.8
WlkTmLcShp	−102.9	−129.0	−650.5	−0.5	−1.5
TrvTmWrBu	−75.3	−94.4	−475.7	−0.4	−1.1

*Note: * Per square feet.*

While land is more expensive in urban areas and therefore units are smaller, there are policies that can increase the attractiveness of such areas. As discussed above, providing parking is the most important attribute for the property value. However, providing parking may be difficult in high-density areas and is also not consistent with the objective of reducing auto travel. The second most important variable in terms of willingness to pay is good and excellent schools with a value of $2,500 to $4,600 for medium-income households. Following in importance is the mix of ownership, with a willingness to pay of $3,000 for a neighbourhood with mostly home ownership in comparison with a neighbourhood with mostly rental units. Safety has a willingness to pay of $2,000, and even attributes like the availability of a bicycle path can increase property value by almost $1,400 for a medium-income household. Policy makers can increase the value of urban neighbourhoods by improving these attributes, thus encouraging people to live in an urban rather than a suburban setting. These kind of policies, together with various zoning laws and related housing and urban development legislation and initiatives, can provide an alternative to suburban sprawl.

14.4 THE PORTLAND ACTIVITY-BASED TRAVEL DEMAND MODEL

This section provides a brief description of the Portland Activity-Based Model System that was used to evaluate the effects of land use policies on regional travel. For more details about this model, see Bowman et al. (1998).

The model was developed as part of a project carried out by Cambridge Systematics, Inc. in collaboration with Mark Bradley Research and Consulting and Portland Metro (Cambridge Systematics 1997). The models were estimated using data from the 1994 Household Activity and Travel Survey in Portland, Oregon. A total of 4,451 households were surveyed in the Portland region during 1994-95. Respondents were asked to report on two consecutive days of activities, with all seven days of the week included in the sample.

The model system is designed as a series of disaggregate logit and nested-logit discrete choice models, assuming a hierarchy of the model components. Lower level choices are conditional on decisions at the higher level, and higher level decisions are informed from the lower levels through logsum (accessibility) variables. The shaded box in Figure 14.1 is a diagram of the model system as currently implemented by Portland Metro. There are five boxes within this shaded area, representing the main decisions explicitly modeled in Portland's system:

- Daily Activity Plan: At the highest level of the system is the full day activity pattern model. This model predicts a person's primary activity of the day as either work/school, household maintenance or discretionary, and as at home or as part of a tour away from home. A major contribution of this approach is that it includes at-home activities. This feature allows the model to treat the entire range of activities throughout the day, including tradeoffs between in-home and out-of-home activities. This level of the model also determines the type of primary out-of-home trip chain defined by the number and sequence of any intermediate stops made between home and the primary activity and the number, purpose and type of additional tours made during the day. Since these tours are predicted simultaneously with the primary tour, the model can capture the substitution between making multiple tours from home versus making additional stops during a single tour.

- Home-based Tour Time of Day - Once the full day activity pattern is determined, a time of day model predicts the combination of departure time from home and departure time from the primary activity for each tour away from home.
- Home-based Tour Mode and Destination - Given the day activity pattern and the time of day, the primary destination and mode of tour are determined jointly. The nine possible main modes are drive alone, drive with passenger, auto passenger, light rail transit (LRT) with auto access, LRT with walking access, bus with auto access, bus with walking access, walking, and bicycle.
- Work-based Subtour - For work tours, this model determines whether or not there are any work-based 'subtours' (trip chains beginning and ending at the workplace) that are made during the day.
- Intermediate Stop Location - The lowest level model in the system determines the locations of any intermediate destinations visited between home and the primary tour destination.

14.5 INTERACTIONS BETWEEN THE RESIDENTIAL CHOICE MODEL AND THE ACTIVITY-BASED TRAVEL MODEL

Traditional transportation analysis processes tend to ignore the interaction between land use and transportation. The allocation of households and jobs by traffic analysis zones (TAZs) are treated as external variables, not sensitive to the transportation system. Land use models attempt to quantify the location decision of households and employers using transportation accessibility measures, thereby creating a two-way interaction between transportation and land use.

In this work, the residential choice model and the travel activity-based model are run in conjunction to analyse the effects of land use policies on regional travel. This section describes the interactions between these two models.

The travel model affects the residential choice through the transportation variables in the residential choice model. These variables include: walking time to local shops; travel time to work by bus; and availability of bicycle paths. Changes in transportation system performance will affect these variables, and therefore will affect residential choice. Some of these variables, such as travel time to shopping, also represent land use variables. Mix land use development will affect travel time to shopping locations, and therefore residential choice. Two other accessibility variables of interest, travel time to work by auto and travel time and fare to local shops by bus, were not included because they were insignificant in the model estimation. In addition, accessibility measures to other activities such as family, friends and different leisure activities should be included. However, such data were not available.

Residential choice is viewed as a long-term decision that, along with principal workplace, appears at a high level in an activity-based model system. Residential choice affects travel through the origin of home-based tours thereby changing the origin-destination pairs. Residential choice may have additional effects on travel through some land use variables in the transportation model. Looking at the Portland activity-based model system, the main travel decisions that may be affected by residential choice (other than changes in the Origin Destination matrices) are the mode of travel and choice of destination through the following variables:

- travel time and cost;
- for transit with walk access mode - households within one-quarter mile of transit in the origin zone; and
- for bicycle and walking - mixed use within one-half mile of the origin zone.

These variables also affect the choice of daily activity pattern and the tour time of day, as both include logsum variables of the mode and destination model.

14.6 THE CASE STUDY

14.6.1 The Policies Case Study

A package of sustainable land use/transportation policies was evaluated that included the following elements:

- Improve land use within the Washington County Urban Growth Area boundary by providing bicycle paths, upgrading the level of available local shops by encouraging entry of specialty shops where only basic shops are now available, and provide a community square where special shops are already available. It is further assumed that the increase in local shops will reduce walking time to these shops by 10 minutes.
- Improve transit service and therefore reduce travel time to work by bus by 10 minutes. This improvement directly affects both the residential choice and the travel model. For the travel model, it is assumed that there is an

improvement of five minutes in vehicle time and five minutes in waiting time.
- Increase safety and school quality in the city centre. Increases from average to above average in safety and from base to good or from good to very good or excellent in school quality are assumed.

14.6.2 Results

Applying the residential choice model to the policies described above shows that improving these attributes increases the number of households in the urban centre by 16 percent (11,000 households) and in the rest of the urban growth area by 13 percent (14,000 households). A total of 25,000 households, or 4.2 percent of the total metropolitan households, move from the suburb to the urban growth area, reducing suburban population by 6.1 percent (25,000 households).

However, applying the activity-based travel model system for both the base distribution of households and for the concentrated land use policy yields only marginal effects on regional travel patterns. There is actually an increase in all type of tours, except work subtours. The main results are:

- Tours by all non-auto modes increased as expected. Transit tours increased by 5.2 percent, walking tours by 7.2 percent and bicycle tours by 7.8 percent. It is interesting to note that the number of auto tours also increased slightly by 2.5 percent, showing that the increased accessibility added more auto tours than the number of auto tours that shifted to non-auto modes.
- Work tours increase by 2.9 percent and maintenance and discretionary tours increase by 2.2 percent. This increase is a result of higher accessibility in the central area and the potential to break a daylong tour into two or more shorter tours by living in the centre. This may also explain the reduction of 2.7 percent in work subtours.
- In terms of vehicle miles of travel (VMT), average trip length decreased by 8.9 percent as a result of shorter trips in the centre area. However, the combination of shorter trips and more trips resulted in an overall increase of 1.4 percent in VMT.

While application of the residential choice model to test the land use policy yields a significant change in the distribution of households in the metropolitan area, the effects on regional travel based on use of the Portland activity-based model are only marginal. Furthermore, the direction of this change is in the direction opposite to that which the policy was intended to achieve, namely an increase in VMT and auto tours. In other words, the move of households from suburban to urban location does not really affect travel and does not contribute to reduced auto use, or may even increase it as in this example. This may be a result of increased accessibility in urban locations. Higher densities mean more activity opportunities and lower cost of reaching those opportunities. The ability of the activity-based travel model to take such considerations into account is one of its main advantages in analysing such policies.

14.7 SUMMARY AND CONCLUSIONS

This chapter presents the integration of a residential choice model, estimated using a recent stated preference survey conducted in the Portland, Oregon Metropolitan Area with a newly developed set of activity-based travel demand models for Portland in order to evaluate the effects of potential land use policies on regional travel.

The estimated stated preference model shows that land use policies can affect people's residential choice in a way that favors urban area growth over suburban growth. The suggested policies tested in this work yield household growth of 16 percent in the city centre and 13 percent within the rest of the urban area growth boundary. In total the model application forecasts that 4.2 percent of the Portland metropolitan area households will move from a suburban location to within the urban growth area boundary under the proposed policies.

Incorporating the results of the residential choice model into the Portland activity-based travel demand model system, however, shows only a marginal if not actually counterproductive effect on regional travel. There is an increase in the total number of tours, with an increase of work tours of 2.9 percent and an increase of maintenance and discretionary tours of 2.2 percent. While transit tours increase by 5.2 percent and non-motorised tours increase by more than 7 percent, auto tours also increase by 2.5 percent. Average trip length decreased by 8.9 percent, but with the increase in the number of tours, there was an overall increase of 1.4 percent in VMT.

While the work presented here shows an important improvement over traditional methods of dealing with transportation and land use policies, the following represents priorities for future work:

- The current residential choice model lacks location-specific indicators and other important variables like property values and neighbourhood characteristics. The model is not calibrated to any revealed preference data. Revealed data of people's current residence could be used to estimate a joint revealed stated preference data model.

- The current model represents people's preferences when choosing a residential location, and redistributes current households by zone based on land use policies affecting residential preference. Further improvement in the model should take into account constraints like available land and housing units and should consider equilibrium between supply and demand.
- Further work is needed to test the applicability of the Portland activity-based model in order to analyse the kinds of policies considered in this chapter.

These limitations are more than offset by the approach taken here combining the stated preference model with the activity-based model system. The results show that stated preference data can be very helpful in assessing innovative policies where a base of existing implementation experience is lacking, and therefore cannot be modelled well through revealed preference data.

The activity-based model system represents an important improvement over trip- and tour-based models in use today and provides behavioural insights that simply are not possible with conventional four-step transportation modelling approaches. The integration of the stated preference residential choice model and the activity-based model system provides the opportunity to test the effect of land use policies on regional travel.

REFERENCES

Axhausen, K.W. and T. Garling (1992), 'Activity-based approaches to travel analysis: conceptual frameworks, models and research problems', *Transport Reviews*, **12** (4), pp. 323-41.

Bagley, M.N. and P.L. Mokhtarian (2000), 'The impact of residential neighbourhood type on travel behaviour: a structural equations modeling approach', Paper submitted for presentation to the XI Pan-American Conference in Traffic and Transportation Engineering, Gramado, Brazil, May 2000.

Ben-Akiva, M. and J.L. Bowman (1998), 'Activity-based travel demand model systems', in *Equilibrium and Advanced Transportation Modeling*, Boston, MA: Kluer Academic Publishers, pp. 27-46.

Bowman, J.L., M. Bradley, Y. Shiftan, T.K. Lawton and M. Ben-Akiva (1998), 'Demonstration of activity based model system for Portland in world transport research', in H. Meersman, E. Van de Voorde and W. Winkelmans (eds), *Selected Proceedings from the 8th World Conference on Transport Research*, July, Antwerp, Belgium: Elsevier Science, Ltd.

Cambridge Systematics, Inc. (1997), *A System of Activity-Based Models for Portland, Oregon*, Draft Report of a Demonstration Project for the FHWA Transportation Model Improvement Program.

Cervero, R. and K. Kockelman (1997), 'Travel demand and the 3Ds: density, diversity, and design', *Transportation Research D*, **2** (3), pp. 199-219.

Dunphy, R. and K. Fisher (1996), 'Transportation, congestion and density: new insight', *Transportation Research Record*, **1552**, pp. 89-96.

Ettema, D. and H. Timmermans (1997), 'Theories and models of activity patterns', in D. Ettema and H. Timmermans (eds), *Activity-Based Approaches to Travel Analysis*, Oxford: Pergamon, pp. 1-36.

Frank L. and G. Pivo (1994), 'Impact of mixed use and density on utilization of three modes of travel: single-occupant vehicle, transit and walking', *Transportation Research Record*, **1466**, pp. 44-52.

Holtzclaw, J. (1990), 'Manhattanization versus sprawl: how density impacts auto use comparing five nay area communities', Proceedings of the Eleventh International Pedestrian Conference, City of Boulder, Bolder, Colorado, pp. 99-106.

Kitamura, R., P. Mokhtarian and L. Laidet (1997), 'A micro-analysis of land use and travel in five neighborhoods in the San Francisco Bay area', *Transportation*, **24** (2), pp. 125-58.

Newman, P. and J. Kenworthy (1989), 'Gasoline consumption and cities: a comparison of U.S. cities with a global survey', *Journal of the American Planning Association*, **55** (1), pp. 24-37.

Newman, P. and J. Kenworthy (1999), *The Cost of Automobile Dependence: A Global Survey of Cities*, Washington: Transportation Research Board.

Shiftan, Y. and J. Suhrbier (1998), 'The contribution of activity-based models to analyses of transportation control measures', in H. Meersman, E. Van de Voorde, and W. Winkelmans (eds), *World Transport Research, Selected Proceedings from the 8th World Conference on Transport Research*, July, Antwerp, Belgium: Elsevier Science, Ltd.

15. Public versus Private Rental Housing in Israel: Public Policy and Tenants' Choice

Elia Werczberger

15.1 INTRODUCTION

15.1.1 The Problem

Most households in Israel own the dwellings in which they live, while less than a quarter live in rental accommodations. This has not always been the case. At its peak in the early 1970s, public housing alone comprised about a quarter of all housing units. Since then, its share has declined to about 6 percent. Similarly, the market rental sector, which before World War II comprised more than 50 percent of the stock, has been shrinking to 10 percent in 1989. It now consists almost exclusively of individual condominium-units owned by small landlords.[1] However, despite the predominance of home ownership, a sizable minority of households continues to depend on renting. Because of the high cost of public housing, almost every Israeli government has in the past attempted to revive the commercial private rental sector, but without success. We hope that a better understanding of the rental housing sector might facilitate the design of a more successful policy.

This chapter examines three facets of the Israeli rental market: the changing government policy, the main characteristics of rental housing, and the demand for renting. The discussion first sets out a simple conceptual model of the rental market and then surveys some of the research about rental housing demand. Next, it discusses the development of Israeli housing policy and the main tenure forms. The following sections compare the different submarkets and estimate a tenure choice model and a simple demand model for private sector housing. The concluding section discusses some policy issues raised by this kind of market.

15.1.2 A Simple Model of the Supply of Affordable Housing

Housing, like many other physical goods, is subject to an only partly reversible process of physical deterioration and depreciation (Malpezzi and Green1996; Grigsby 1987). The decline in quality is typically associated with a decrease in economic value and the replacement of the residents by lower income groups. This development, usually denoted as a filtering process, can be conceptualised by assuming a hierarchy of housing quality levels, through which individual units and neighbourhoods filter down while households filter up. Buildings and neighbourhoods may experience temporary revitalisation and renovation, but the final stage of the process is inevitably demolition and redevelopment. Building age consequently correlates with many undesirable housing and neighbourhood characteristics such as a lack of amenities, inadequate maintenance, nuisances and a low socio-economic status of the residents, but also with more affordable prices and rents.

From the point of view of housing policy, the main problem of the private rental market is that, because of the high cost of land and construction, low-income households generally cannot afford socially acceptable new housing (Downs 1983; Gilderbloom and Appelbaum 1988). They have to rely on older units, which must significantly depreciate before they become affordable (Lowry 1960). Equally problematic is that the supply of low-cost rentals depends on the demand by those who can afford new housing. Thus the greater the ratio between the demand for rental housing by the poor and the demand for new rentals by the middle class, the greater the housing problem at the lower end of the market. The quality of maintenance also tends to be related to the rental level. Thus by the time housing has sufficiently depreciated, its quality is likely to have become socially unacceptable (Lowry 1960). Almost everywhere the competitive market has therefore failed to insure an affordable and satisfactory supply of rental housing for low-income groups, except when heavily subsidised or complemented by public housing.

In Israel, the problem is exacerbated because of the predominance of home ownership and the sharply reduced supply of new public housing. Since home ownership has become the normative form of tenure, households choose renting only if ownership is either not affordable or clearly inappropriate. As a consequence, the commercial development of rental housing has ceased to be profitable. During the past half century, additional private rental housing has been produced only through the conversion of individual dwelling units, located mostly in condominiums. To be affordable to the typical renter, these converted units must have considerably depreciated. Being older they are likely to be located in older neighbourhoods near the urban centre. For the same reason, they tend to be smaller and of lower quality than the average owner-occupied dwelling unit.

15.1.3 The Demand for Rental Housing

Factors affecting the choice between the various forms of tenure have been examined from a variety of perspectives, each adding a different insight to the understanding of the issue. From the economic point of view, the decision of whether to own or rent primarily depends on user costs and the household's economic resources, that is income, wealth and access to financing. Therefore, owners are likely to be more affluent, older, and more stable in their employment than renters (see, for example, Mills 1990; Henderson and Ioannides 1983). Renting is attractive mainly to households, who lack the necessary equity or access to financing. Thus, renters are likely to have a lower income or to be younger than homeowners. Moreover, because of the high transaction costs of buying, ownership is favoured by households expecting to stay in the dwelling for a number of years. This reduces the annual cost of initial outlays for search, sales taxes and so on, as well as commissions for lawyers and real estate agents (Pines and Weiss 1974). Compared with homeowners, the typical renter therefore tends to be more mobile and younger. A large proportion of students who are both young and mobile are thus likely to rent.

Cultural and social forces affect tenure choice as well (Kemeny 1981). In many, if not most, societies, home ownership provides a feeling of security and serves as an important symbol of achievement and status contributing thus to satisfaction with housing and life in general. Hence ownership may be politically attractive, even if it is inferior from the economic or social point of view. Many governments will therefore support owner occupancy through economic incentives or tax discrimination in order to achieve political objectives and voter support.

15.2 HOUSING POLICY AND TENURE FORMS IN ISRAEL

15.2.1 The Development of Housing Policy in Israel

Since the establishment of the State of Israel in 1948, the social and economic absorption of immigrants and the provision of shelter have been considered central obligations of the state, second only to national security.[2] Housing, therefore, served until the late 1980s as a primary instrument in immigrant absorption. Only later it became part of general welfare policy.

During the first years after the establishment of the State of Israel, 1949-53, immigration doubled the population of Israel leaving no alternative to direct government involvement. In fact, most of the immigrants had initially to be accommodated in emergency shelters located in transition camps. Permanent housing was provided by the government only later and slowly, mostly in public housing projects built in new neighbourhoods and in some thirty new towns (Carmon and Czamanski 1991).

With the gradual improvement of the economy during the 1960s, an increasing number of households were able to accumulate the equity necessary to become homeowners. The government in turn supported ownership in order to finance new construction, to reduce current consumption, and to strengthen the economic interest of households in their home and neighbourhood. It did so through a variety of programmes such as savings schemes and government sponsored construction, as well as through direct and indirect subsidies granted to owner occupants. These included, in particular, low-cost public land, low-interest mortgages, exemption from income tax on imputed rents, and last but not least, the subsidised sale of public housing to sitting tenants.

For political and administrative reasons, however, the Ministry of Housing has been concerned mostly with the provision of housing solutions to specific target groups, rather than with the management of the housing stock as a whole. This policy bias resulted, for example, in a failure to deal with rent controlled housing and in a lack of maintenance of the stock of social housing. One of the major consequences was the physical and social decline of most public housing projects, which eventually deteriorated to a residual sector for the poor.

Similar to developments elsewhere, housing policy in Israel during the past thirty years has experienced a neo-conservative policy drift toward reduced government involvement. It involved a shift from the direct provision of housing to producer and then consumer subsidies, and more recently to an increasing emphasis on personal entitlements and grants (Carmon 1999). Yet, the emphasis on the provision of housing solutions to specific target groups has remained. Nevertheless, while housing programmes were in the past offered only to new immigrants, they are now available to a wider range of households in need: the poor, single parent families, the elderly, the homeless and so on.

At the same time, the responsibility of government offices gradually shifted from the development and construction of new housing to policy formation, the provision of subsidies and the promotion of large projects. The decision of whether to build a housing project is now made by the private sector based on its anticipated profitability. The Ministry of Housing takes the initiative only during emergencies, such as during the 1990s, when almost a million new immigrants arrived (mostly from the former USSR). Public involvement then took the form of land allocation and the commitment to buy dwelling units which developers could not sell.

15.2.2 The Different Types of Tenure

The Israeli housing market currently comprises four basic forms of tenure (Table 15.1): owner occupancy, market rental, public housing and rent-controlled apartments. The remainder of this section briefly describes the different tenure categories and the effect of housing policy on their development.

Table 15.1   Distribution of households by tenure type in 1995

Tenure type	1995 Population Census[2]			Housing Ministry 2000[1] (%)
	Respondents	Percentage	Net percent	
Owner occupancy	195,721	71.9	76.2	70.5
Market rental	41,292	15.2	16.1	15.4
Public housing	15,820	5.8	6.2	5.7
Rent control	3,904	1.4	1.5	1.6
Other types of rental	1,974	0.7	-	1.3
Other tenure types	13,502	5.0	-	5.5
Total	272,213	100.0	100.0	100.0

Notes:
[1] Estimates by the Housing Ministry and updated from the 1995 Population Census.
[2] The data were obtained from the 20 percent sample of the 1995 Population Census. They exclude households and individuals living in institution, collective settlements (Kibbutzim), as well as those respondents for which the type of tenure could not be identified.

Owner-occupied housing: Israel has one of the highest proportions of home ownership among developed nations. Between 1957 and 1995 the percentage of owner occupants increased from 51.9 percent to 76.2 percent (Table 15.2). Home ownership has thus become the normative form of tenure. For the vast majority of households the various forms of renting are considered only if ownership is not affordable or unsuitable. Most of the owner-occupied units are located in multifamily buildings. Differences in housing quality between owner occupants and renters are thus not the result of the building type but of differences in the maintenance quality or the initial standard of amenities, materials and finish.

Table 15.2   The change in market share of the different tenure categories

Year	Households	Owner Occupants (%)	Market rental (%)	Public housing (%)	Rent control (%)
1957	514,000	51.9	25.5	22.6	-
1963	594,000	60.5	17.0	22.5	-
1969	694,000	62.1	15.6	22.3	-
1974	824,000	67.2	10.5	18.3	5.4
1983	1,104,270	72.9	10.7	13.8	2.2
1991	1,228,000	73.0	13.0	12.0	2.0
1995	1,361,000	76.2	16.1	6.2	1.5

Note: No information available.

Source: Werczberger (1990, 1993); *Statistical Abstracts of Israel.*

Rent-controlled housing: The predominance of home ownership is a relatively recent phenomenon. Before 1948, rental housing was the prevalent form of tenure, at least for the Jewish population. Yet, after the outbreak of World War II, the British Mandatory Government enacted a strict first-generation type of rent control regime (Werczberger 1990). Following the establishment of the State in 1948, some of the more draconian regulations were modified, exempting in particular new construction from controls. Nevertheless, practically no new rental housing has been built since 1940. As a result of demolition and of the decontrol of units repossessed by landlords, rent-controlled dwellings now comprise only about 1.5 percent of the total stock (Table 15.1, Table 15.2). We believe that the sector is likely to disappear within a decade or two, so that this type of tenure will be ignored in most of the remaining discussion.

Public housing: Most of the immigrants, who came to Israel after the War of Independence, lacked the income or equity required to purchase housing in the market.[3] In the absence of private rental construction, subsidised public housing was the only feasible alternative to makeshift shelter provided initially in the transition camps (Werczberger 1991). By 1949 more than 200,000 social housing units had been built, which comprised by 1970 almost a quarter of the total housing stock (Werczberger 1988). However, the share of social housing has during the past 30 years declined to about 6 percent of the housing stock (Table 15.2) and now provides shelter almost exclusively for the lowest income groups.

There are number of reasons for this development. First of all, since the construction of the first public housings units, the government has pursued a persistent, though not always consistent, privatisation policy. Thus by 1990 most of the units which ever had been publically-owned had already been sold to tenants at discounts which amounted up to 75 percent of the market price (Werczberger 1991). In 1998, the Knesset passed the 'Public Housing Bill' which, if implemented, would provide even greater discounts to sitting tenants than has been the case until now. Its implementation is still uncertain, but it seems that it will not make a great difference. The rate of sales which varied in the past between 3 percent and 5 percent (Werczberger 1993) is unlikely to change a lot, because most of the households interested in buying their dwelling have already done so, except for new immigrants. Second, the construction of new projects has been seriously curtailed and is now far below the rate of privatisation.

Some of the difficulties of public housing are the result of its institutional structure (Werczberger 1993). For example, from the beginning construction has been financed from the current government budget completely separating the cost of land and capital from management and maintenance. The construction of public housing has thus been constrained by budgetary short-run considerations often creating slums right from the start. Rents, which are set according to social criteria such as income, size of household, age and so on, amount now to between 5 percent and at most a third of market rents and in fact do not cover even administration costs, let alone the costs of upkeep. Responsibility for maintenance has thus in effect been transferred to tenants, who for the most part are neither able nor willing to pay for it.[4] Moreover, similar to the experience, for example of Great Britain, low initial quality, the lack of adequate maintenance, and privatisation have resulted in the social residualisation of public housing through selective outmigration.

The new private rental sector: There remains in any case a non-negligible need for rental accommodation by households, for whom owning is not affordable or not suitable, but who do not qualify for the limited supply of public housing. The commercial private rental sector (PRS), which elsewhere supplies most of the demand, seems to be beyond salvation for three reasons (Kurtz 1995). Because of the high cost of land, financing and building, households who depend on renting cannot afford the rent of new housing. Taxes (in particular capital gains taxes) discriminate against commercial landlords and developers who build for rent rather than for owner occupation. Moreover, the long-run profitability of commercial rental housing critically depends on financing. Yet, interest rates have been and continue to be high by any standard, inflating the cost of rental housing compared with development for sale.

During the 1990s, three developments critically changed the profitability of renting at least to amateur landlords. (a) More than 800,000 immigrants from the former USSR arrived in Israel, most of which had to rely, at least during the first years, on rental housing. (b) Generous rental assistance was provided to the new immigrants after their arrival. (c) Private landlords were exempted in 1990 from taxes on their income from renting. Given a marginal tax rate between 40 percent and 50 percent for the average small landlord, this exemption amounted to a very significant subsidy to the PRS. It certainly explains the expansion between 1985 and 1995 in the supply of privately rented dwellings by about 80,000 units and the increase in the proportion of households in the PRS from 10.7 percent in 1983 to 16.1 percent in 1995.

15.3 RENTAL HOUSING IN ISRAEL: THE CURRENT STATE

15.3.1 The Stock of Rental Housing

The four tenure types - owner occupancy, market rental, public housing and rent-controlled units - seem to correspond to distinct submarkets. The first question is, then, whether and how much the three markets differ regarding their physical characteristics and spatial distribution. The following is based on the recently released 20 percent sample of the 1995 Population Census (Table 15.3). Because of space limitations, a qualitative summary of the results must suffice.

Table 15.3   Indicators of dwelling quality and housing conditions

Indicator	Owner occupants	Market rental	Public housing	Rent control	Total
Median number of rooms	3.0	2.6	2.6	2.1	2.8
% of dwellings with two rooms or less	13.4	37.7	38.0	50.8	20.6
% of dwellings built before 1970	47.1	57.4	58.7	89.7	50.0

Note: Households with density (persons/room) exceeding 1.

Age of the building: Dwellings in the rental sector (private and public) are indeed older than those in owner-occupied housing. The proportion of dwellings built before 1970 was 57.4 percent in privately rented units and in public housing 58.7 percent. In contrast, only 47.1 percent of the owner-occupied dwellings had been constructed before 1970. Since the quality of new dwelling units has been rapidly improving during the last decades (in particular regarding amenities and finish), rental housing tends to be inferior in quality compared with the average quality of the owner-occupied stock.

Size of rental units: With the increasing standard of living, the average floor area of new dwelling units increased between 1955 and 1991 from 58 m^2 to 146 m^2 (Werczberger 1994). Therefore rental dwellings (public and private), being older than owner-occupied units, also tend to be smaller in size. For example, the median number of rooms in public housing and market rentals is 2.6 (compared to 3.0 in owner-occupied units) and the percentage of very small dwellings (2 rooms or less) is 37.6 percent (compared to 13.4 percent for owner-occupied units).[5]

15.3.2 The Spatial Distribution of Tenure Types

We would expect private rental housing to be concentrated in larger urban centres, in which there is a supply of older housing and of activities and amenities which attract the young and mobile. Public housing, on the other hand, would be more likely in peripheral development towns where most of the housing was built by the government as social housing. In addition, privatisation was far less successful in development towns than in the centre, where housing prices are significantly higher and hence the discounts offered are far more attractive to potential buyers.

Indeed, the proportion of households renting in the PRS clearly increases with the size of the settlement or city (Table 15.4).[6] In the Arab sector, the trend is the same, except that the proportion of renters is lower because of the more rural character of the Arab population and their lower level of income. The proportion of tenants in public housing, on the other hand, is larger in smaller settlements, most of which are located in the periphery (Table 15.4).

15.4 DEMAND FOR RENTAL HOUSING: TENURE CHOICE

If the different tenure categories really serve distinctive submarkets, then it should be possible to differentiate between their residents. This section focuses therefore on the differences in demographic and socio-economic characteristics between households that choose the four tenure types. Using the 20 percent sample of the 1995 Population Census we estimate a multinomial logit model, which predicts the choice of tenure, if household characteristics are known.[7]

Table 15.4   Tenure by population size and type of settlement in percent[1]

Settlement type or size	Owner-occupier	Key money	Private rental	Public housing[1]	Key money	Total house-holds[2]
Jerusalem	65.9	2.5	23.9	3.5	2.5	114,325
Tel-Aviv	58.7	5.9	28.1	3.7	5.9	121,870
Haifa	70.9	4.7	18.9	3.3	4.7	81,660
Jewish: 100,000-200,000	74.8	0.5	17.3	5.0	0.5	336,750
Jewish: 50,000-100,000	74.9	1.2	14.7	6.7	1.2	140,055
Jewish: 20,000-50,000	72.4	0.7	12.7	11.6	0.7	26,190
Jewish: 10,000-20,000	72.3	0.6	12.0	12.7	0.6	60,840
Jewish: 2,000- 10,000	79.0	0.4	9.9	7.7	0.4	50,385
Arab: 50,000-100,000	83.8		11.0	0.9		9,550
Arab: 20,000- 50,000	94.1		4.0	0.3		17,805
Arab: 10,000- 20,000	95.0		2.1	0.1		40,105
Arab: 2,000- 10,000	93.8		2.1	0.1		49,895
Moshavim[2]	74.4	0.2	9.7	1.5	0.2	41,839
Rural settlements	78.9	0.1	5.5	7.9	0.1	33,990
Total[3]	71.9	1.4	15.2	5.8	1.4	1,361,065

Notes:

[1] The rows do not add up to 100 percent, since households living in unidentified or other tenure forms were excluded.

[2] Agricultural settlements with limited cooperation.

[3] The total excludes households in institutions and members of Kibbutzim (communal settlements).

Logit models are appropriate when the variable to be explained is categorical as in the case of tenure choice models. For each of the alternatives (public housing, private renting and so on) the dependent variable is defined as the logarithm of the odds that the particular tenure form is selected instead of the contrast (ownership).[8] It is then easy to show that the exponential function $\exp(b_i)$ of the coefficient b_i equals the factor by which the odds of an alternative must be multiplied if the independent variable is increased by unity (Menard 1995). Since the coefficient b_i has not simple intuitive meaning, the results are discussed in terms of the exponential function $\exp(b_i)$. Note also that if the value of any b_i is negative, then $\exp(b_i) < 1$, so that any increase in X_i reduces the probability of the respective choice.

After the exclusion of variables whose coefficients are insignificant for each of the tenure categories, only seven variables remained in the final equation: age of household head, his/her education, marital status, ethnic background, religion, labour force participation, student and district.[9] The final equation shown in Table 15.5 is highly significant and all coefficients included in the equation have the correct signs. Nevertheless, the pseudo R^2 (Nagelkerke) is only 0.203. But given the structure of the sample, we believe that this does not affect the validity of the results.[10]

Demographic characteristics: Two demographic characteristics entered the equation: age and marital status. Households are more likely to rent in the PRS than to own if they are younger $[\exp(b_i) = 0.840]$ and to live in rent-controlled dwellings than to own if they are older $[\exp(b_i) = 1.146]$. The choice of public housing, on the other hand, hardly seems to be affected by age $[\exp(b_i) = 0.951]$. Marital status also affects the tenure choice. Compared with home-ownership, renting is significantly more likely for unmarried household heads (than for married ones), regardless if he or she is divorced, widowed or single. It is presumably easier for couples to accumulate the equity required for buying than for household heads living alone. Compared with married couples, divorcees are most likely to rent. They are followed by single household heads, and then by widow(er)s, many of whom have presumably inherited an apartment.

Social characteristics: Since most housing programmes focus on specific population groups, it should not be surprising that the proportions of households in the different tenure types vary with the background of the household head. Two background variables entered the equation: ethnic origin and religion. Compared with households of Israeli origin, household heads of Asian (Yemen, Iraq, Iran and so on) origin are, *ceteris paribus*, significantly more likely to own than to rent $[\exp(b_i) = 0.740$ and $\exp(b_i) = 0.703]$. The tendency is weaker among household heads of (North-)African origin, which are more likely to live in public housing $[\exp(b_i) = 1.091]$. On the other hand, households of European or American extraction tend to rent in the PRS $[\exp(b_i) = 1.214$ and $\exp(b_i) = 1.740]$. The tendency to own rather than to rent is even greater among Moslems and Druze families $[\exp(b_i) = 0.578$ and $\exp(b_i) = 0.177]$. Among Christian households, on the other hand, there is a greater likelihood to rent in the private sector than

Table 15.5   A tenure choice model with owner occupancy as contrast[1]

Indicator		Market rental	Public housing	Rent control
Age of Household head		0.840	0.951	1.146
Marital Status:	Divorced	3.081	2.964	3.497
	Widowed	1.546	1.532	1.414
	Single	1.877	2.369	3.519
Contrast:	Married			
Years of education		1.131	0.866	0.910
Ethnic Origin:	Asia	0.740	0.703	0.558
	Africa	0.889	1.091	0.674
	Europe	1.214	0.895	0.797
	The Americas	1.740	2.106	0.634
Contrast:	Israel			
Religion:	Moslem	0.578	0.131	(1.140)
	Christian	1.814	0.455	5.181
	Druze	0.177	0.131	0.274
Contrast:	Jewish			
Labour force:	Does not work	2.052	1.621	(1.108)
	No employment	1.921	1.607	1.667
Contrast:	working			
Student:	Student	1.279	1.094	(0.977)
Contrast:	Not studying			
District:	Jerusalem	1.232	2.177	(1.061)
	North	0.359	5.615	0.077
	Haifa	0.640	1.785	0.577
	Centre	0.676	1.437	0.149
	South	0.579	3.729	0.063
Contrast:	Tel-Aviv			
Number of valid observations		264,426		
Goodness of Fit:	Significance	0.0000		
Pseudo R^2:	Cox and Snell	0.162		
	Nagelkerke	0.203		

Notes:
[1]   Values of coefficients are given as exponential function of *b* Exp(*b*).
All coefficients are significant at the 5% level, except those in parenthesis.

among Jewish households [exp(b_i) = 1.814].[11] Note that 33.3 percent of the new immigrants live in the PRS. Nevertheless, probably because of multi-collinearity, the corresponding variable did not enter the equation.

Economic conditions: Only three indicators of the economic situation of the household head remained in the equation: the number of school years completed, participation in the labour force and whether the household head is a student. Income and occupation had to be excluded because of the very large number of missing values. Education and participation in the labour force thus serve as indicators of economic conditions. Educated households are more likely to rent in the private market [exp(b_i) = 1.131] and less likely to live in public housing [exp(b_i) = 0.866]. Household heads who are permanently or temporarily unemployed have a lower income than those who are working and are therefore twice as likely to rent, particularly in the private rentals sector [exp(b_i) = 2.052 and exp(b_i) = 1.921]. Students are very mobile and may not be able to realise the full earning potential expected based on their formal education. They are thus more likely to rent in the private market than to own [exp(b_i) = 1.279].

Geographic differences: When the other factors affecting tenure choice are kept constant, location also influences tenure choice. Compared with households living in the Tel-Aviv district, the odds to rent in the PRS are significantly higher in Jerusalem [exp(b_i) = 1.232], perhaps because of the large population of temporary residents. It is much lower in all other Districts, especially the North with its large Arab population [exp(b_i) = 0.359]. Compared with the Tel-Aviv district, public housing is more likely to be chosen than ownership in every other district, including Jerusalem [exp(b_i) = 2.177] and particularly the North with its Arab population and development towns [exp(b_i) = 5.615].

15.5 THE DEMAND FOR RENTAL HOUSING: WILLINGNESS TO PAY

In public housing and in rent-controlled dwellings, the rent is determined not in the market but by administrative decision. The relevant decision is therefore the choice of tenure and not the price or user cost of the dwelling. This section, which is concerned with the willingness to pay, therefore focuses on demand in the private sector only.

Data and methodology: As a data source we used the 1997 household expenditure survey of the IBS (Israel Bureau of Statistics), which provides extensive information on income and expenditures and also selected data on the socio-economic characteristics of the households included in the survey (n = 5,230). After eliminating variables for which too many observations were missing, we used OLS to estimate a log-linear equation. As the dependent variable we used the natural logarithm of the rent per room paid by the tenant. It is regressed on the variables listed in Table 15.6.[12] As in log-linear models, the coefficients of the independent variables can be interpreted as demand elasticities.

Table 15.6   Factors affecting the demand for market rental in 1997

Variable	Unstandardised coefficient b	Standardised coefficient beta	Level of Significance
Constant	3.698		0.000
Rooms in the apartment (log)	−0.717	−0.262	0.000
Age of household head (log)	−0.497	−0.158	0.000
Net income (log)	0.363	0.223	0.000
Years of formal schooling (log)	0.670	0.221	0.000
Self-employed (dummy)	0.292	0.086	0.009
Small town (2k-50k population)	−0.469	−0.200	0.000
Jerusalem (dummy)	−0.380	−0.118	0.000
Haifa (dummy)	−0.397	−0.109	0.001
Dependent Variable:	Log of rent/room		
Number of observations (N)[1]	870		
Standard error of estimate	0.891		
Adjusted R^2	0.231		
ANOVA	Df regression: 9	F = 26.87	0.000
	Df residual: 752		

Note: The sample size includes only renters.

Results: Consider first the coefficient associated with income. By definition it equals the percentage change in rent per room for a 1 percent increase in income. Since the coefficient is positive ($b_i = 0.363$) but small, the demand for rental housing is quite inelastic and not much affected by the income of the tenants. In contrast, the coefficient associated with the number of rooms ($b_i = -0.717$) is negative, fairly large, although less than unity. The rent per room thus declines with the size of the apartment. It seems that the typical tenant in market rentals cannot afford a large apartment for himself, and instead has to share with other renters, which means less privacy. Hence the rent paid for additional rooms declines with the size of the apartment. The smaller size of privately rented apartments may thus be explained by the lack of demand rather than the lack of supply of larger flats. Older tenants pay less per room ($b_i = -0.497$). However, it is not clear, whether this is the effect of the location of their dwelling or of the duration of their tenancy, as landlords are typically willing to accept a lower rent from long-standing reliable tenants.

We have no information on the quality of the neighbourhood in which the dwellings are located, except for indicators of socio-economic status of the tenants themselves. Formal schooling has indeed a positive effect on the demand for rental housing (b_i = 0.670). The same holds for self-employed household heads who are also willing to pay more (b_i = 0.292).

Finally there is the effect of living in specific cities; in particular, the effect of the (population) size of the settlement. Compared with Tel-Aviv, which serves as the comparison, the rent per room is significantly lower in Jerusalem (b_i = –0.380), Haifa (b_i = –0.397) and the most in small towns (b_i = –0.469). The variable for medium-sized towns with a population of 50,000-200,000 is not significantly different from the rent in Tel-Aviv, presumably because most cities included in this category are suburban satellites of Tel-Aviv.

15.6 DISCUSSION

15.6.1 Summary

Despite continuing efforts by Israeli governments to encourage home ownership, there remains a substantial demand for renting by households, who cannot afford buying or for whom home ownership is clearly not suitable. Two housing sectors mainly provide shelter for this population: public housing and the private rental sector.

The provision of public housing represents a considerable financial burden for the government. During the past decades it has been socially and quantitatively residualised because of low initial quality, a lack of maintenance, social stigmatisation and privatisation. It contributes now only about a quarter of all rental housing and caters mainly to the poor. Given current government policy, the share of public housing is unlikely to contribute to the expanding need for rentals for single-parent households, divorcees and other non-standard households.

The remainder of the demand for rental housing is supplied by the private rental sector and comprises now almost exclusively converted condo-units rented by small landlords. It provides indispensable housing services for a significant part of the population: in particular, the young, the mobile, new immigrants, the unmarried and other non-standard households, and this largely in the main urban centres of the country. The demand is for older and smaller units, which offer privacy at an affordable price. The income elasticity of demand is low. Therefore, the premium paid for apartments by the young, the educated, many of which may be students, and the self-employed, probably reflects differences in the character and the socio-economic status of the neighbourhoods. This is supported by the considerable differences in rents between cities, which by and large parallel general housing price variations.

15.6.2 What are the Alternatives?

There is a broad consensus that the private rental sector is too small to meet the potential demand created by fluctuations in immigration and by young households who have not yet been able to accumulate savings for buying. Government programmes to support and revitalise the commercial rental sector have hitherto been based on reducing the tax burden to the developer during the first decade after construction (Kurtz 1995). Afterwards, they are allowed to sell the units with a full or partial exemption from capital gains tax. This means that the new dwellings are taken off the rental market before they can become affordable for the typical tenant. Nevertheless, benefits granted to developers did not offset the tax disadvantage compared with builders of housing for sale, so that all these programmes failed. The success of the new rental sector, on the other hand, implies that a policy intended to strengthen private renting should focus on the conversion of older condominium units.

There appear to be two approaches to expand or at least to stabilise the new private rental sector. First, measures could be taken to encourage more small landlords to invest money in the rental market. The most important step would be to reduce uncertainty by making existing tax exemptions on rental income permanent. Currently they are temporary measures, which can be revoked at any time, as suggested in recent tax reform proposals. The alternative is to create conditions which would make the new rental market attractive to investors and make long-term investment in older rental housing profitable also to commercial landlords. This could be achieved, for example, by providing similar tax exemptions on rental income as those which are available to private landlords, and by refraining from taxing the back conversion to condo-units. Commercial landlords would be able to create scale economies in management and maintenance by assembling large portfolios of rental units. This would reduce the cost of management and administration and lead to higher profits than available to the petty landlord. Moreover, without the current exemptions on capital gains taxes the emphasis will be on long-term investment rather than quick profits, and this is really what is necessary for creating a viable private rental market.

ACKNOWLEDGMENT

I am greatly indebted to Erez Lenchner, who was responsible for data processing, programming and statistical analysis. His contribution has been invaluable. The data of the Population Census and of the Household Expenditure Survey were obtained from the Social Science Data Archive at the Hebrew University. Their assistance is greatly appreciated.

REFERENCES

Carmon, N. (1989), 'Israel's project renewal: describing and explaining its relative success', in N. Carmon (ed.), *Neighborhood Policy and Programs - Past and Present*, London: Macmillan Press.

Carmon, N. (1999), 'Housing policy in Israel: the first 50 years', in D. Nachmias and G. Menahem (eds), *Public Policy in Israel*, Tel-Aviv: Am Oved, Israel's Institute for Democracy (Hebrew).

Carmon, N. and D. Czamanski (1991), 'Housing policy and practice in Israel', in W. van Vliet (ed.), *International Handbook of Housing Policies and Practices*, Westport, CT: Greenwood Press, pp. 517-36.

Christensen, R. (1997), *Loglinear Models and Logistic Regression*, New York: Springer.

Downs, A. (1983), *Rental Housing in the 1980s*, Washington, DC: The Brooking Institution.

Gilderbloom, J.I. and R.P. Appelbaum (1988), *Rethinking Rental Housing*, Philadelphia: Temple University Press.

Grigsby, W.G. (1987), *The Dynamics of Neighborhood Change and Decline*, Oxford: Pergamon.

Henderson, J.V. and Y. Ioannides (1983), 'A model of housing tenure choice', *American Economic Review*, 73, pp. 98-113.

Israel, Central Bureau of Statistics (1997), *Statistical Abstracts of Israel*, Jerusalem: CBS.

Kemeny, J. (1981), *The Myth of Homeownership: Private and Public Choices*, Routledge and Kegan Paul.

Kurtz, I. (1995), 'Rental housing: cost-benefit analysis for the economy and examination of the economic profitability', Final report to the Ministry of Construction and Housing, Tel-Aviv (Hebrew).

Lowry, I.S. (1960), 'Filtering and housing standards: a conceptual analysis', *Land Economics*, pp. 362-70.

Malpezzi, S. and R.K. Green (1996), 'What has happened to the bottom of the US housing market?', *Urban-Studies*, 33 (10), pp. 1807-20.

Menard, S. (1995), *Applied Logistic Regression*, Sage: Thousand Oaks.

Mills, E.S. (1990), 'Housing tenure choice', *Journal of Real Estate Finance and Economics*, 3 (4), pp. 323-31.

Norman H.N. et al. (1967), *SPSS*, N.Y.: McGraw Hill.

Pines, D. and Y. Weiss (1974), 'Homeowner, the rental market and the cost of housing in Israel', Working Paper, Tel-Aviv: The Center of Urban and Regional Studies, Tel-Aviv University.

Werczberger, E. (1988), 'The experience with rent control in Israel. From rental housing to condominiums', *The Journal of Real Estate Finance and Economics*, 1, pp. 159-74.

Werczberger, E. (1990), 'Social and economic consequences of the law for the protection of tenants in Israel', Discussion paper No. 5-90, Tel-Aviv: Tel-Aviv University, The Sapir Centre for Development (Hebrew).

Werczberger, E. (1991), 'Public housing in Israel', Discussion paper No. 5-91, Tel-Aviv: Tel-Aviv University, The Sapir Centre for Development (Hebrew).

Werczberger, E. (1993), 'Protected tenants in the Tel-Aviv district according to the 1983 population census', in D. Nachmias and G. Menachem (eds), *Social Processes and Public Policy in Tel-Aviv Yafo*, Tel-Aviv: Ramot, Tel-Aviv University (Hebrew).

Werczberger, E. (1994), 'Housing in Israel for the 21st century', in N. Carmon (ed.), *Planning for 'Quality of Life' for Everybody, Israel 2020*, The National Masterplan for 21st Century, Haifa: Technion. Ch. 7.

NOTES

1. During the 1990s the percentage has been rising again to about 16 percent as a result of the large-scale immigration from the former USSR.
2. For a detailed discussion of Israeli housing policy, see, for example, Carmon and Czamanski (1991) or Carmon (1999).
3. The immigrant population comprises at that time mostly survivors of the Holocaust from Europe and refugees from North African or Mid-Eastern nations. Both groups arrived in the country practically penniless.
4. Project Renewal, initiated during the late 1970s, represented a major effort to halt the continuing decline by combining a variety of policies ranging from renovation, to the enlargement of apartments and social programmes (Carmon 1989). However, it failed to solve the underlying causes and the problems created by the spatial concentration of low-income and under-employed households in low-quality housing and neighbourhoods.
5. The median is calculated by following the procedure suggested in Norman et al. (1967).
6. The relatively large proportion in Moshavim (9.7 percent) is presumably due to demand for a rural residential environment among young affluent households.
7. For an excellent introduction to the logistic regression model, see, for example, Menard (1995) or Christensen (1997).

8. Instead of a formal specification, an informal description will have to suffice. Assume that Y, the dependent variable, is a categorical random variable. It can take the values $R = 0, 1, 2, 3$ corresponding to the four alternative tenure forms, where 0 stands for owner occupancy. If the household chooses tenure type R, then $Y = R$. Let $P(Y=R)$ equal the probability that $Y = R$. The ratio $[P(Y = R)]/[P(Y = 0)]$ is then the odds that the household chooses $Y = R$ instead of $Y = 0$. The logit $\log\{[P(Y = R)]/[P(Y = R)]\}$ is defined as the logarithm of the odds. In logit analysis, this logit is used as the dependent variable of a linear function of the independent variables X_i.

$$\log\{[P(Y = R)]/[P(Y = 0)]\} = a + \Sigma_i b_i X_i + e$$

where a is a constant, X_i is the value of the ith independent variable, b_i is the coefficient associated with the ith variable and e is the error term.

9. The excluded variables are: country of birth, income, occupation, year of immigration, years studied in a Yeshiva (Talmud academy) continent of origin and gender. Occupation and income had to be omitted because of the large number of missing values.

10. Since 75 percent are homeowners, by guessing for all observations owner occupation as tenure, we would err only in 25 percent of all cases. The improvement in the proportion of correct prediction possible by adding the information on household characteristics is thus far more limited than achievable in regressions with continuous dependent variables.

11. We suspect that many of the Christian renters are new immigrants from the former USSR and not Israeli Arabs.

12. Stepwise regression was used to eliminate variables, whose coefficients would not have been significant.

Index

Printed and bound by CPI Group (UK) Ltd, Croydon, CR0 4YY

23/04/2025

14661002-0004